IMAGES
of America

OXFORD

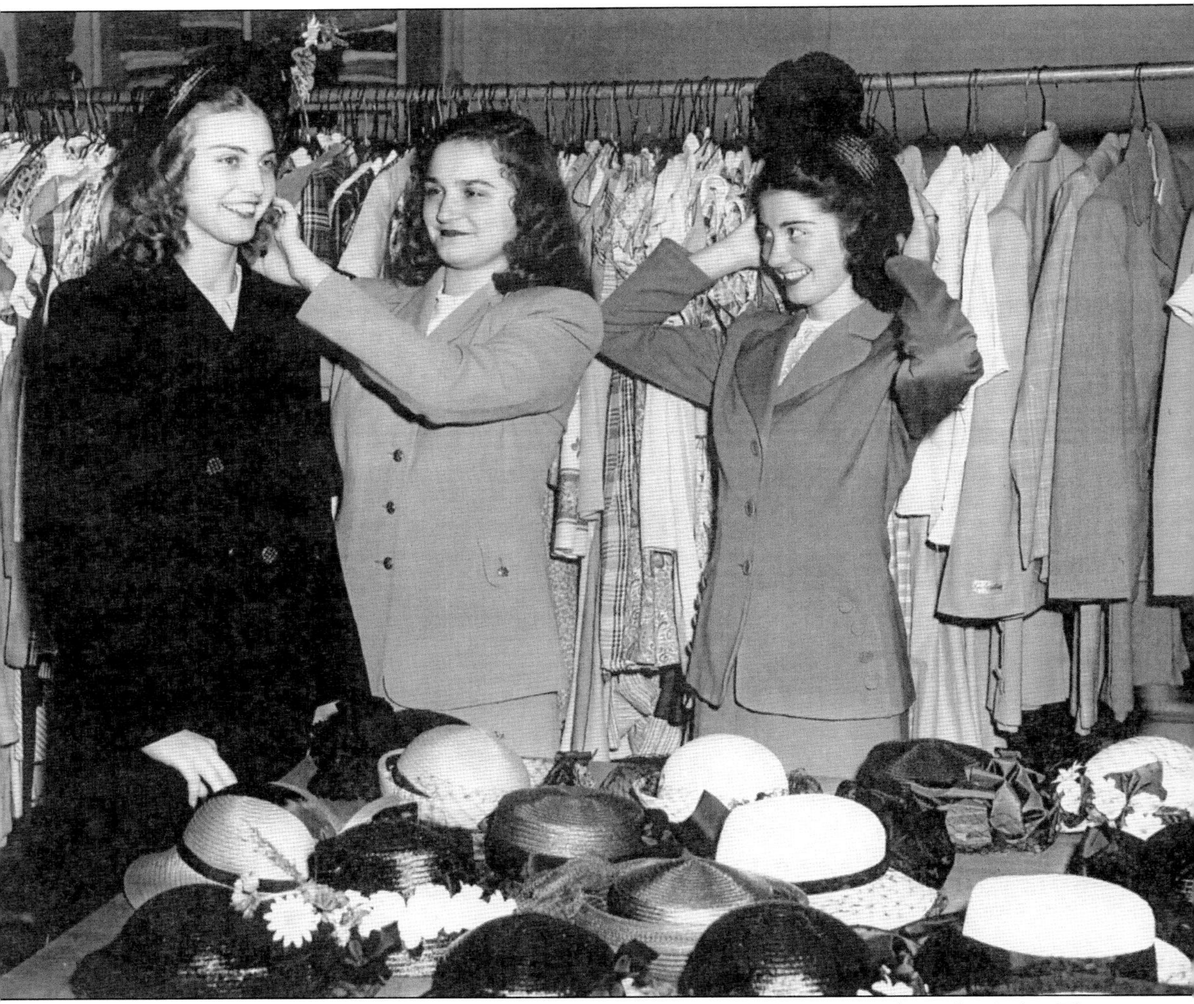

From left to right are Georgia Throckmorton, Bobbie Halliburton, and Emily Cole. These young ladies are shopping in downtown Oxford in the 1950s.

IMAGES
of America

OXFORD

Lewis Bowling

ARCADIA
PUBLISHING

ISBN 978-0-7385-1780-3

Published by Arcadia Publishing
Charleston, South Carolina

Printed in the United States of America

Library of Congress Catalog Card Number: 2004117439

For all general information contact Arcadia Publishing at:
Telephone 843-853-2070
Fax 843-853-0044
E-mail sales@arcadiapublishing.com
For customer service and orders:
Toll-Free 1-888-313-2665

Visit us on the internet at www.arcadiapublishing.com

This book is dedicated to the people of Granville County.

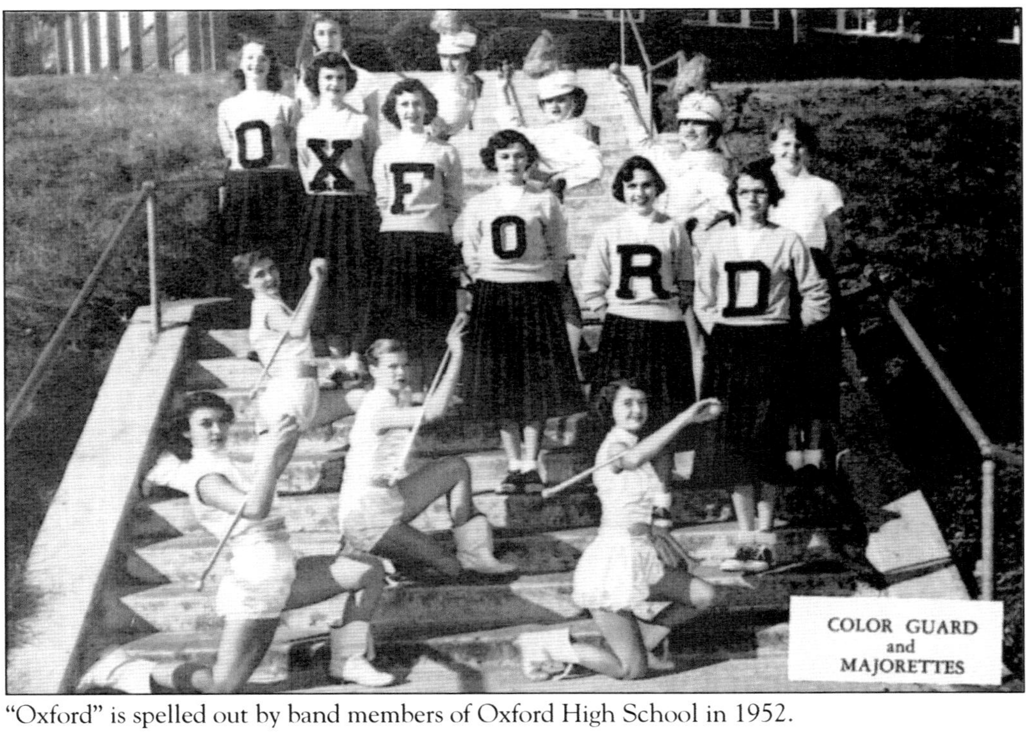

"Oxford" is spelled out by band members of Oxford High School in 1952.

Contents

ACKNOWLEDGMENTS

I would like to thank Edythe Day, Phyllis Beck, A.S. Woodlief, Teresa Parham, Woody Breedlove, Kevin King, Francis Hart, Sigma Finch, Harold Slaughter, Mary Bowling, Beth Harward, Carolyn Moss, Danny Bowling, Linda Bowling, Brin Wilkins, Mildred Harris, Jim Boring, Cindy Boring, Fann Montague, Sharon Mullen Watts, Ronald Ragland, Rachel Thomas, Jean Gill, Liz Falkner, Hart Curl, Herbert Grissom, Barbara Wilkerson, Opal White, Kathy Judd, Shirley Currin, Becky Currin, Josephine Currin, Rowena Wheeler, Nettie Dickerson, Birk Lunsford, Mike Alston, Bob Hunt, Judy Hunt, Pat Colenda, Isabel Brummitt, Lisa Oakes, Pam Thornton, Amy Bowen, Ruth Dean, Sam Currin, Clessie Thomas, Betty King, Arthur Ray Currin, Al Woodlief, Elaine Breedlove, Lee Bowling, Rosalyn Crews, Jennie Schilagi, John Wilson, Mary Wayne Bowling, Emily Champion, and Josh Mangum.

I would also like to acknowledge the use of facilities at the Granville County Historical Society Museum, the Central Children's Home Archives, the Masonic Home for Children Archives, and the Richard H. Thornton Library. Kathy Judd of the *Oxford Public Ledger* was very helpful in letting readers know about this book.

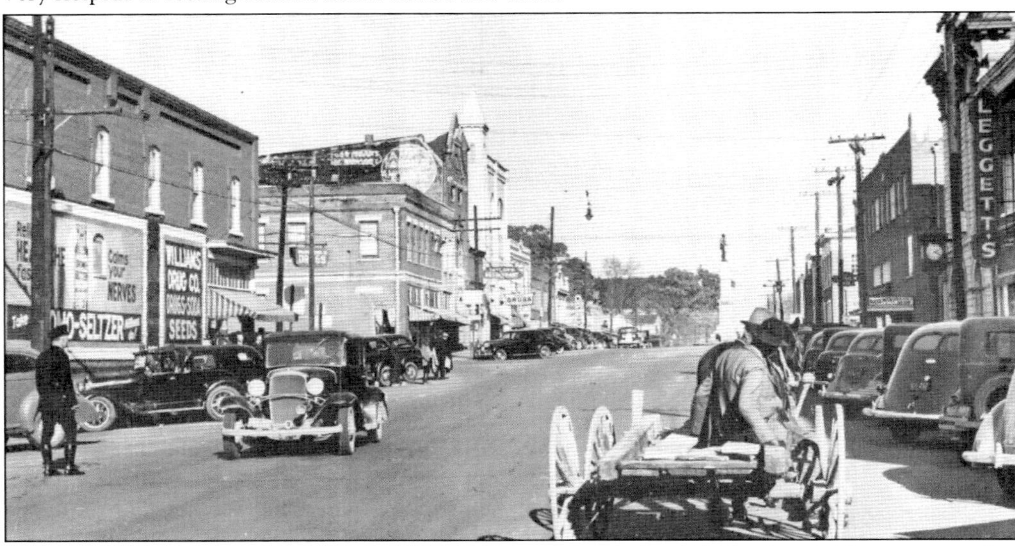

This picture looks down Hillsboro Street in Oxford in the late 1930s. It is 2:20 p.m. according to the clock at the right. Leggett's Store and the Basement Barber Shop can also be seen on the right. On the left is Williams Drugs, Taylor's Restaurant, and the Orpheum Theatre sign. (Courtesy of Southern Historical Collection, University of North Carolina at Chapel Hill.)

Introduction

4 March 1812—Thomas B. Littlejohn of Granville Co. to Robert Burton, Charles Eaton, John Hare, Robert Jeter, Benjamin Hilliard, Commissioners in trust for the county of Granville $2,636.00 by virtue of an act of the General Assembly of the State of North Carolina passed at Raleigh in the session of 1811 entitled an act to appoint Commissioners to contract with Thomas B. Littlejohn for fifty acres of Land to erect a Town. . . . the said Robert Burton, Charles Burton, John Hare, Robert Jeter, and Benjamin Hilliard were appointed Commissioners to carry the said act . . . being a part of the tract of Land called the Court House or Oxford tract . . . beginning . . . near where the former Jail stood, ninety feet from the west end of the Court House designated in the annexed plan by the letter A.

That is how the town of Oxford got started. In 1760, Samuel Benton acquired title to 200 acres of land, which he called Oxford Plantation. Eventually Thomas Littlejohn bought some of this land, and Granville County bought the 50 acres from Littlejohn, as described above. Littlejohn developed lots around the present courthouse and established a hotel himself. Oxford was incorporated in 1816. The town began to grow and expand slowly. In 1830, the first local newspaper, *The Oxford Examiner*, was established. In 1840, the Granville County Courthouse was completed, and this building remains the center of Oxford today. By 1850, there were 669 people in Oxford. Agriculture has through the years been the driving force of the economy in Oxford and throughout the county, with tobacco being the main crop. The first warehouse in the county was built in 1866 by L.C. Taylor. With the railroad arriving in town in 1881, business in Oxford really started to increase. In 1911, the Oxford Tobacco Research Station was established, and this facility has contributed much to agricultural life in the country, such as with the discovery of a wilt-resistant tobacco plant.

Oxford became famous in the mid- to late 1800s for its educational institutions, being referred to as the "Athens of the South." Oxford Female College was formed in 1850, St. Johns College in 1857, the Oxford Orphanage in 1873, the Central Children's Home in 1883, Horner Military School in 1851, and Mary Potter School in 1888. Many people have contributed to the educational fabric of Oxford, such as John Chavis, C.G.Credle, J.F. Webb, Franklin Hobgood, James Horner, G.C. Shaw, Henry Cheatham, John Mills, Lizzie Hilliard, and Nettie Bemis.

Culture has also been a strong contributor to the growth of Oxford. In 1888, the Opera House was opened, providing entertainment and education to citizens. Plays, musicals, and lectures were held at the Opera House for many years. This building served several purposes. It provided entertainment on the second floor, such as Shakespeare plays. On the first floor was a market for people to sell meat and vegetables. Many literary clubs have been a part of Oxford's history as well, and they continue to be, such as the Shakespeare Club, the Oxford Choral Society, and the Tuesday Musical Club. In 1908, a group of women organized the Village Improvement Society, which later became the Oxford Woman's Club. This club has been very instrumental in improving the culture of the town. Today the Granville County Historical Society Museum is also very active in preserving our past.

Oxford was advertised in the early 1900s as "an ideal seat of learning. The existence in it for well nigh a century of schools of high grade has developed culture and refinement in its citizens to an unusual degree. It is one of the prettiest towns in all the country, with wide and well shaded streets paved and parked, granolithic walks, large lawns and elegant residences. It is one of the healthiest towns in the state. All the conditions of health—pure air, good water, mild but invigorating climate are found here."

Serving as the county seat of Granville County, Oxford has a population of 8,338. It has the allure of small town life, and with its proximity to Raleigh and Durham, and lower land costs and tax rates than many other towns in the area, the population is sure to continue to grow.

Today, Oxford remains a town that holds onto its past while still moving forward into the 21st century. It is a good place to call home or just to visit. The Oxford of today still has elegant old homes, wide shaded streets, and many remembrances of its past. Most of all, it has good people. It is a town most of us will always remember fondly.

One

Downtown Oxford

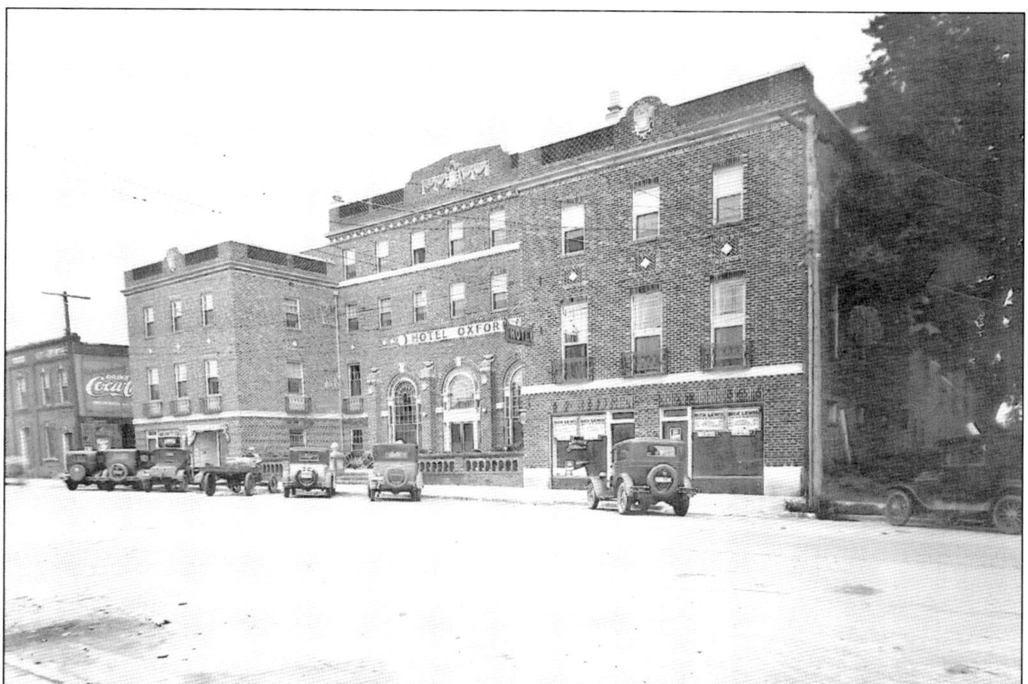

Hotel Oxford stands proudly along Hillsboro Street in 1927. Many residents of Oxford still fondly recall memories of this downtown attraction. This building was torn down in 1967. (Courtesy of A.S. Woodlief.)

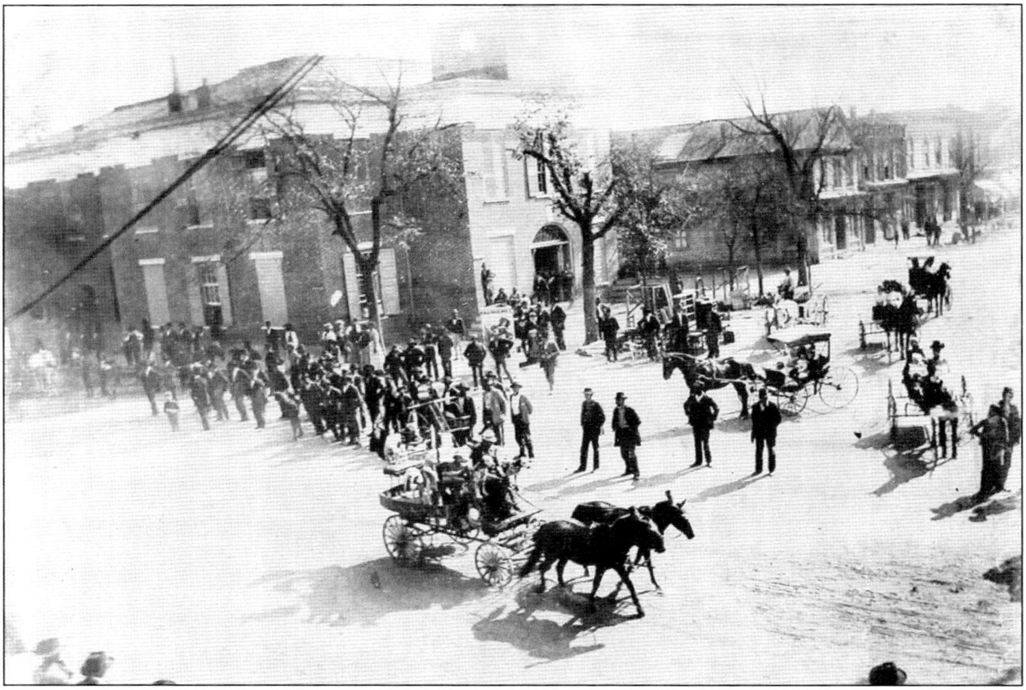

People of Oxford enjoy a parade in the early 1900s. The Granville County Courthouse can be seen in the background, with part of Main Street to the right.

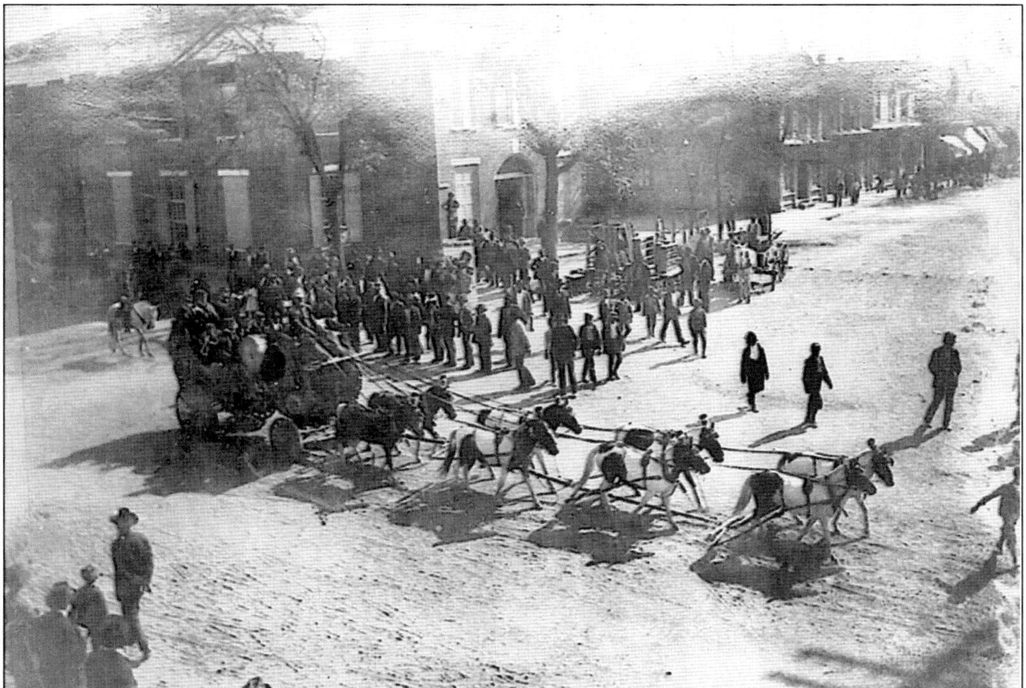

The parade continues, with a loaded wagon being pulled by eight ponies.

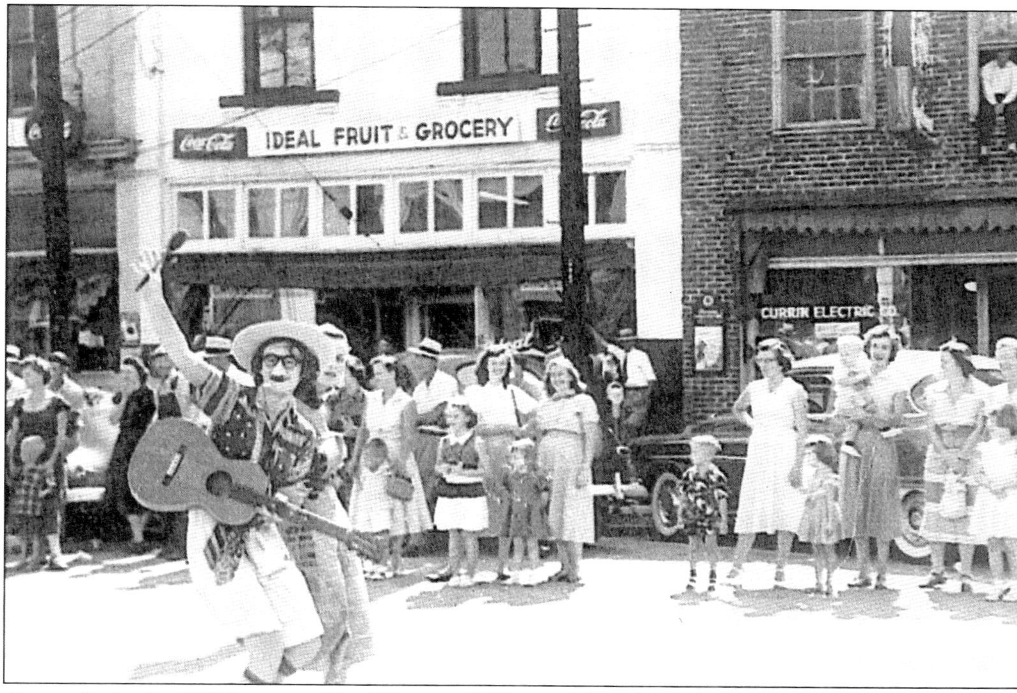

A parade in the 1950s passes Ideal Fruit and Grocery (on the left) and Currin Electric (on the right). Notice the grand view of the parade watcher in the upper right corner.

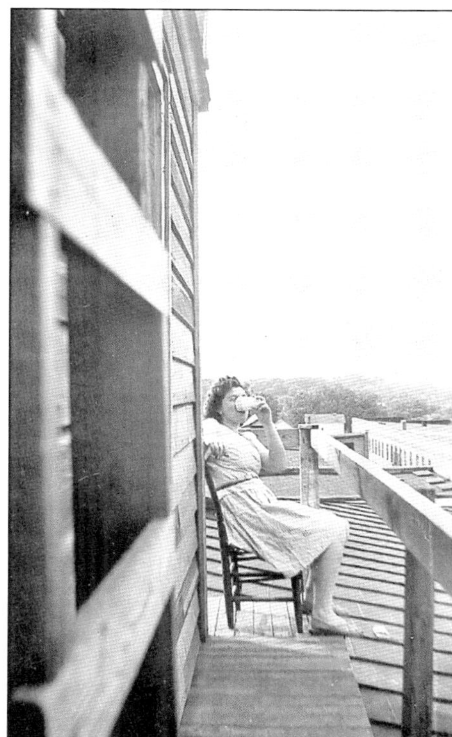

A young lady sits atop a building in downtown Oxford to watch for enemy planes during World War II. (Courtesy of Mildred Harris.)

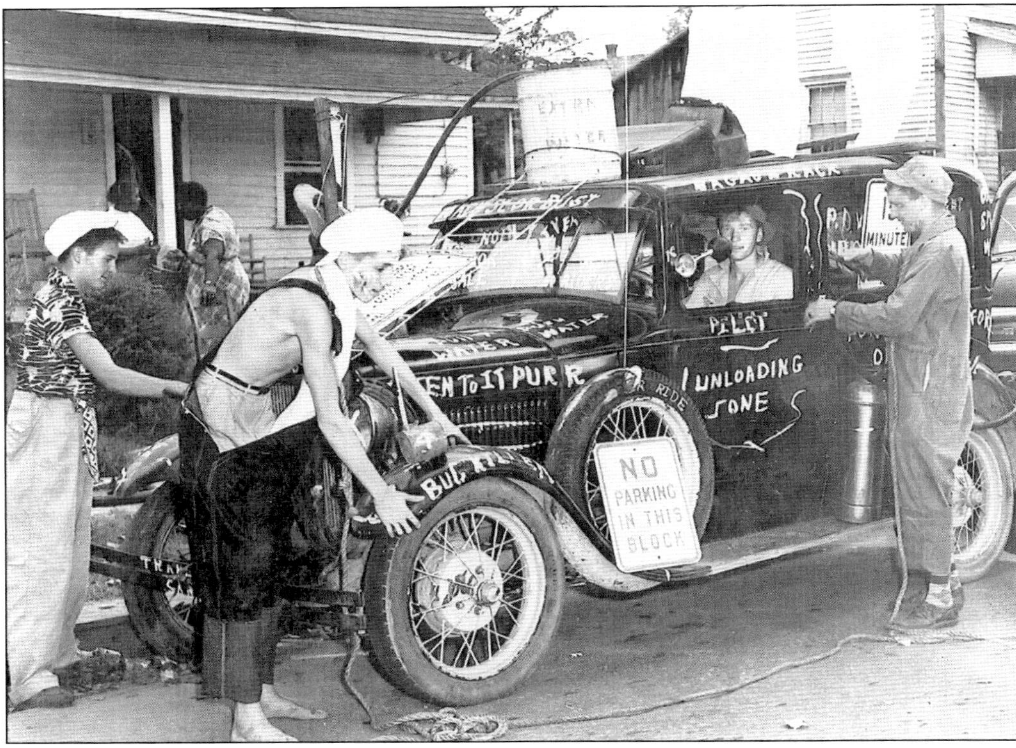

Preparing their vehicle for a parade are, from left to right, Ronnie Talley, Bobby Watkins, driver Francis Hart, and Bobby Talley. (Courtesy of Francis Hart.)

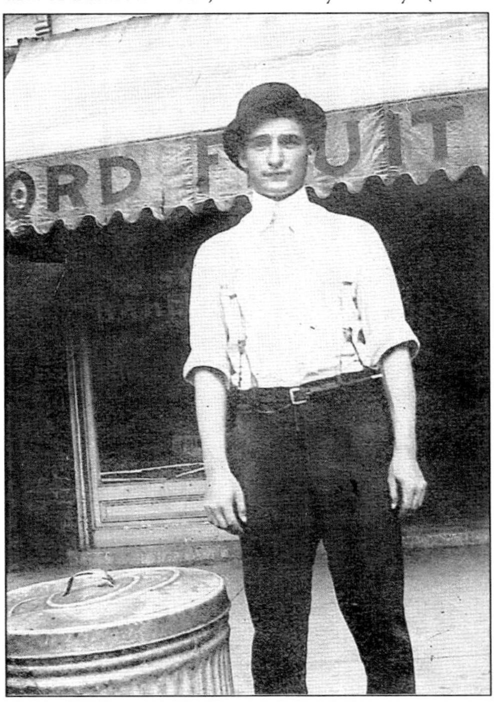

Herbert Knight stands in front of the Oxford Fruit Store in 1920. Herbert was a veteran of World War I. (Courtesy of Teresa Parham.)

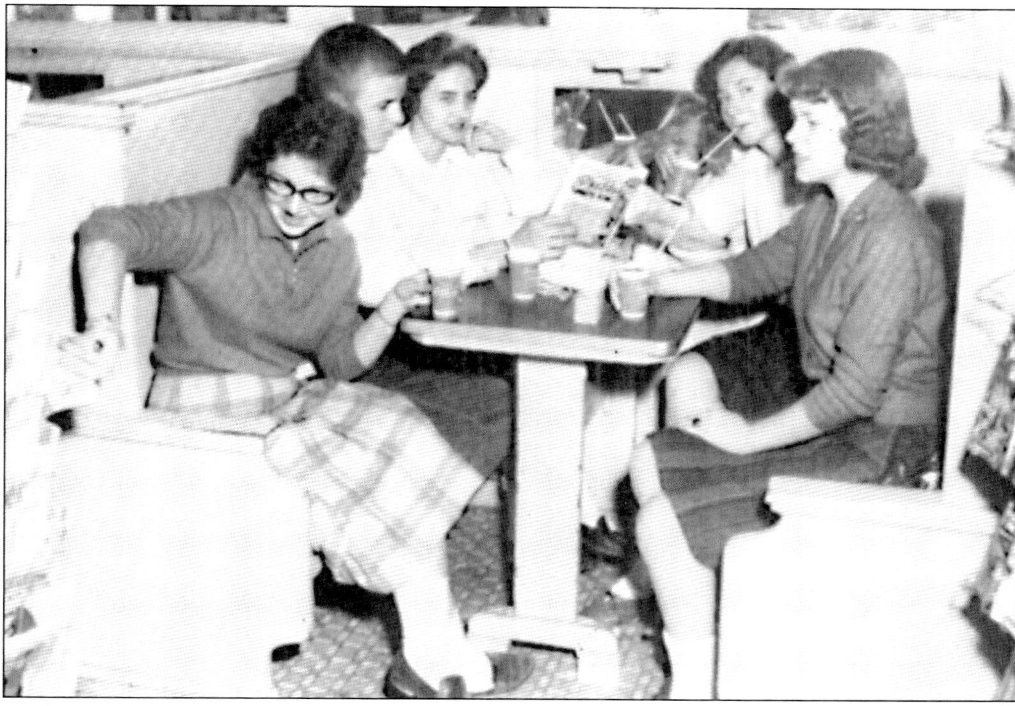

In the 1950s, one lucky young man enjoys the company of four ladies at Lyon's Drugstore after a day of classes at Oxford High School. Located in Oxford, Lyon's was a popular place among locals.

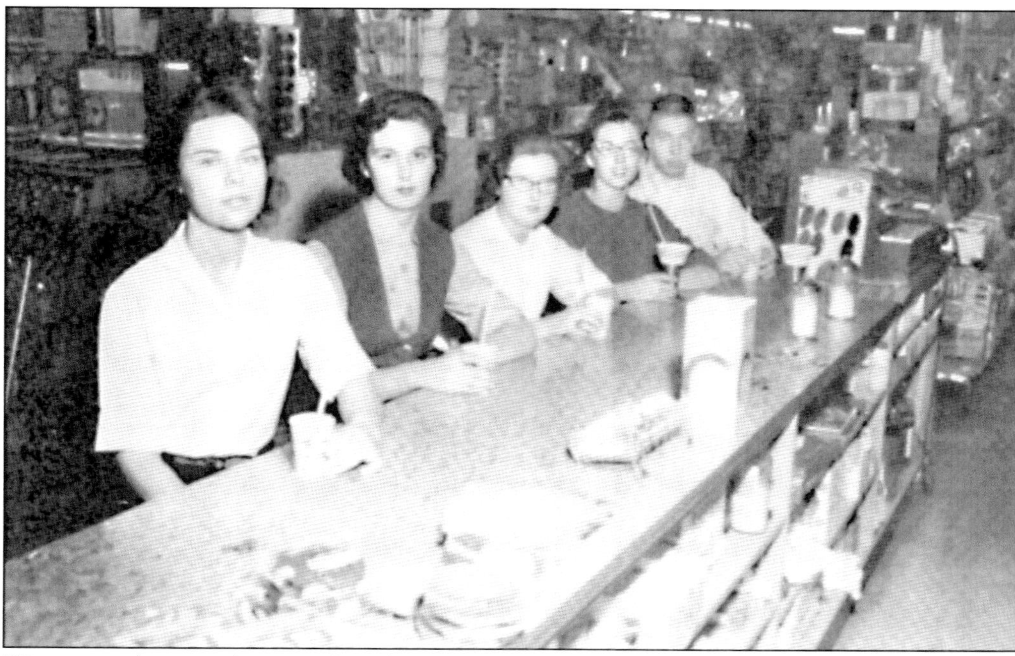

Waiting to be served in another drugstore in Oxford are five young people. Hot dogs and fountain drinks could be enjoyed while catching up on the local news of Oxford.

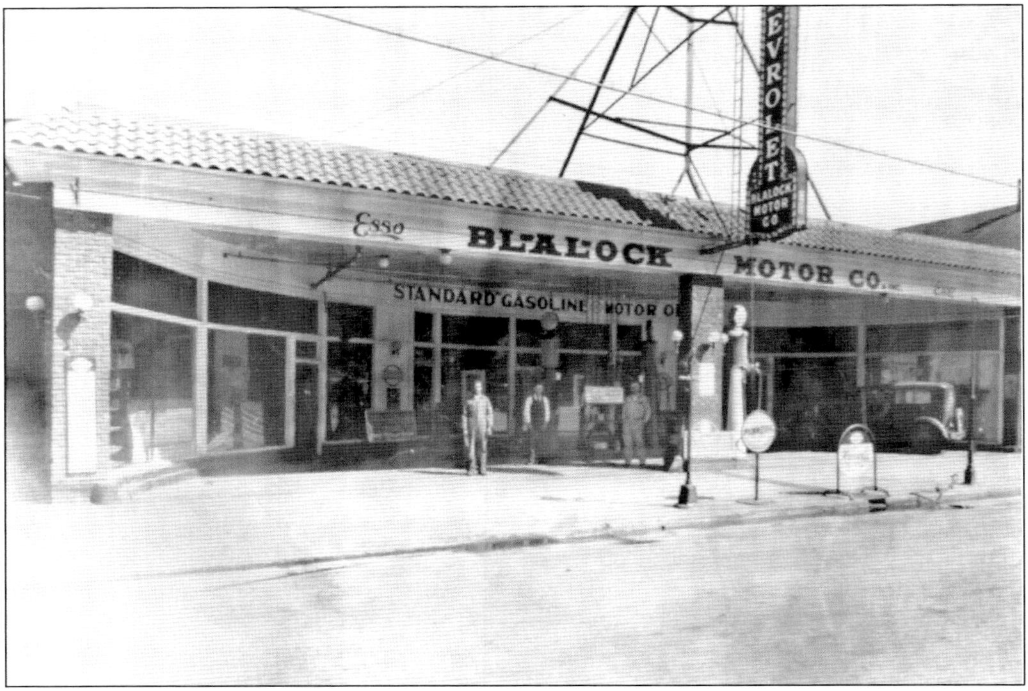

Employees of Blalock Motor Company step outside for a moment in the 1930s. This downtown establishment was located on Hillsboro Street.

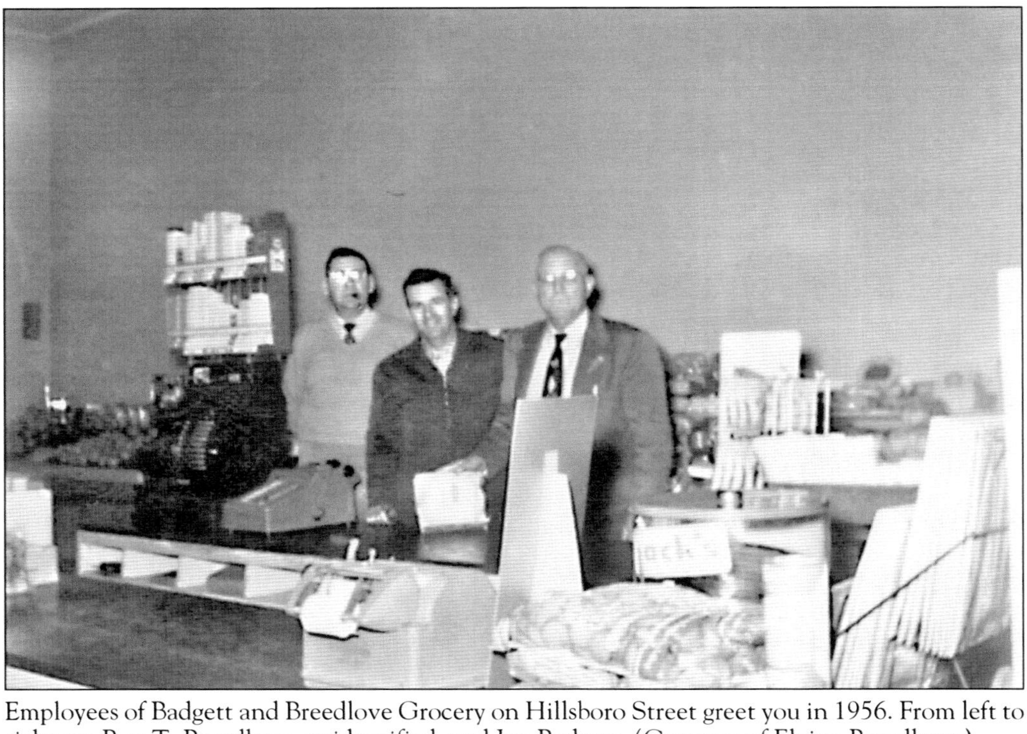

Employees of Badgett and Breedlove Grocery on Hillsboro Street greet you in 1956. From left to right are Roy T. Breedlove, unidentified, and Joe Badgett. (Courtesy of Elaine Breedlove.)

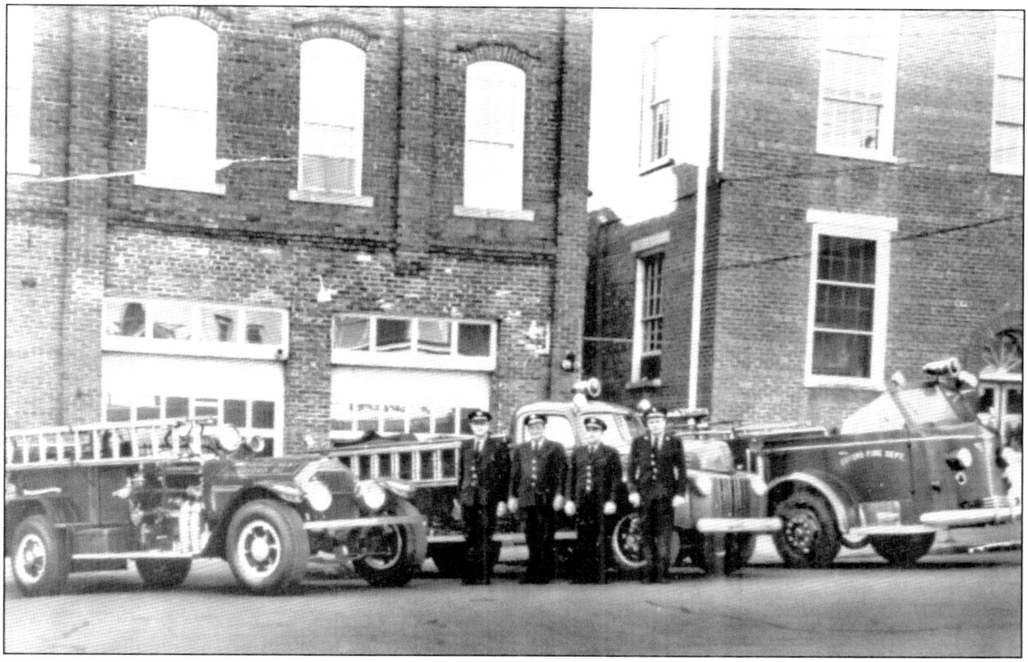

Members of the Oxford Fire Department proudly display their trucks in the 1940s. Included in the picture are Oscar Chappell, Norman Sizemore, Buck Mann, and Allen Cozart.

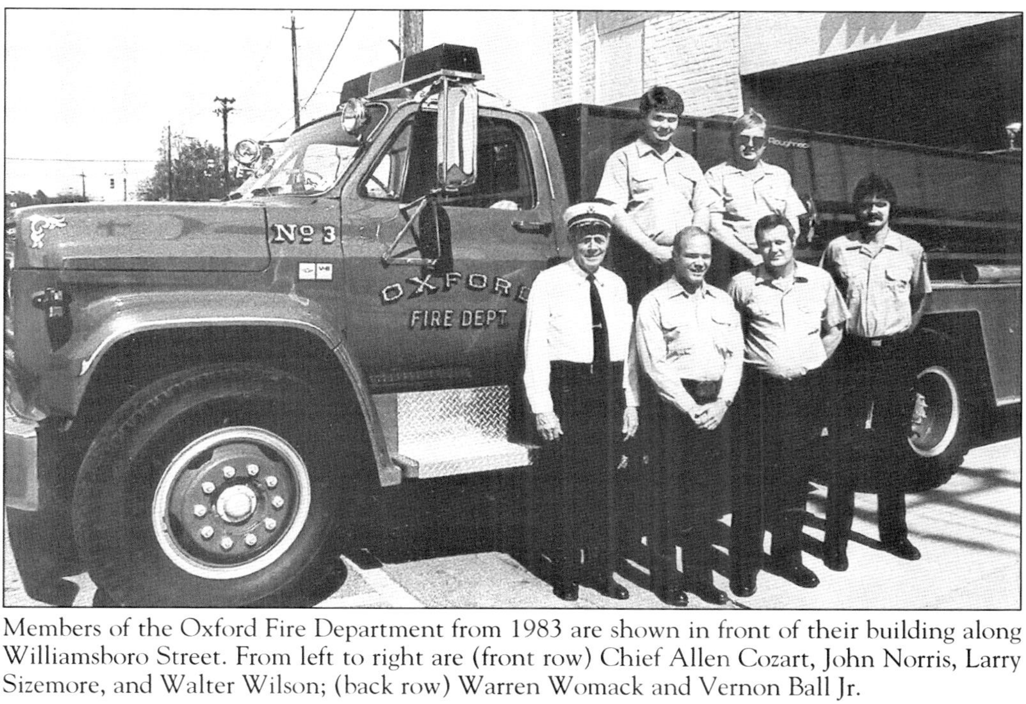

Members of the Oxford Fire Department from 1983 are shown in front of their building along Williamsboro Street. From left to right are (front row) Chief Allen Cozart, John Norris, Larry Sizemore, and Walter Wilson; (back row) Warren Womack and Vernon Ball Jr.

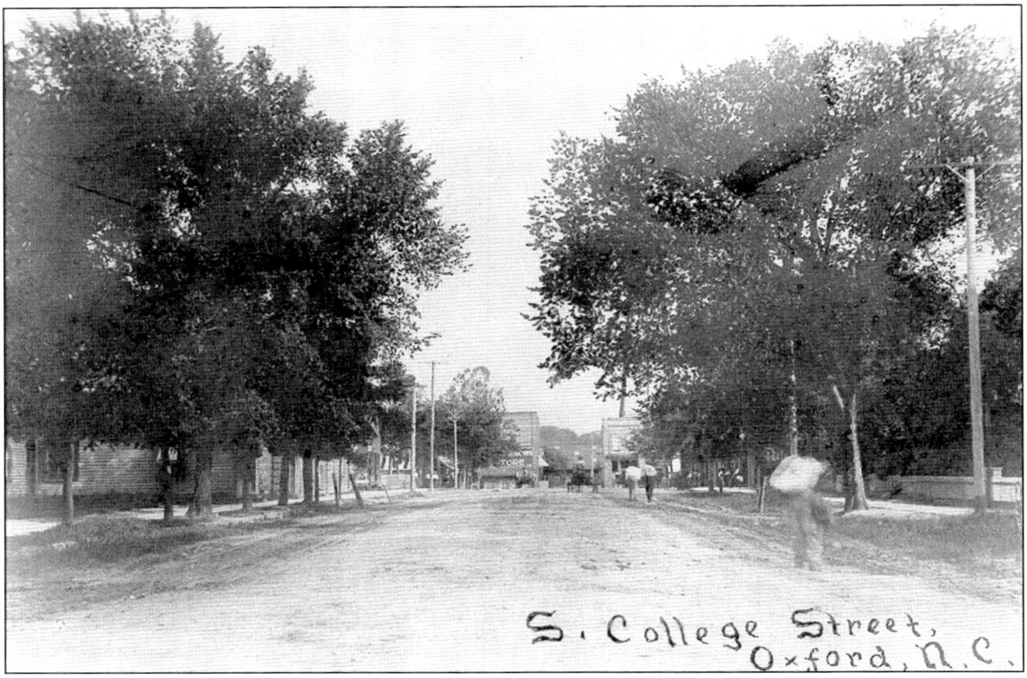

If you were driving down South College Street in Oxford in the very early 1900s, as this view shows, the wide, shaded street beckons you downtown.

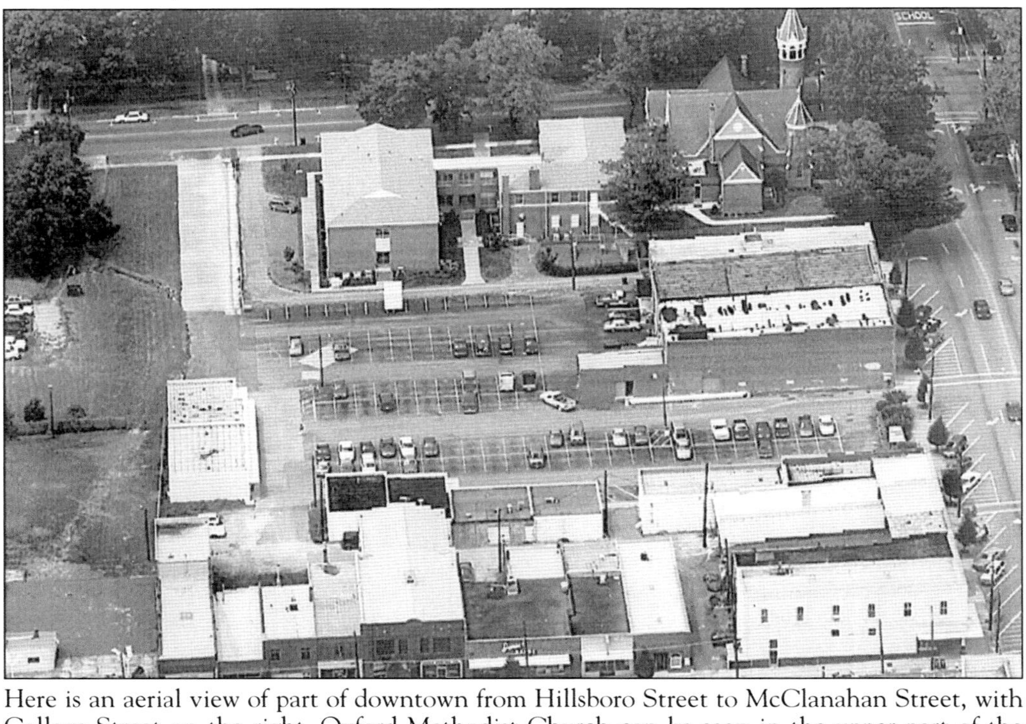

Here is an aerial view of part of downtown from Hillsboro Street to McClanahan Street, with College Street on the right. Oxford Methodist Church can be seen in the upper part of the picture. (Courtesy of Kevin King of Coble Printing Co.)

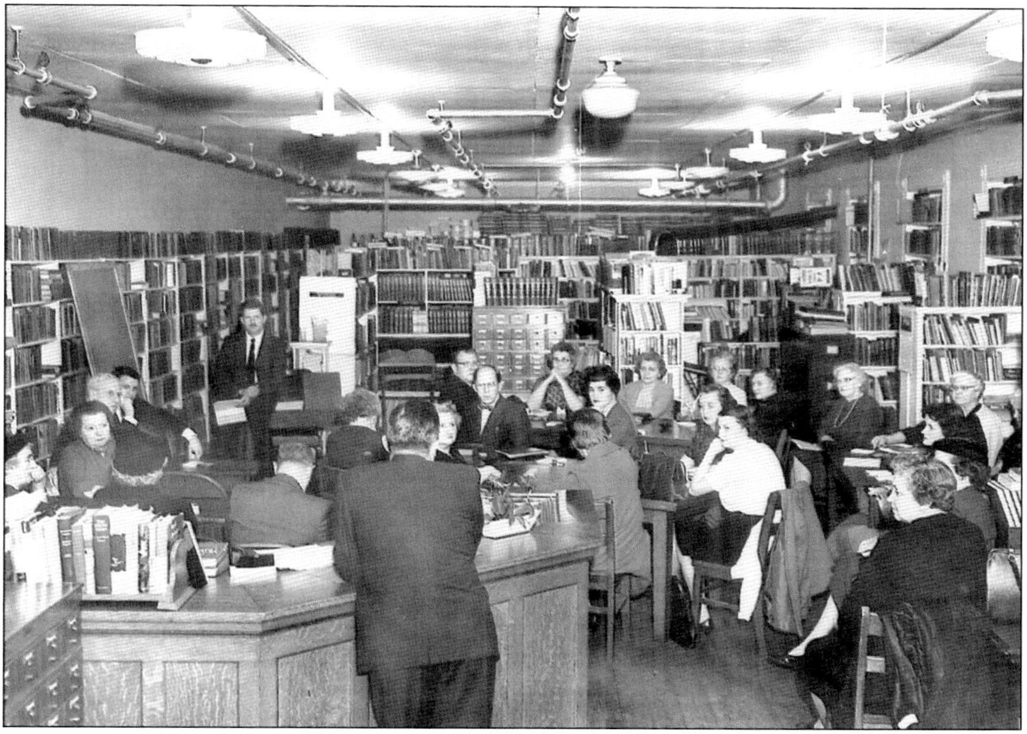

A meeting takes place in the Granville County Library in the 1950s at its location on Williamsboro Street in Oxford. Book clubs and other organizations often gathered here for their meetings. In 1964, the library was moved to Main Street and is now the Richard H. Thornton Library.

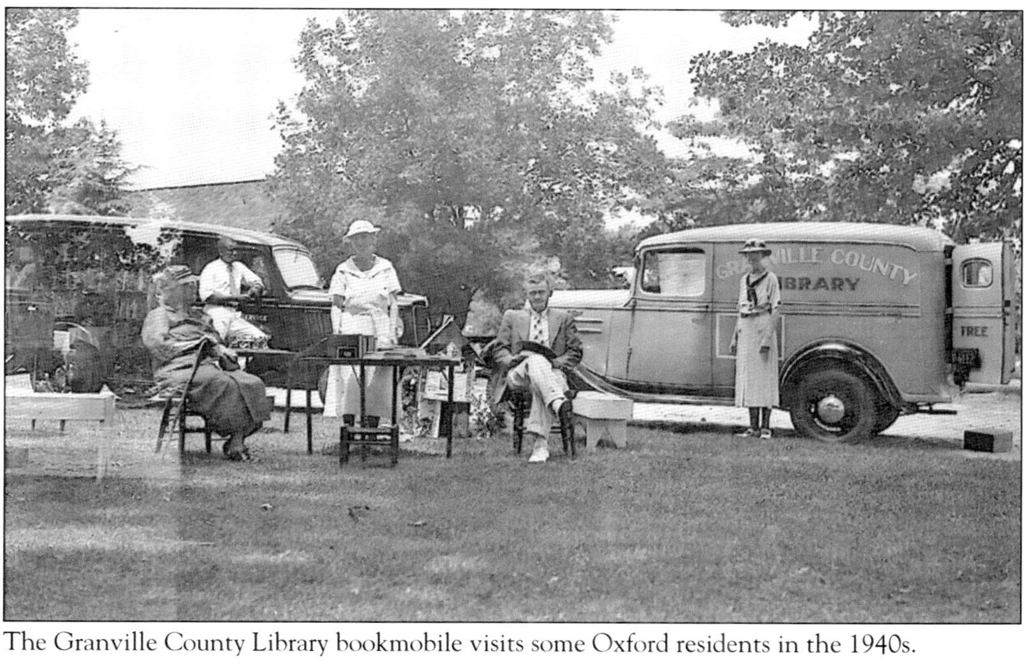

The Granville County Library bookmobile visits some Oxford residents in the 1940s.

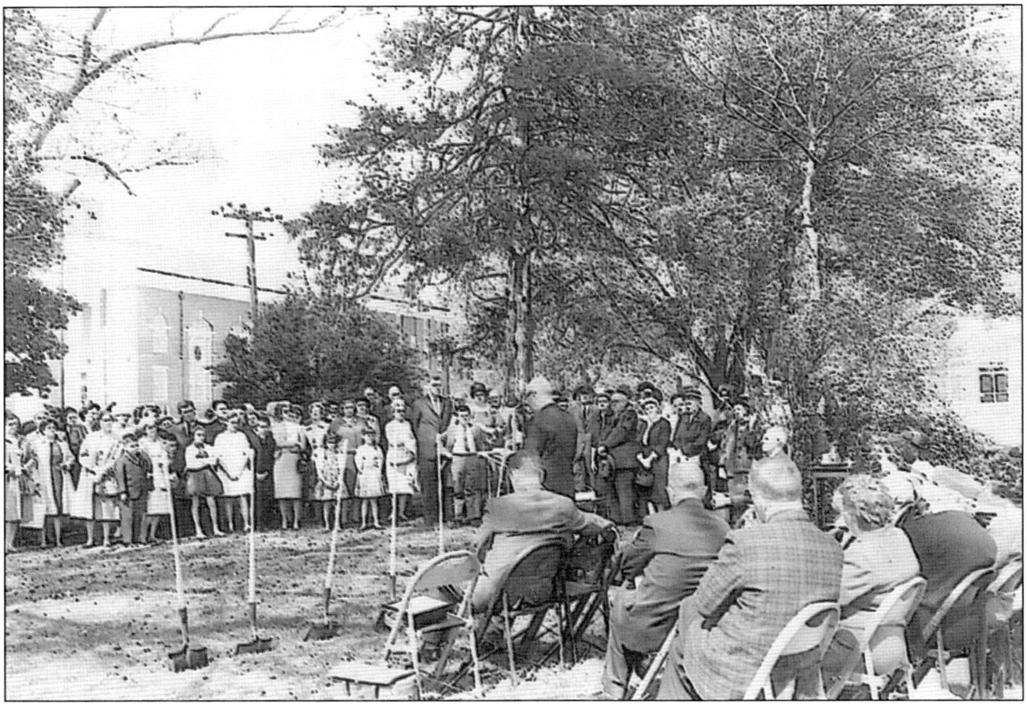

Groundbreaking takes place in 1963 for the Richard H. Thornton Library. Oxford Baptist Church can be seen in the background.

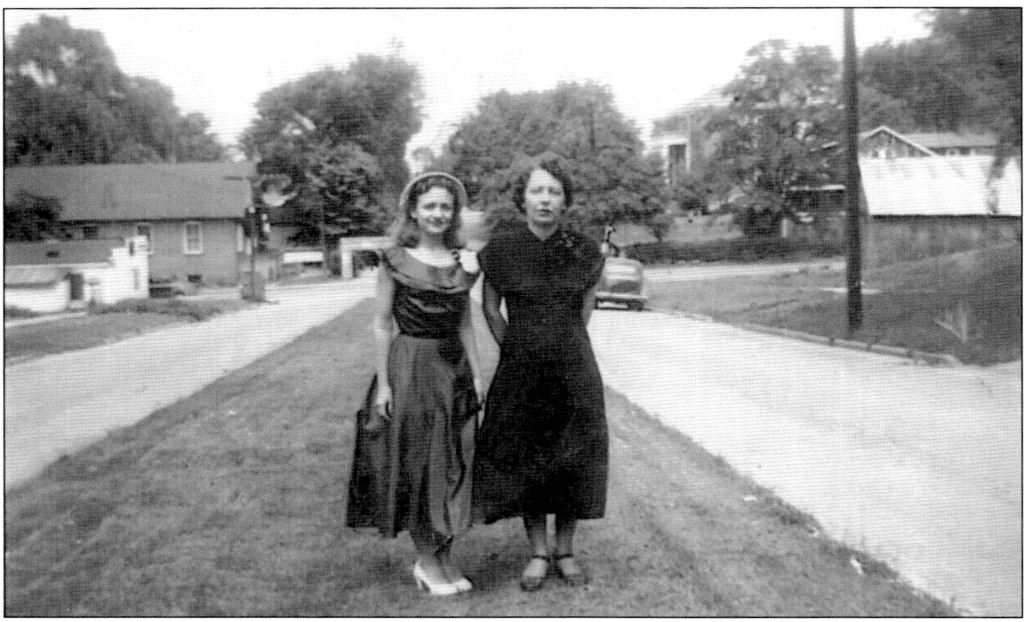

Mary Francis Hart (left) stands with Thelma Faucette on the grass divider of McClanahan Street in the early 1950s. This is between the present location of the Oxford Fire Department and Lowe's Grocery Store. The large building in the upper right corner is part of Mary Potter School. (Courtesy of Betty King.)

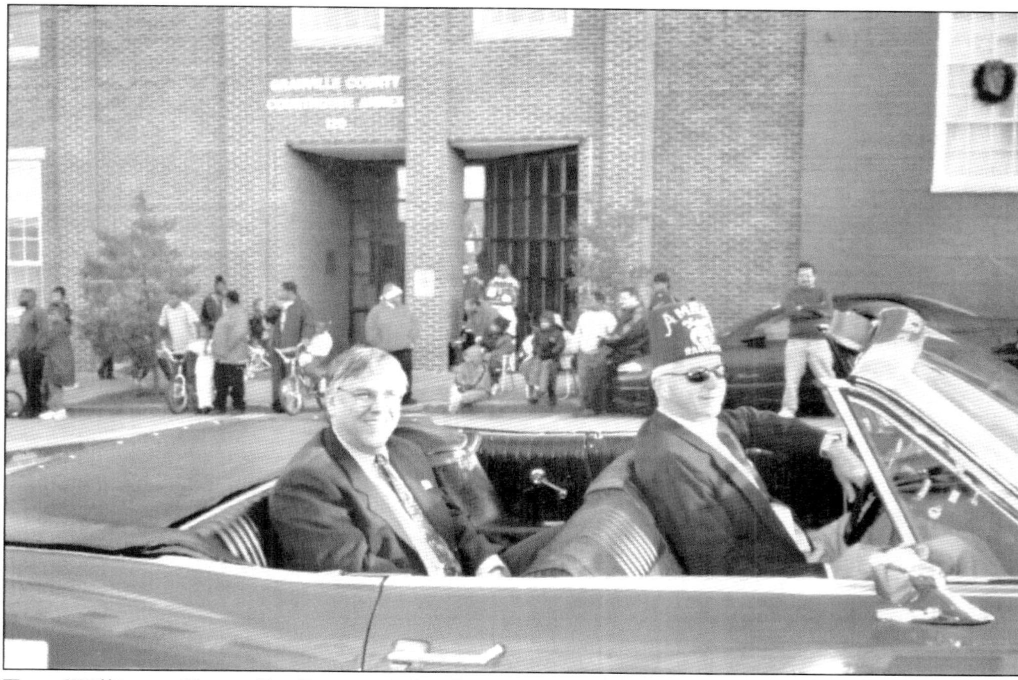

Tom Williams, Granville County Schools superintendent (seated in the back), is part of a Christmas parade in Oxford. The Courthouse Annex is in the background.

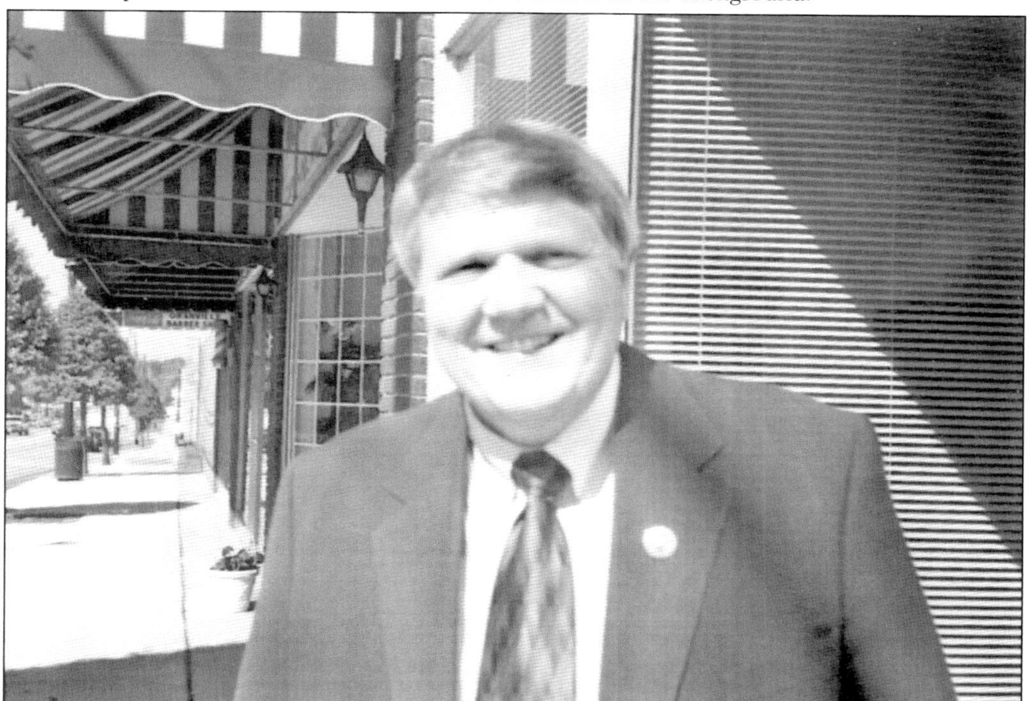

David Smith, Granville County sheriff, meets people downtown. Part of Hillsboro Street can be seen over his right shoulder.

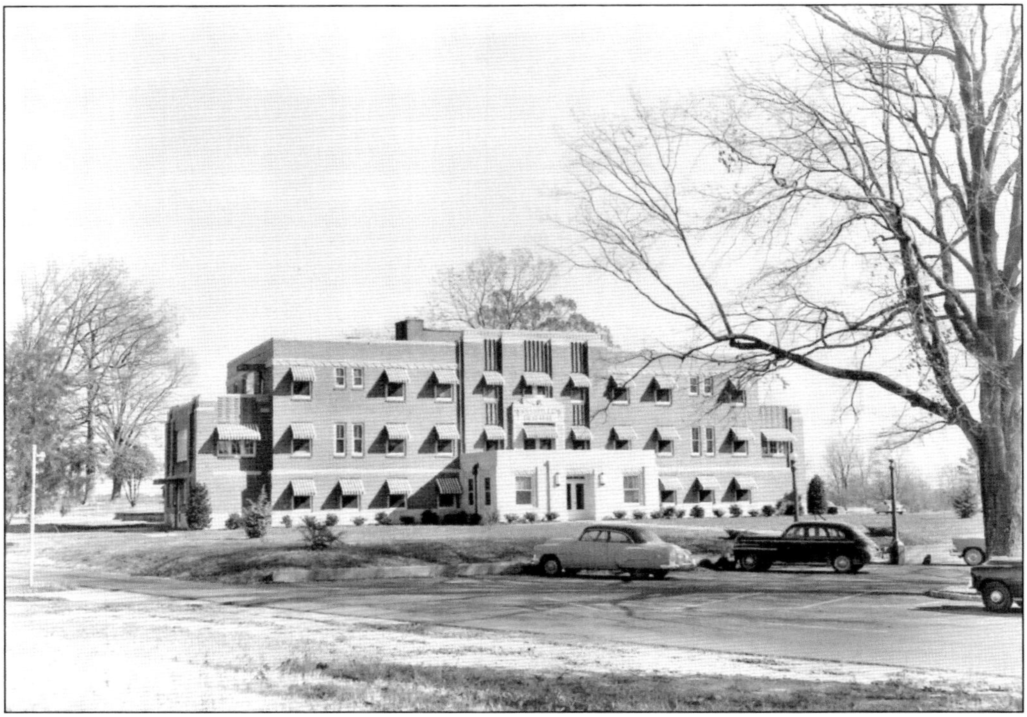

Granville Hospital has been a proud part of Oxford's and the surrounding area's history. This scene is from 1938, shortly after the hospital was constructed.

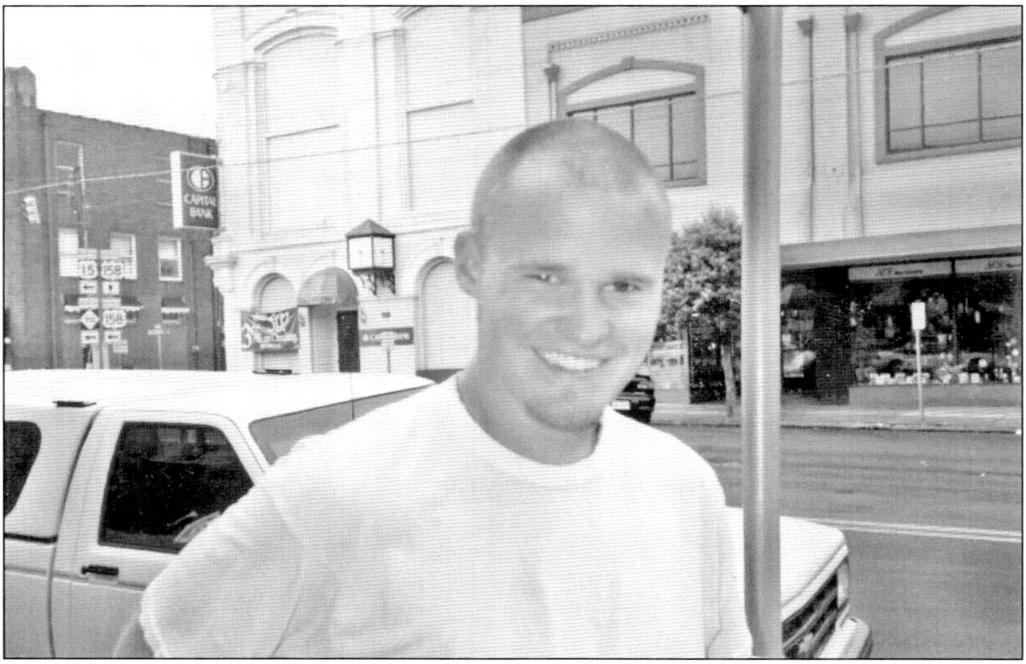

An unidentified young man smiles as he passes through downtown. Capital Bank and Oxford Ace Hardware can be seen also. (Courtesy of Sigma Finch.)

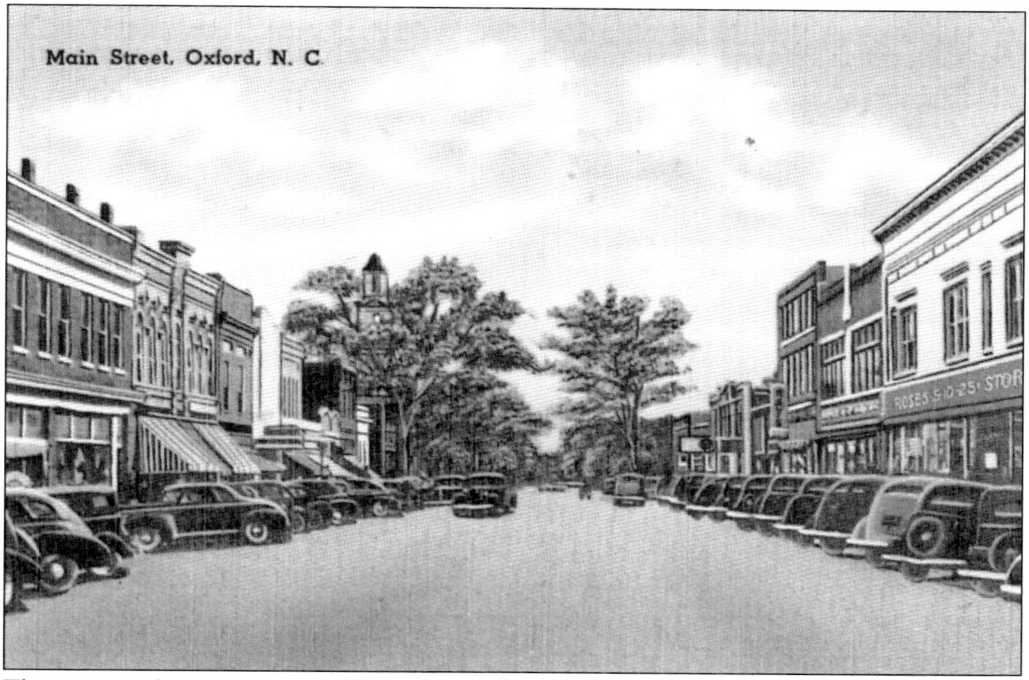

This scene is from a postcard of Main Street from the 1940s. Rose's Store can be seen on the right, while the Carolina Theatre and Hall's Drug Store are on the left. The steeple of Oxford Baptist Church rises in the background.

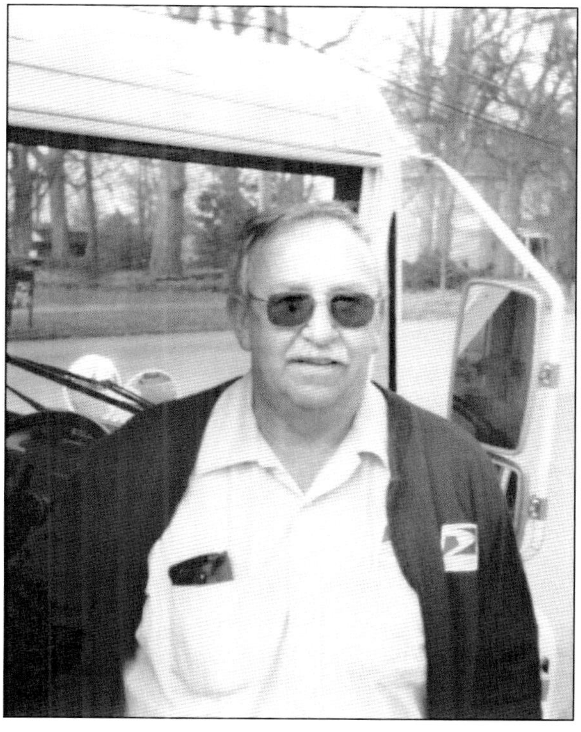

Charles Hight delivers the mail in Oxford. The town's post office is located on Main Street.

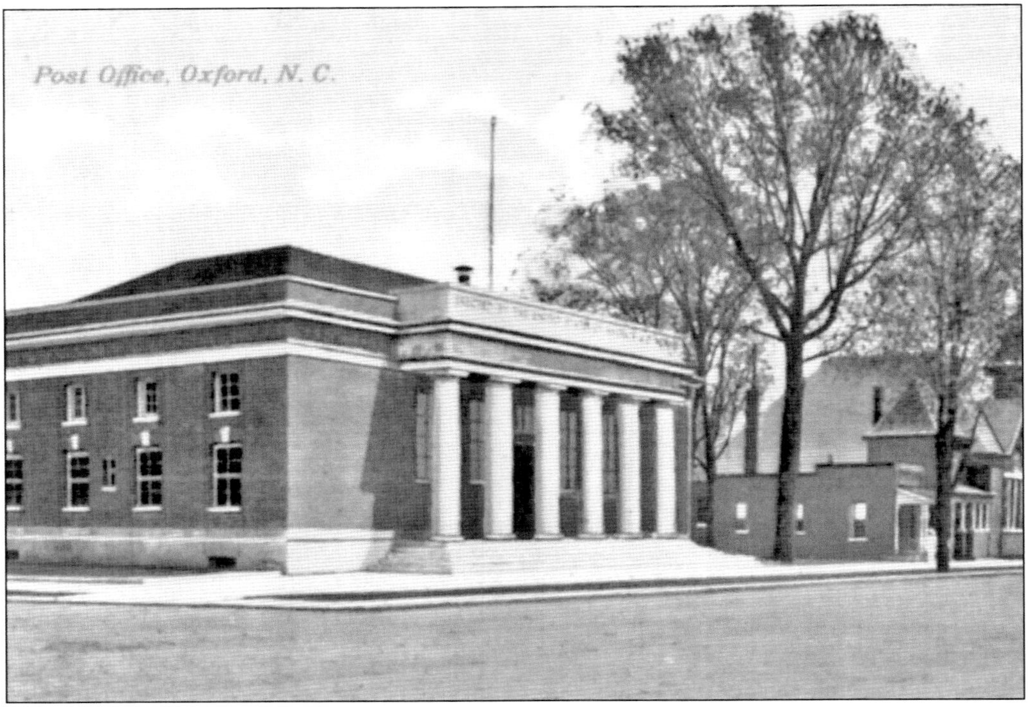

The Oxford Post Office can be seen here in its previous location beside Oxford Baptist Church. It is now on the other side of Main Street.

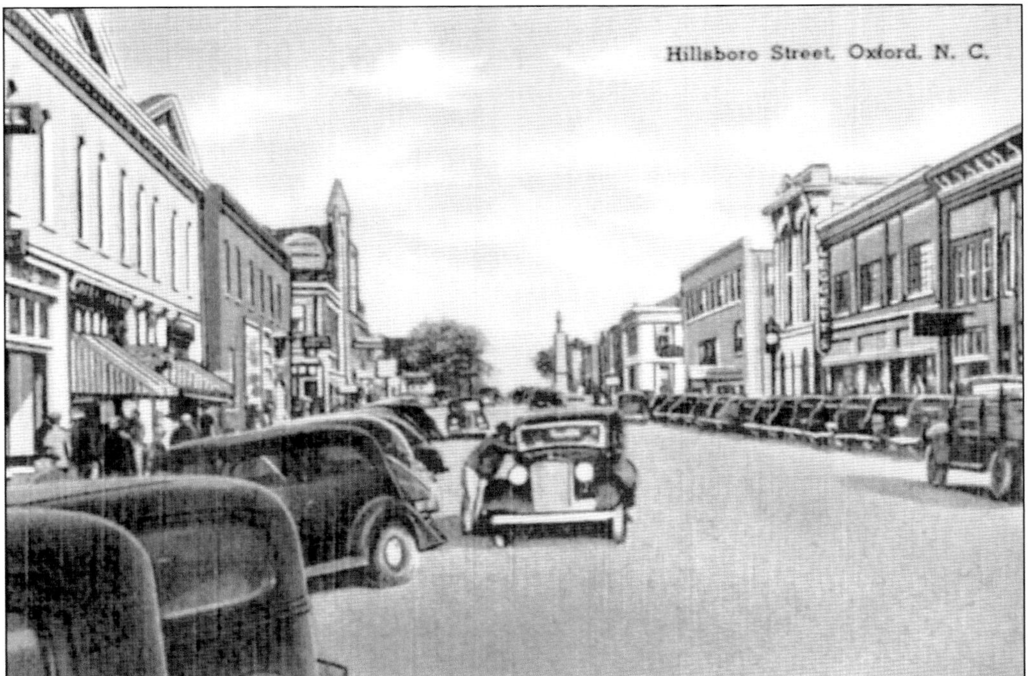

This is a scene from a postcard on Hillsboro Street in Oxford around 1940.

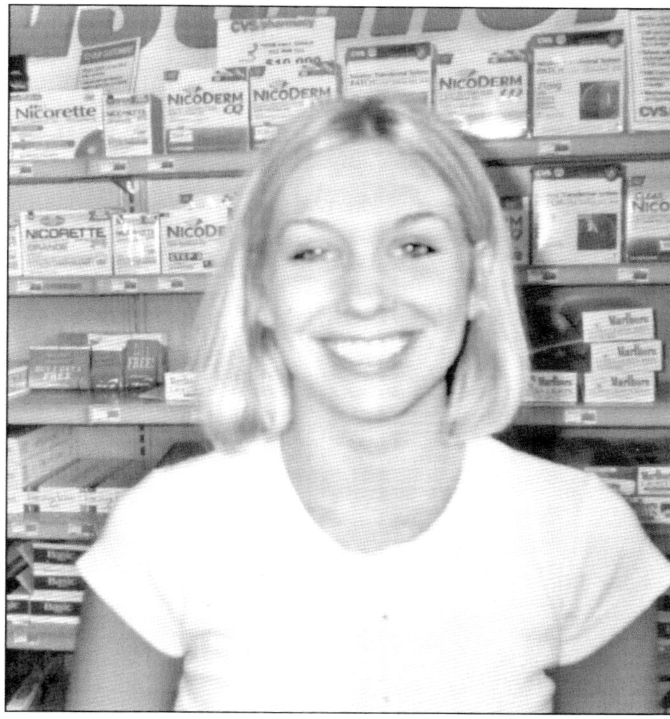

Crystal Roberts is shown greeting customers inside CVS Pharmacy on Williamsboro Street. Her pleasant smile will probably cause them to come again. (Courtesy of Sigma Finch.)

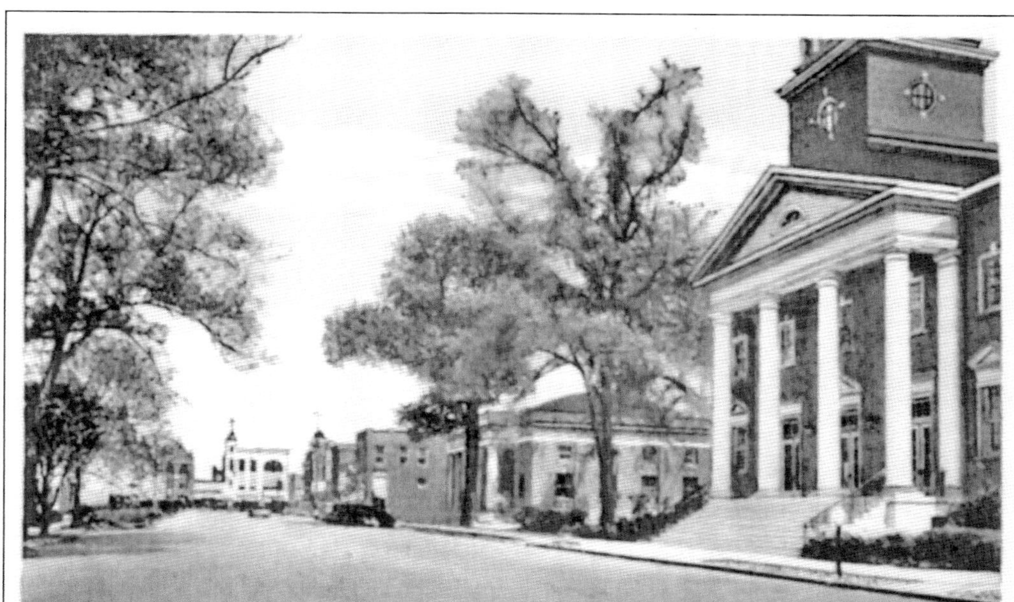

This postcard view looks down Main Street facing north. Oxford Baptist Church, built in 1928, is on the far right.

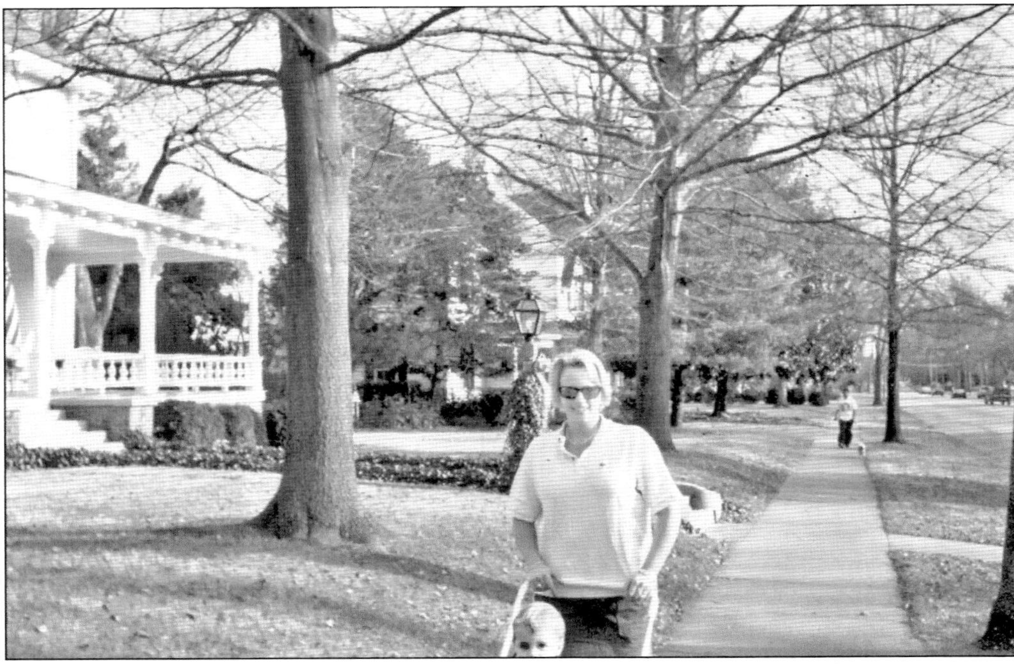

Walking the sidewalks around downtown is a favorite pastime of Oxford residents.

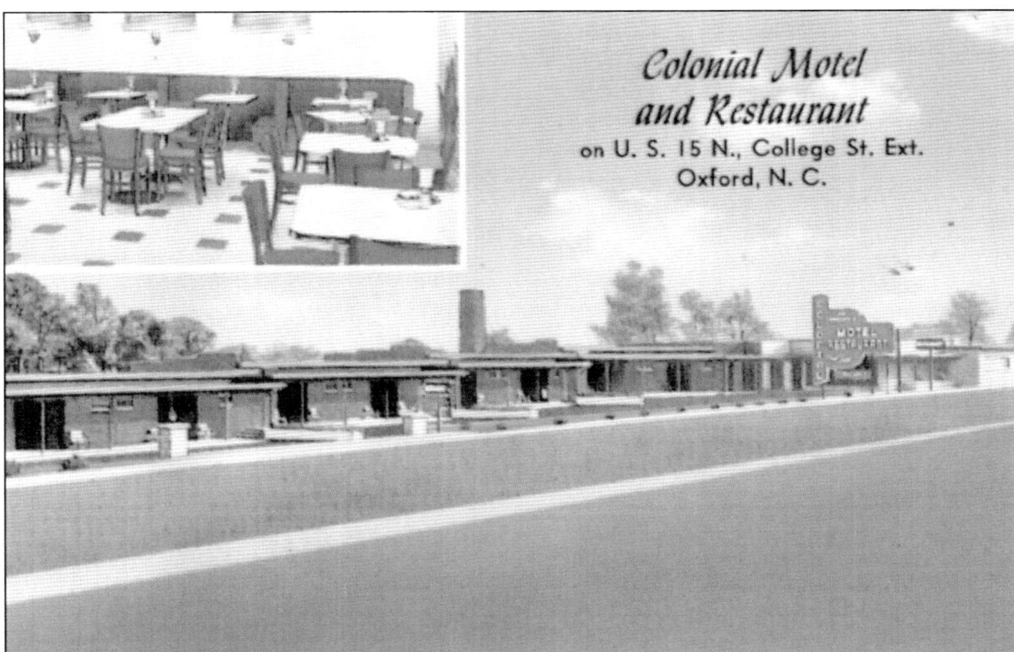

This view looks across College Street at the Colonial Motel and Restaurant in Oxford. A portion of the restaurant's interior can be seen in the upper left corner.

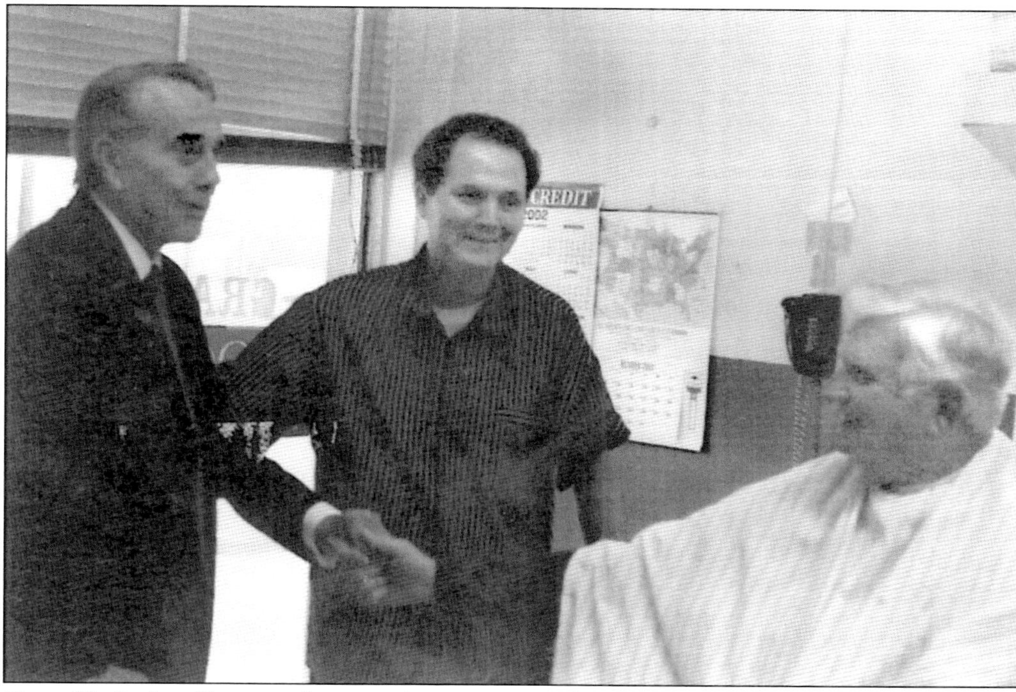

Granville Barber Shop is a favorite place to visit in downtown Oxford. Sen. Bob Dole, on the left, pays Harold Slaughter (center) a visit. Harold, the operator of Granville Barber Shop, cuts hair to a customer's satisfaction. Jerry Whitfield is seated.

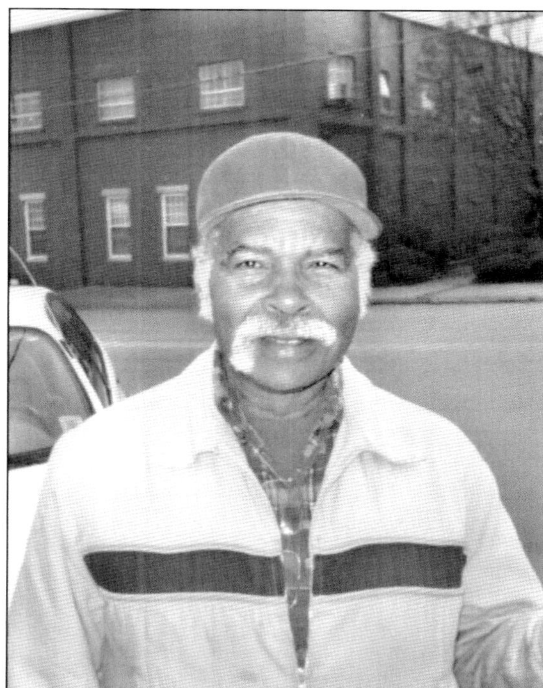

Irvin Hawkins walks along Williamsboro Street in Oxford.

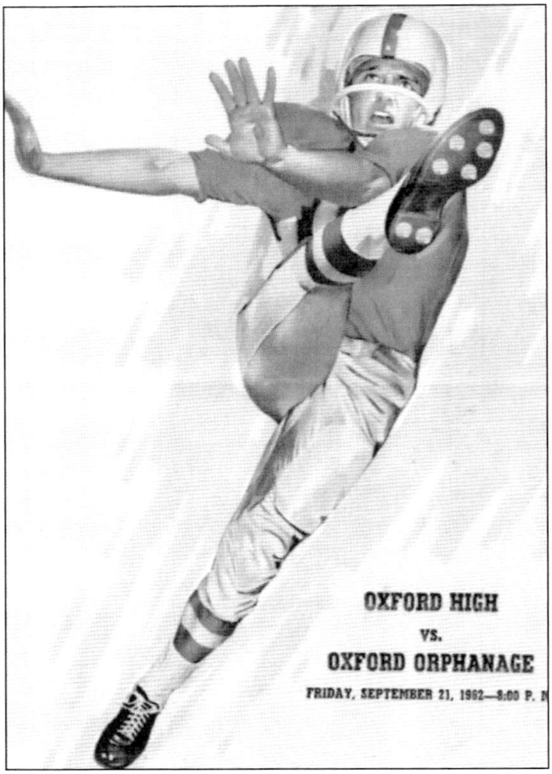

This is from an advertisement in 1962 for a football game between Oxford High School and Oxford Orphanage.

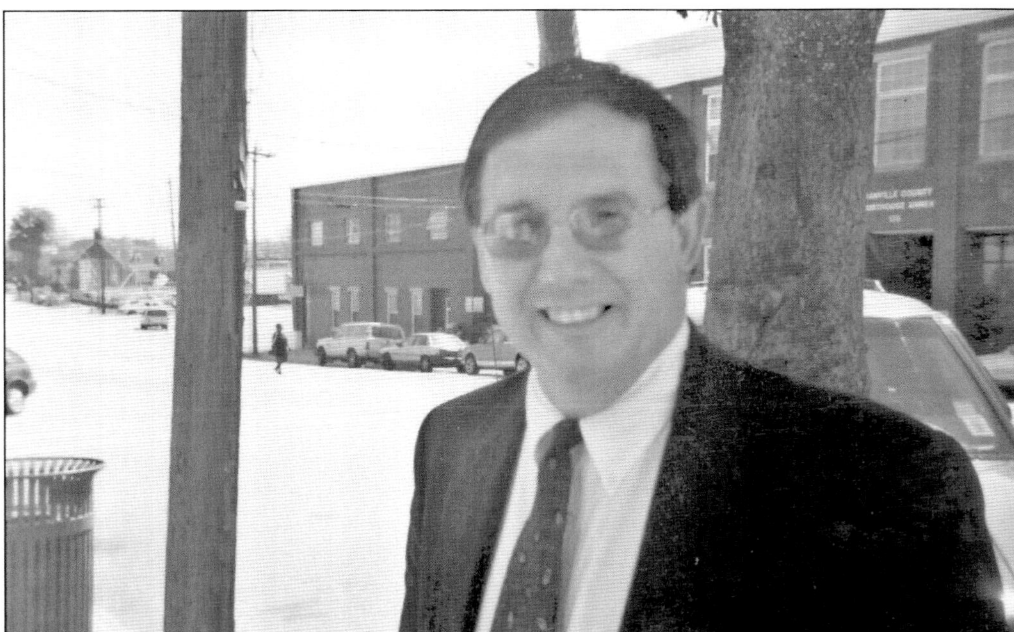

Jim Cross takes time from his law practice to enjoy a snowy day in Oxford. The Granville County Courthouse Annex can be seen over his left shoulder.

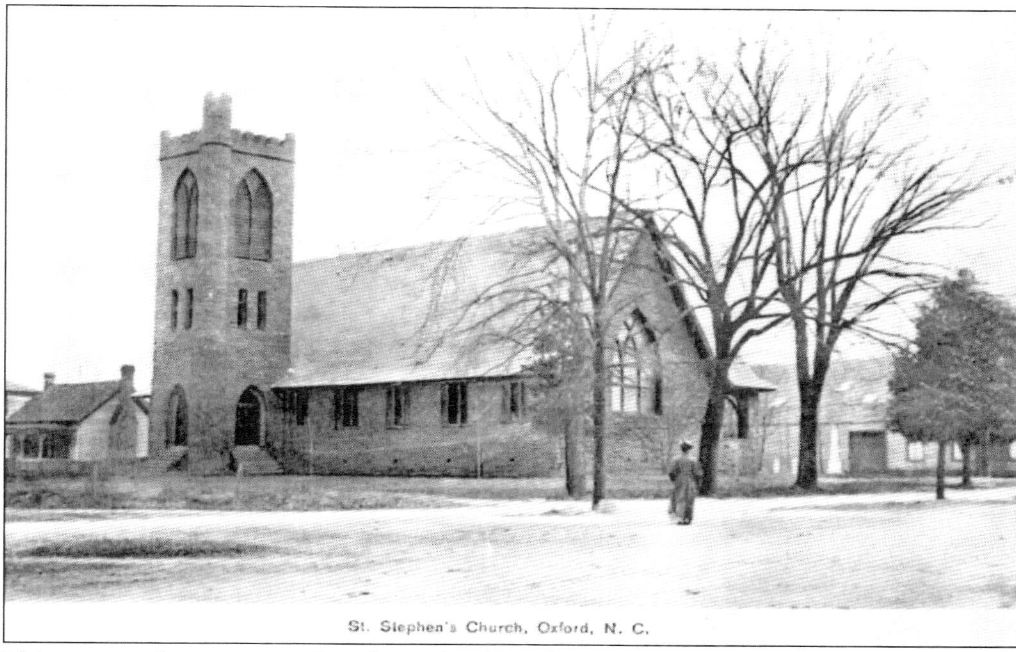

This scene is from a postcard in the early 1900s showing St. Stephen's Episcopal Church on College Street in Oxford.

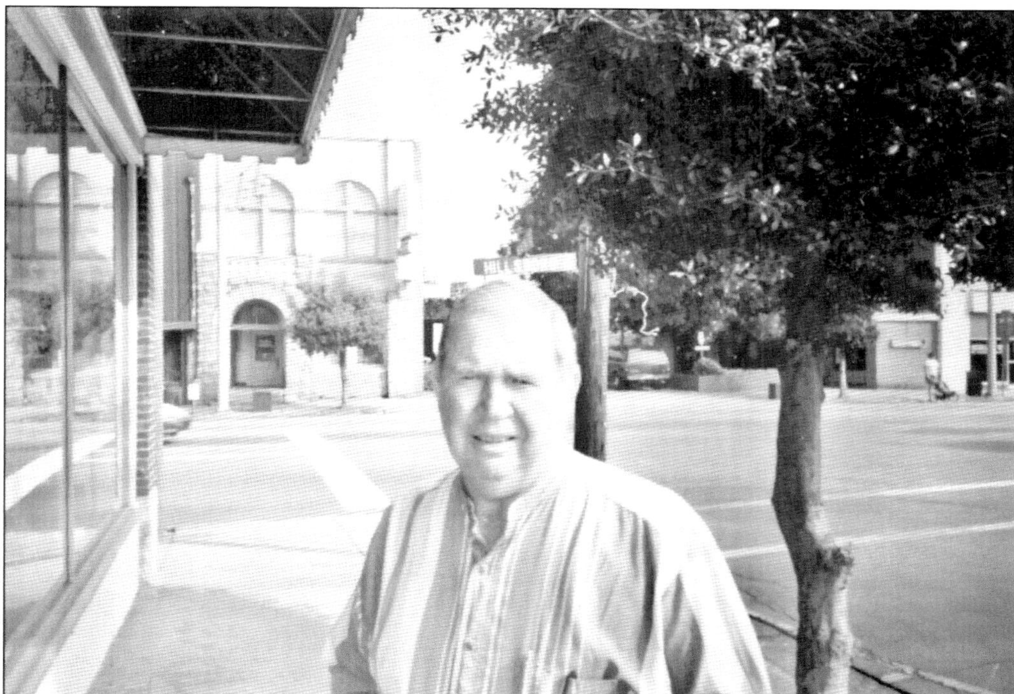
Dan Stovall stands in front of Stovall's Gift Store on the corner of Main Street and Hillsboro Street. The Granville County Chamber of Commerce office can be seen across the street. Stovall's is a popular destination for downtown shoppers in Oxford.

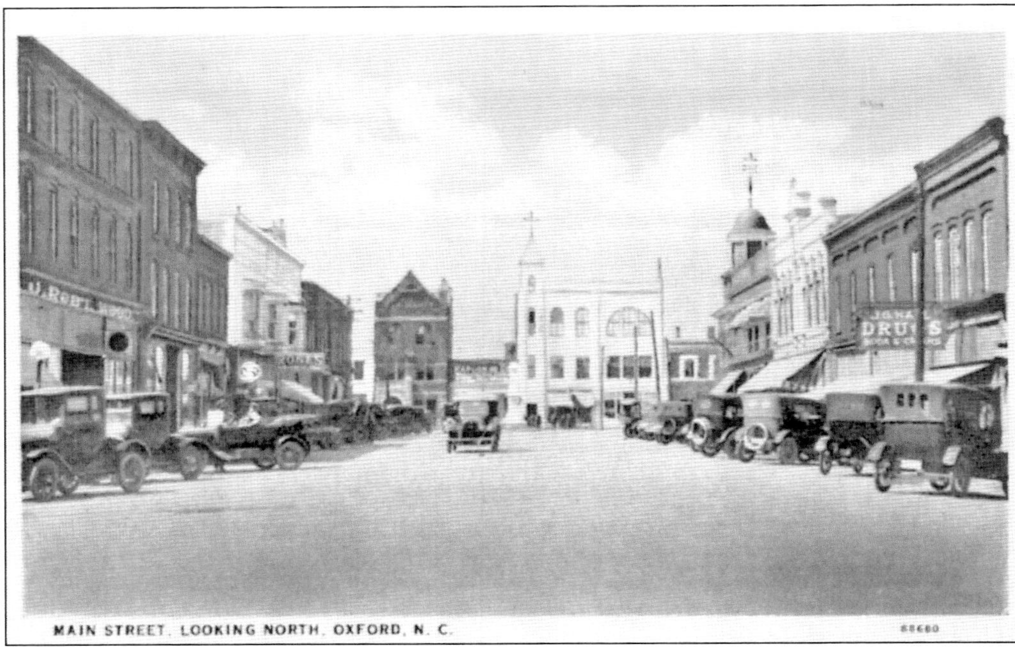

Main Street in Oxford sure looks busy in this postcard picture from the 1910s. J.G. Hall's Drug Store can be seen on the right. Hall's Drug Store opened in 1879 and celebrated its 100th birthday in 1979. Residents of Oxford remember this institution fondly.

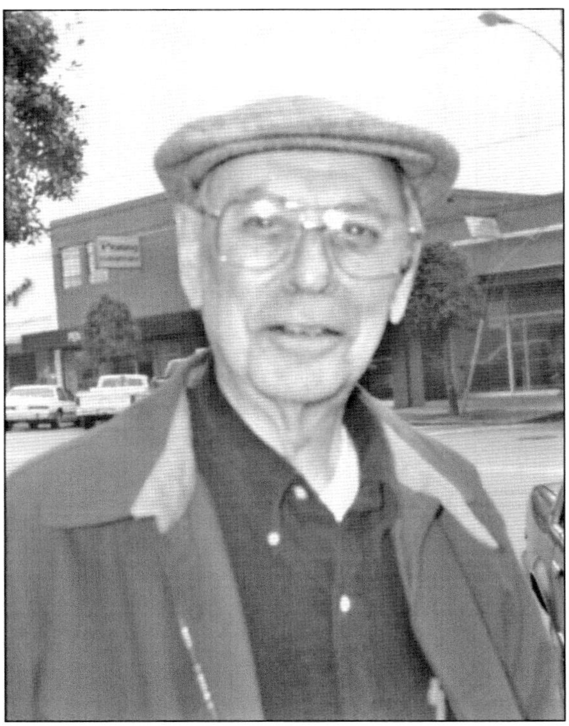
John Mackie walks along Hillsboro Street. Penny Furniture can be seen over Mackie's right shoulder.

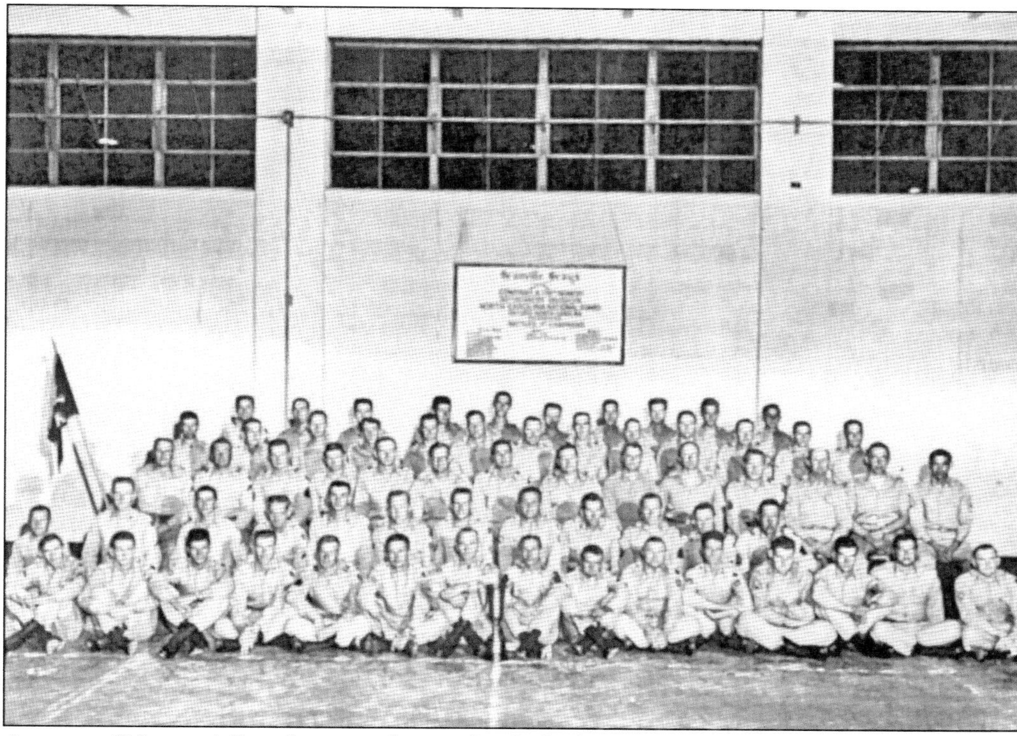

A group of National Guardsmen gather in the Oxford Armory in the 1950s.

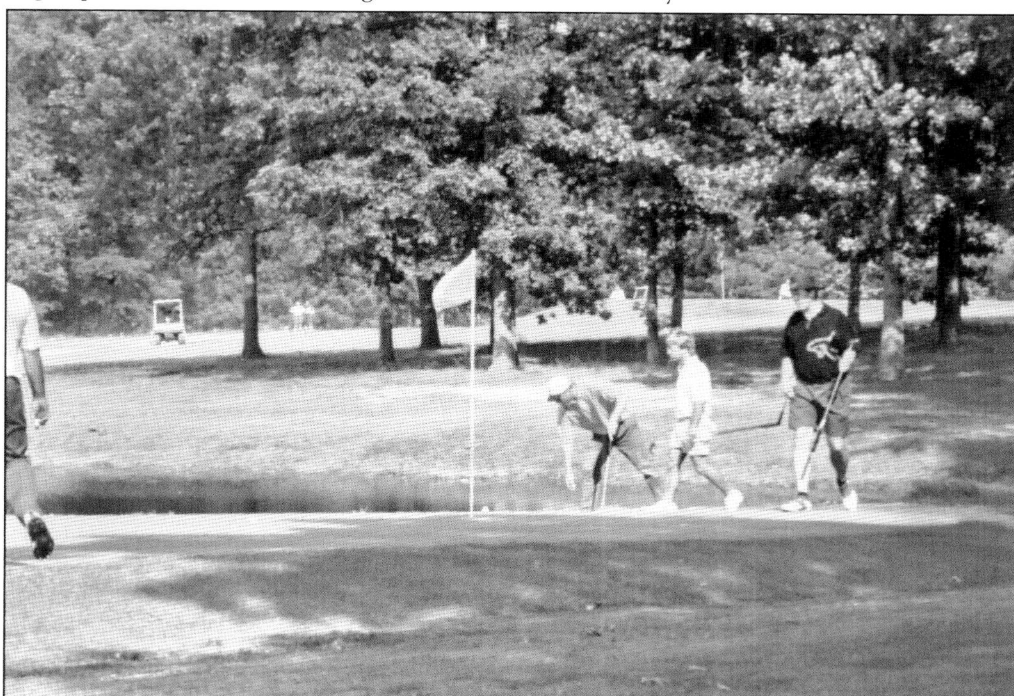

Golfers enjoy an outing at Thorndale Country Club in Oxford.

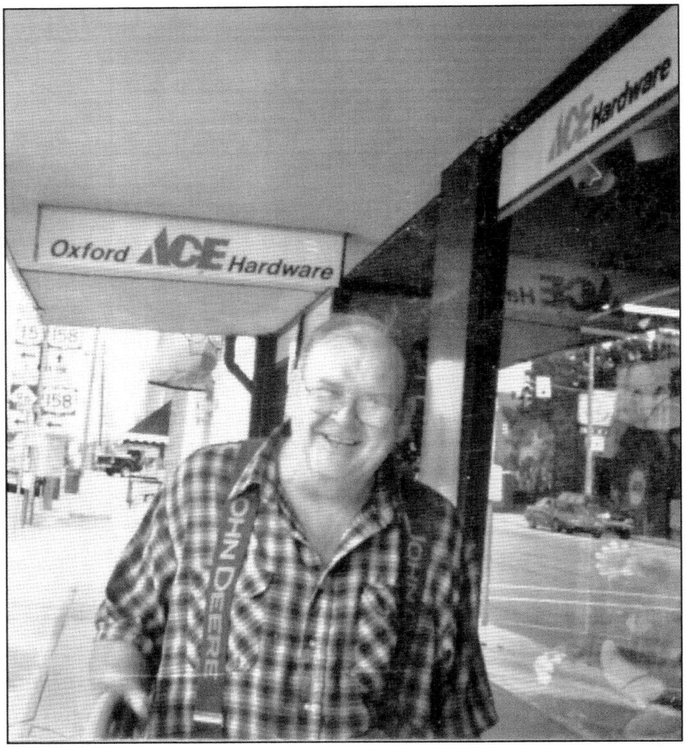

Marvin Dease gives a friendly smile in front of Oxford Ace Hardware.

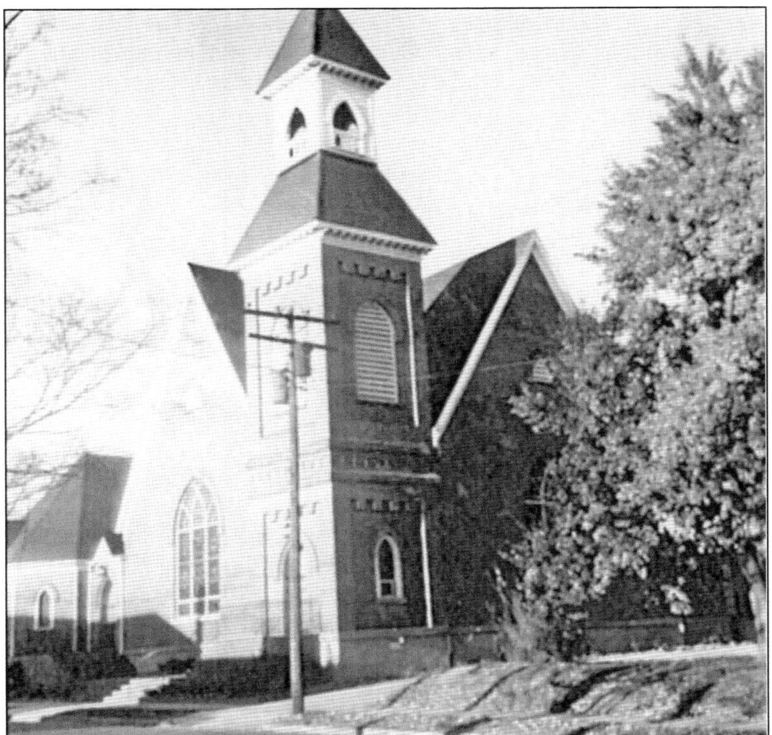

Oxford Presbyterian Church is pictured in November of 1960. Located on Gilliam Street, this church was dedicated in 1892.

Pat and Frank Strickland greet you on the streets of Oxford. The law office of John Pike can be seen in the background.

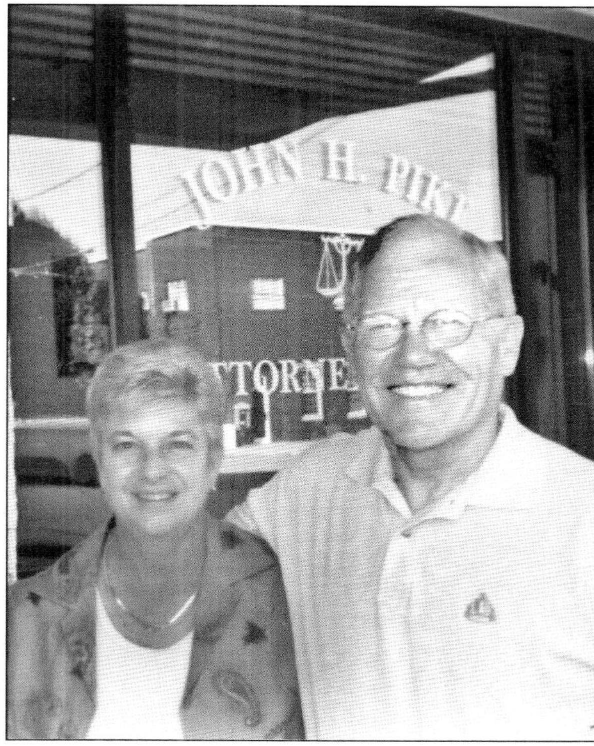

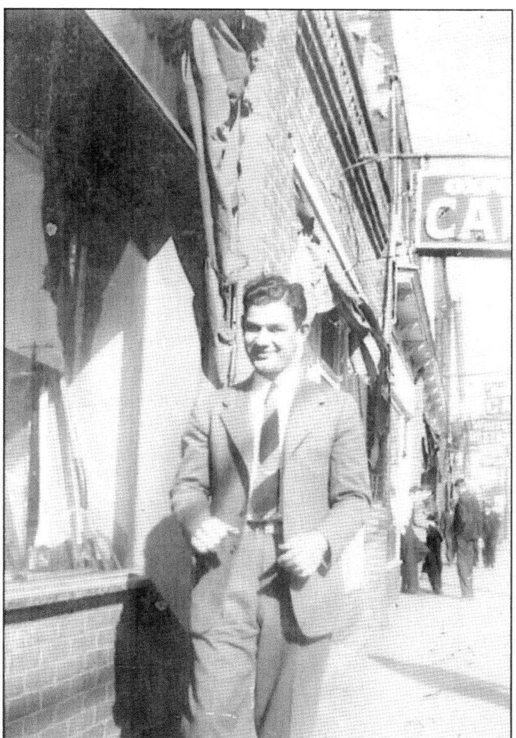

William Oakley walks down Hillsboro Street in the mid-1940s. Oakley is in front of Montague's Hardware. Behind him is the Oxford Cafe, Wilson Cafe, and White Way Restaurant. White Way Restaurant is where Jones Drug Store is now located. (Courtesy of Betty King.)

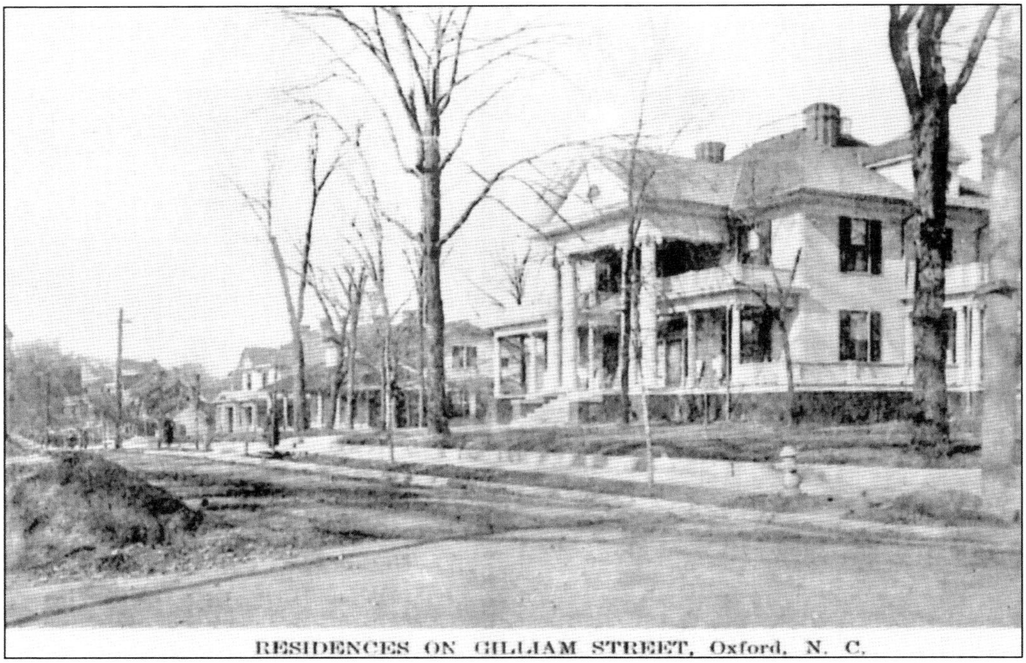

Residences on Gilliam Street in Oxford are shown on this postcard from the very early 1900s.

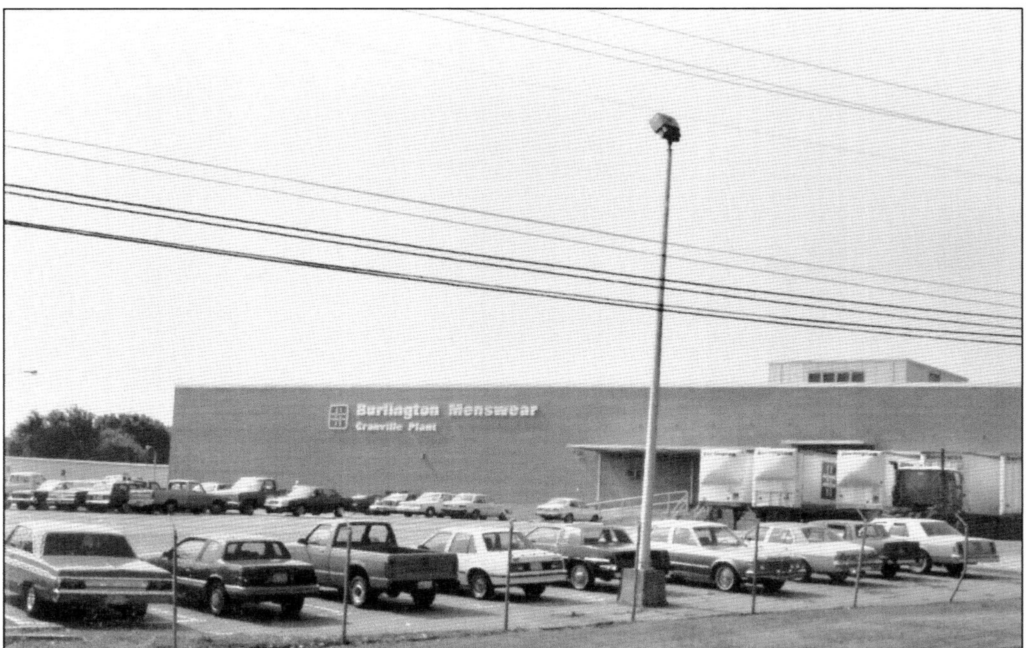

Manufacturing, such as Burlington Menswear, has played a large role in the economic development of Oxford.

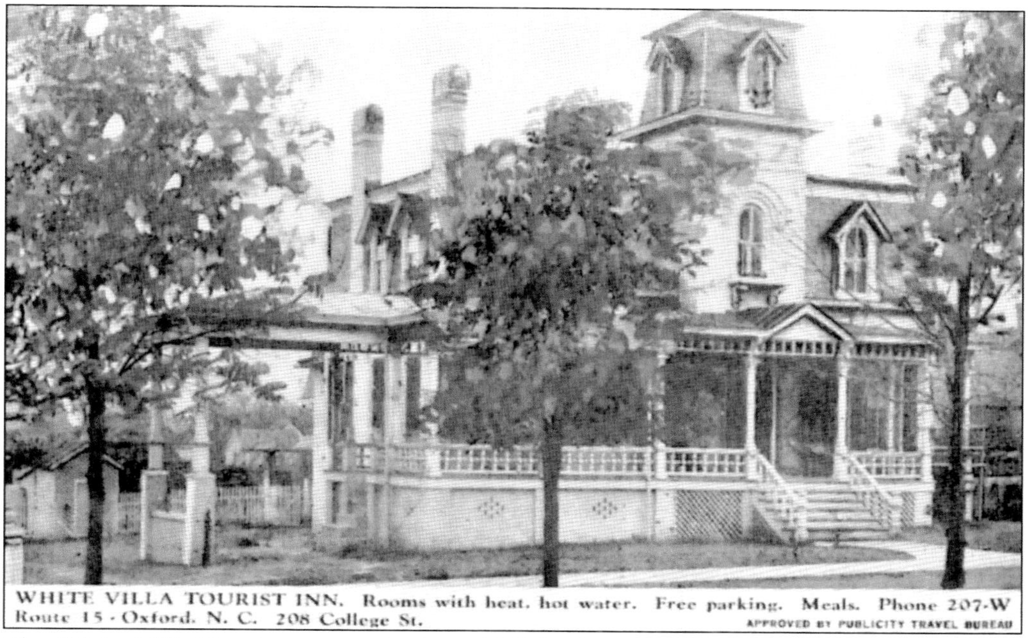

The White Villa Tourist Inn was built in 1889 by George Hundley on College Street. The phone number is listed as 207-W.

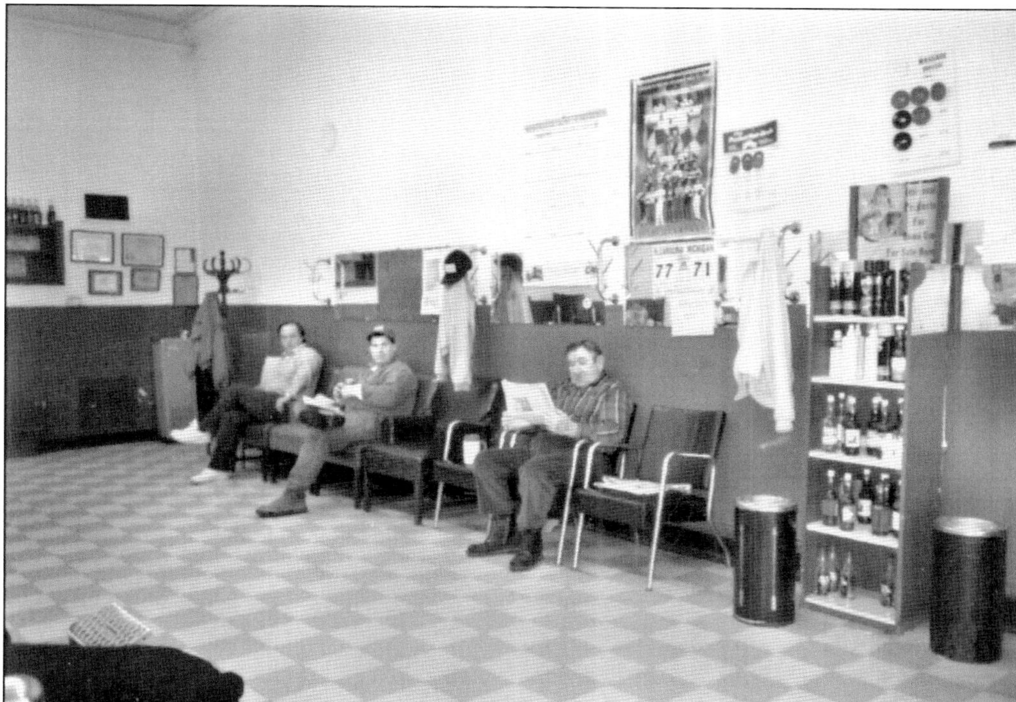

Patrons in Granville Barber Shop await their turn by enjoying each other's company and reading the newspaper.

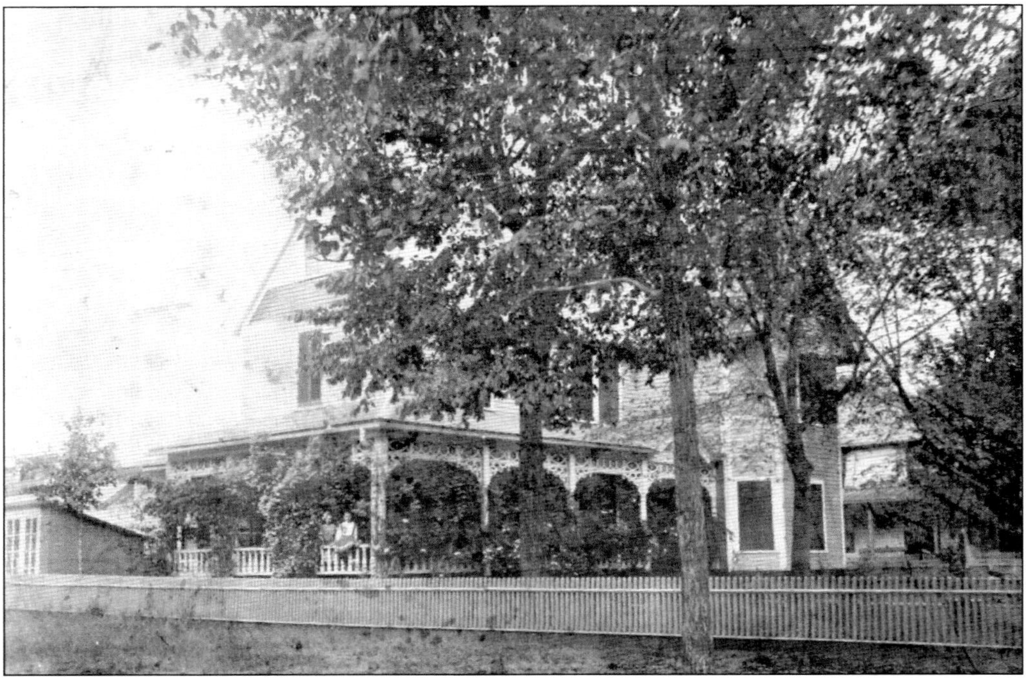

This large house once stood next to C.G. Credle School on College Street. (Courtesy of Carolyn Moss.)

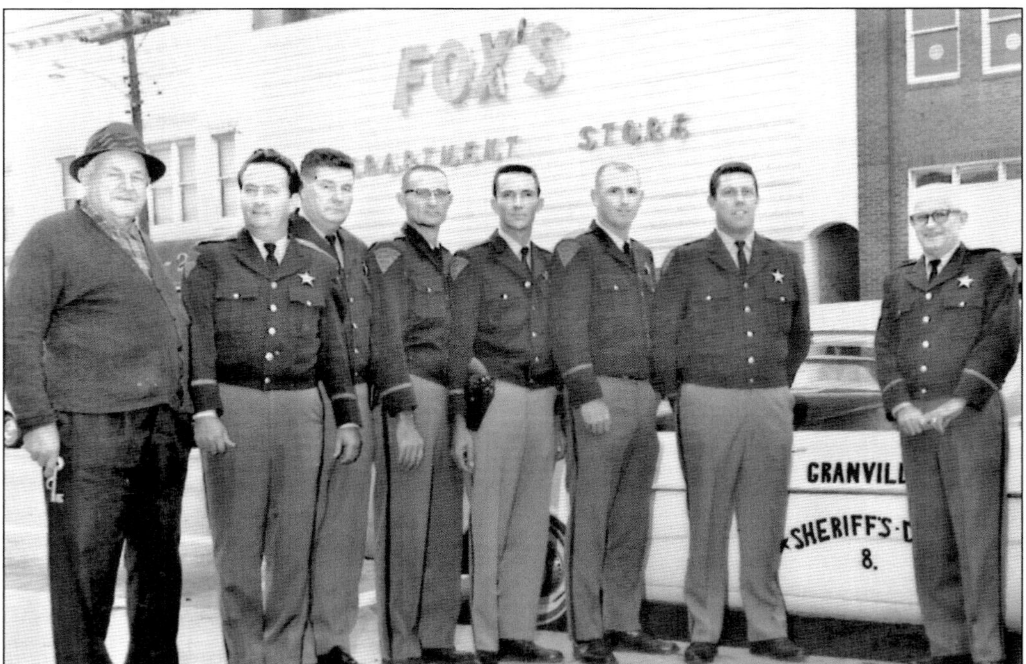

The Granville County Sheriff's Department stands in front of Fox's Department Store in 1968. From left to right are Joe Pruitt, George Currin, Jim Matthews, H.T. Brame, Jack Parrish, Donald Campbell, Bunny Thompson, and Sheriff J.C. Cash. (Courtesy of Brin Wilkins.)

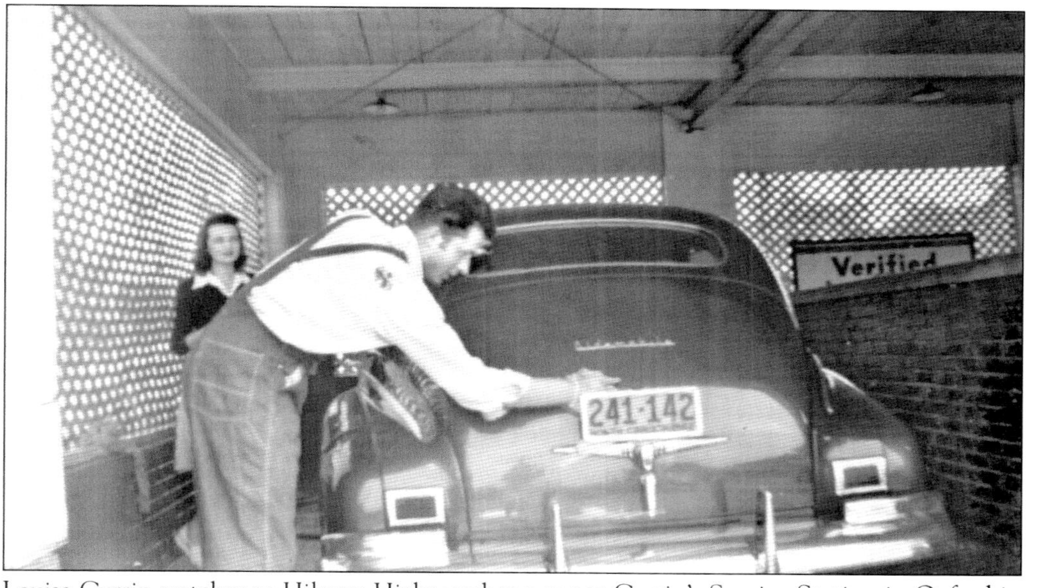

Louise Currin watches as Hilman Hicks washes a car at Currin's Service Station in Oxford in the 1940s. (Courtesy of Mildred Harris.)

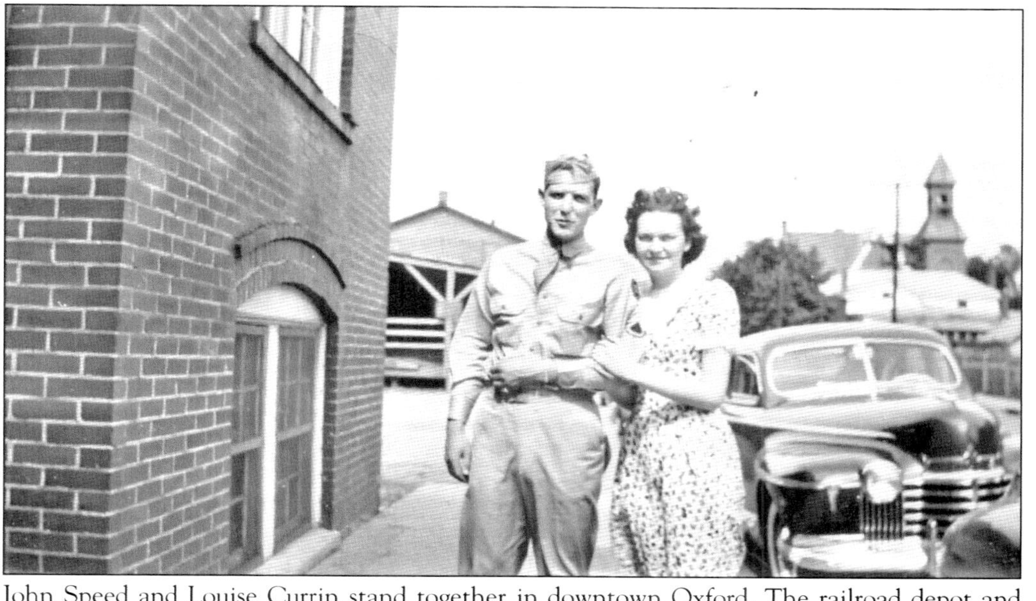
John Speed and Louise Currin stand together in downtown Oxford. The railroad depot and Oxford Presbyterian Church can be seen in the background of this 1940s photo. (Courtesy of Mildred Harris.)

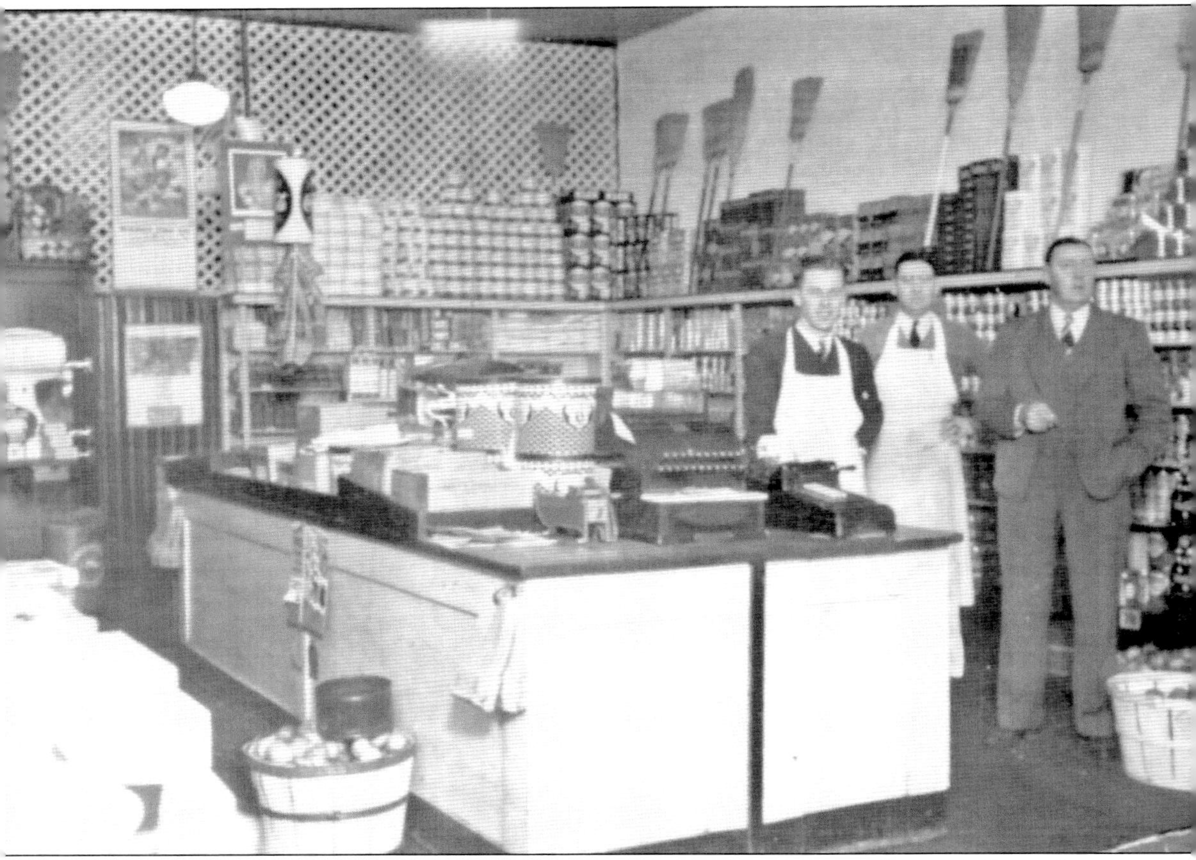

Let's go inside Ideal Fruit and Grocery Store, which was located on College Street. From left to right are Elbert Parrott, Roy Breedlove, and Lonnie Breedlove. (Courtesy of Woody Breedlove.)

Two

People of Oxford

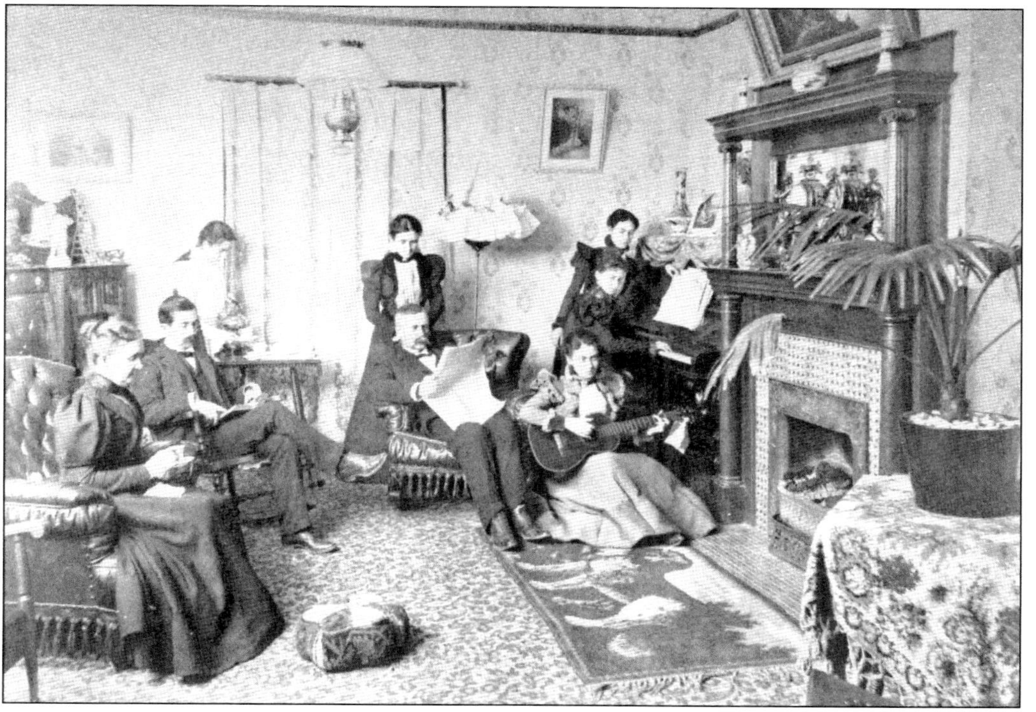

This is a view inside the Currin house on High Street in 1902. Matt Currin reads a newspaper while his family enjoys a relaxing evening by a warm fire. Also in the picture are Cornelia, William, Nelle, Margaret, Leonie, Eva, and Mary Currin. (Courtesy of Jim and Cindy Boring.)

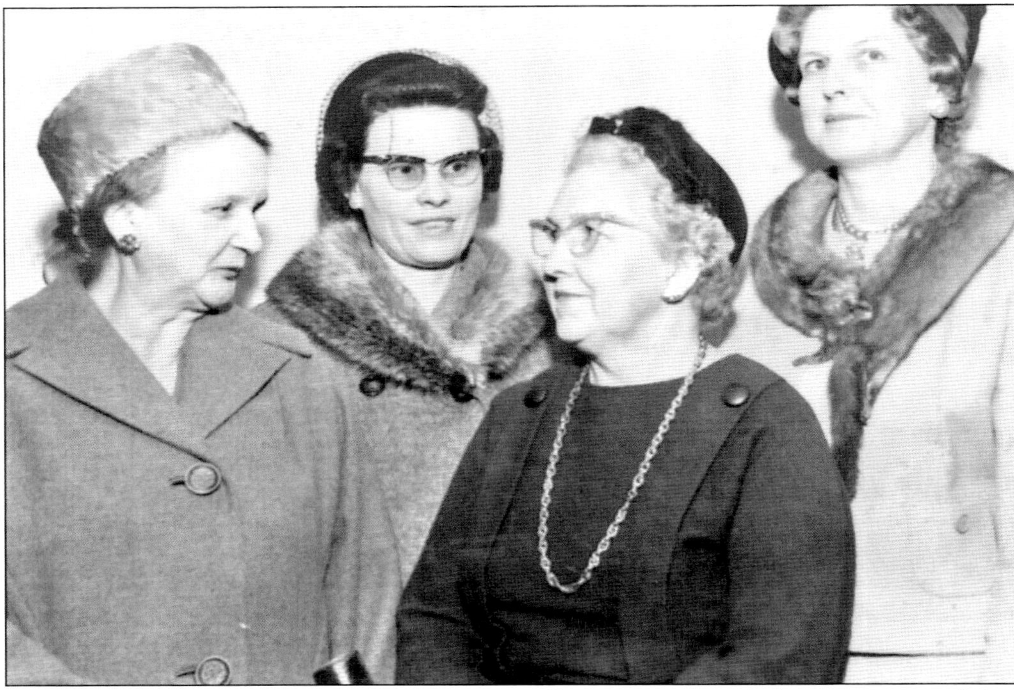

A group of Granville County Home Extension officers meet in Oxford in 1963. From left to right are Mrs. Josephine Burell, Mrs. Frances Floyd, Mrs. Foy Norwood, and Mrs. Edythe Day. (Courtesy of Edythe Day.)

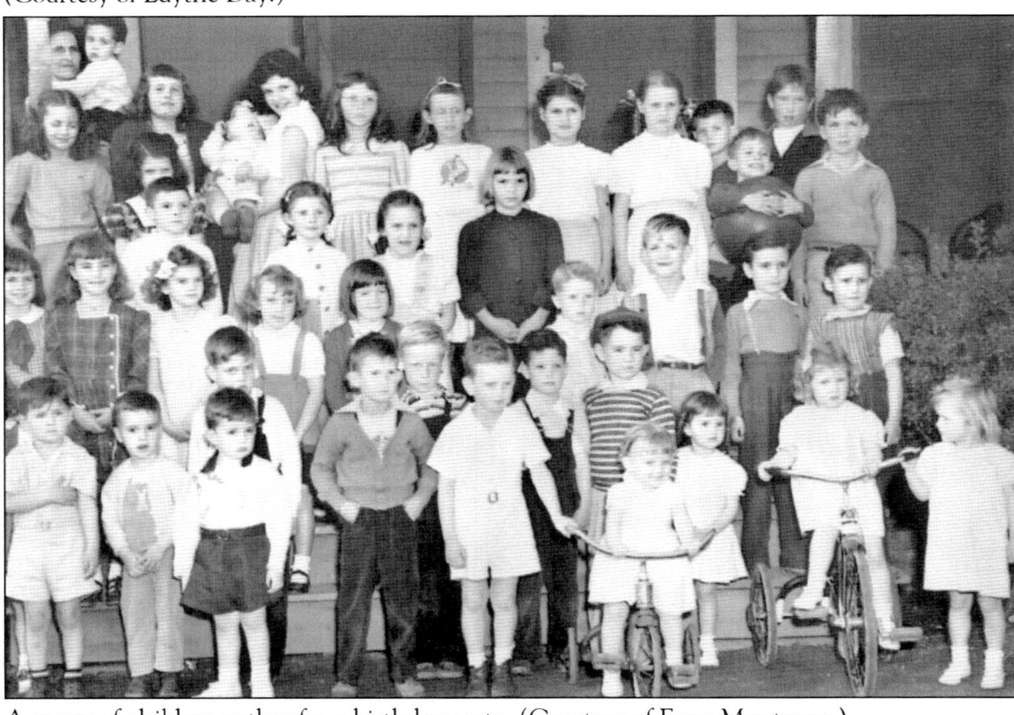

A group of children gather for a birthday party. (Courtesy of Fann Montague.)

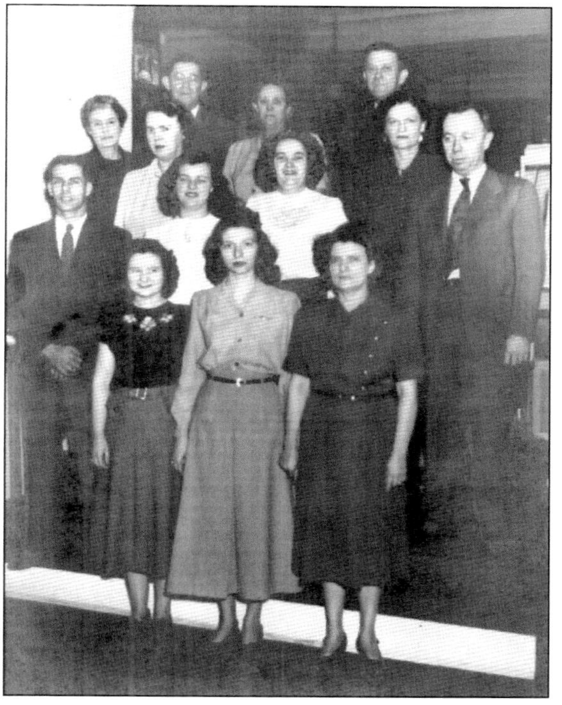

Williams and Breedlove Store employees take a break in the 1940s. From left to right are (first row) Christine Noblin Strickland, Lou Eddie Howard Freeman, and Magie Harrison; (second row) Walter Hughes, Irene Boykin, Kathryn Dillehay Hobgood, and Garland Averette; (third row) Isabell Parham, Lucille Ellington, Mrs. ? Elam, and Fannie Harris; (fourth row) Oscar Breedlove and Allie Hart. (Courtesy of Fann Montague.)

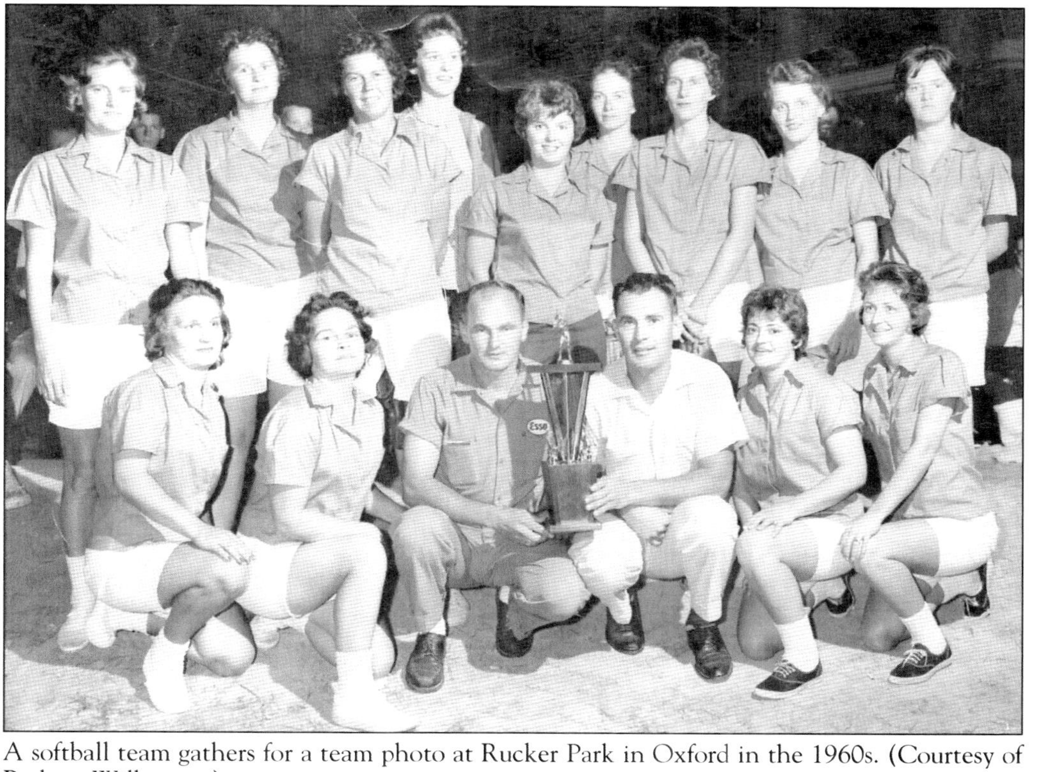

A softball team gathers for a team photo at Rucker Park in Oxford in the 1960s. (Courtesy of Barbara Wilkerson.)

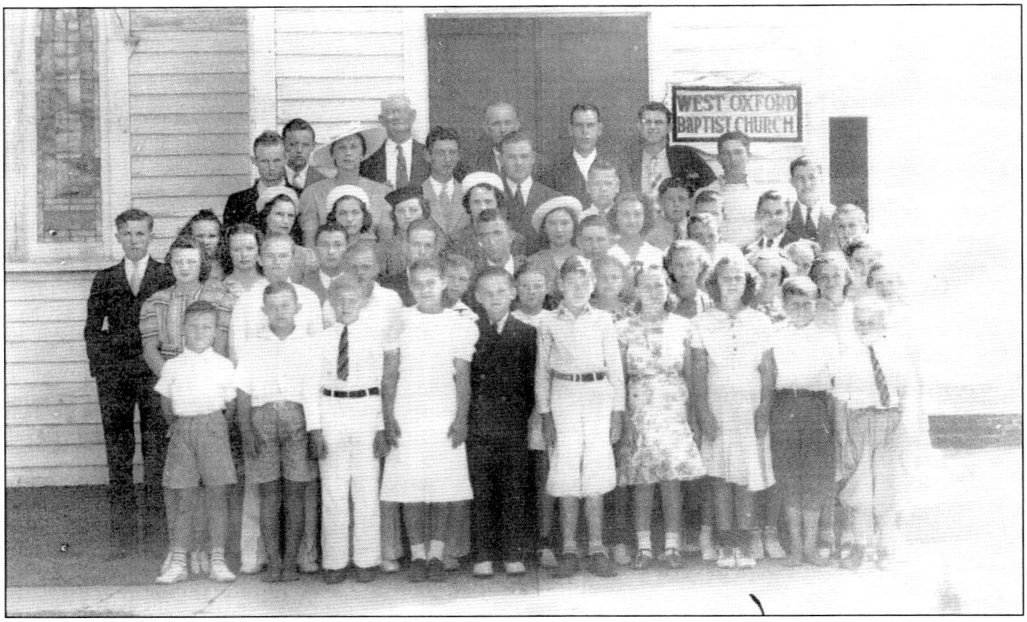

Taking a break from church services, people gather in front of West Oxford Baptist Church.

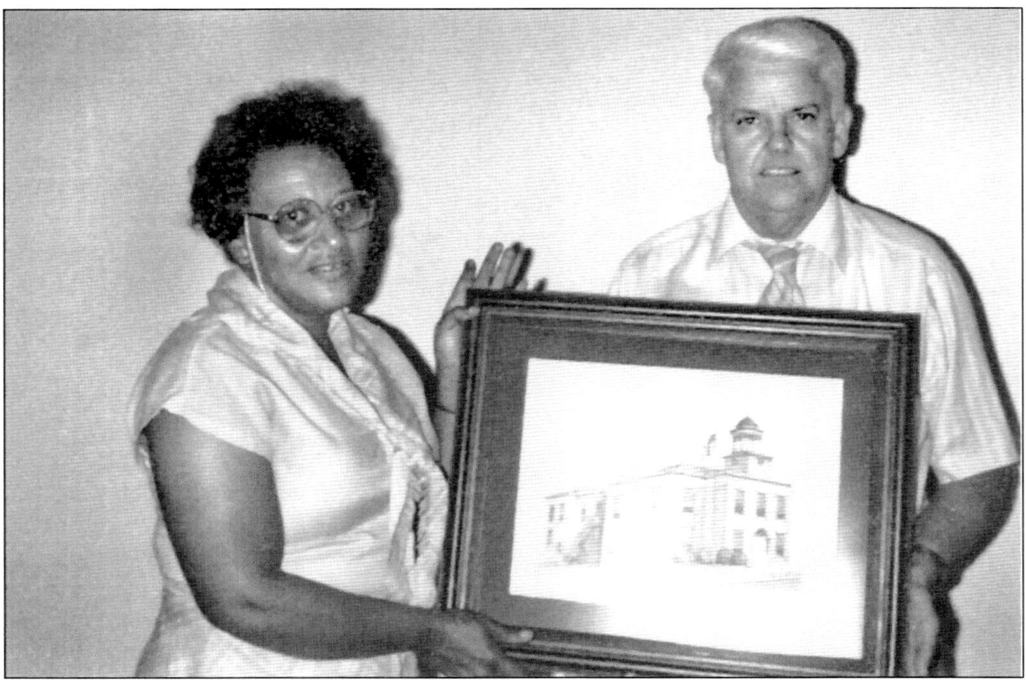

W.W. Mullen, director of Social Services, is honored for 30 years of employment in 1981. Esther Carter, a social worker, presents Mullen a print of the Granville County Courthouse, the location of his first office. Mullen was the longest serving director in county history. (Courtesy of Sharon Mullen Watts.)

Martha Hilton enjoys a walk around Oxford.

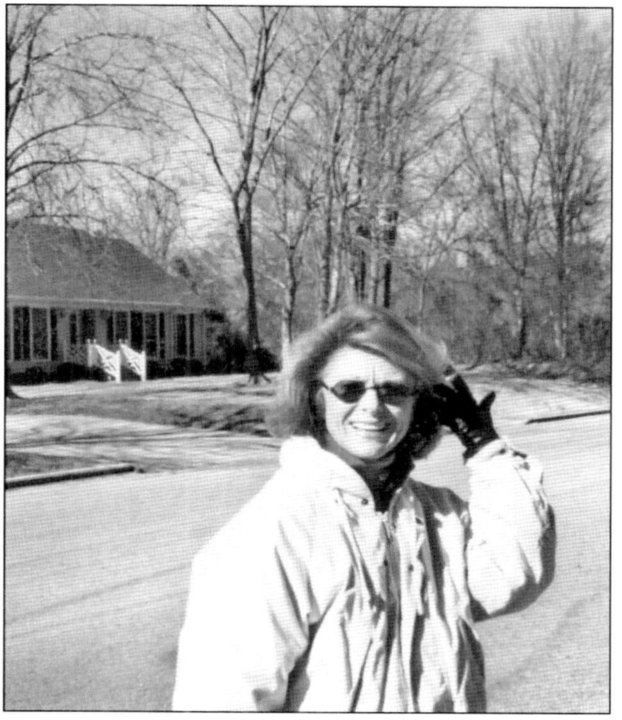

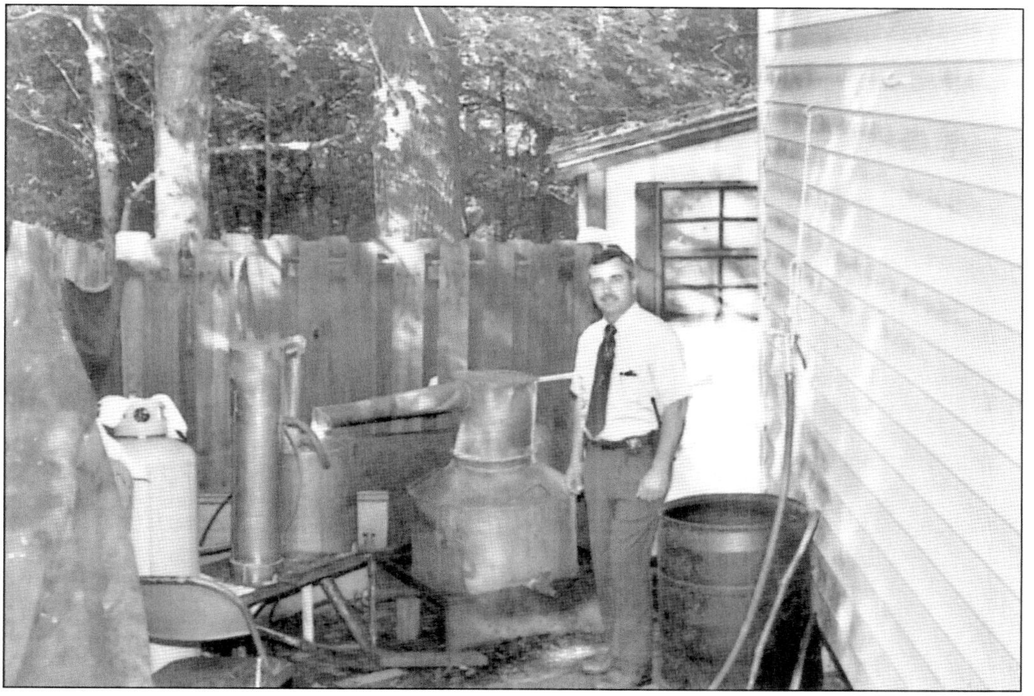

Brin Wilkins, Granville County chief deputy sheriff, stands next to a whiskey still in the southern part of the county.

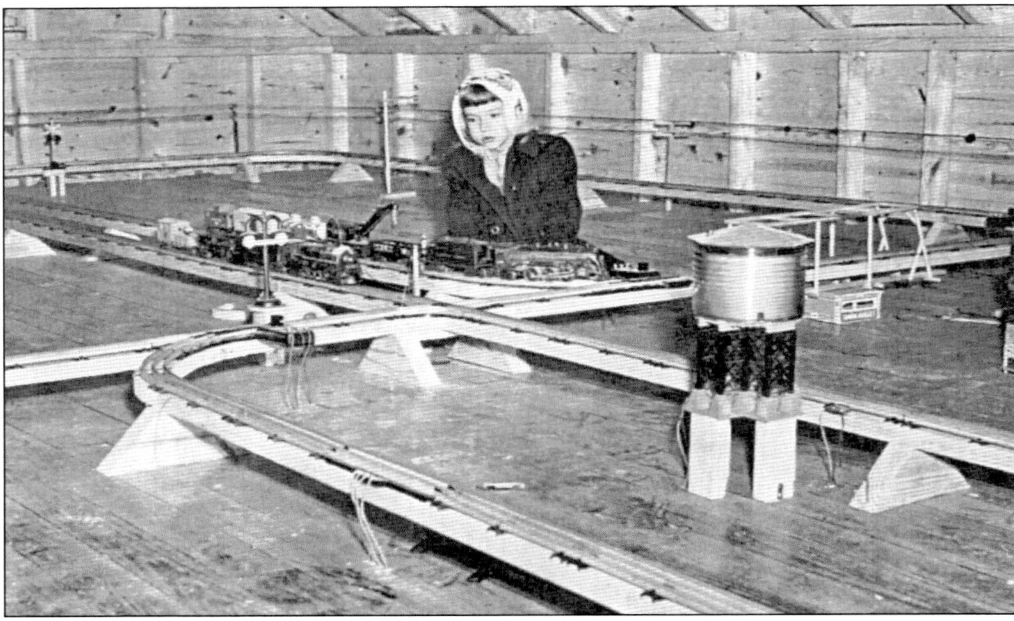

Jane Ensley enjoys her huge train track in the attic of her Oxford home in the 1950s.

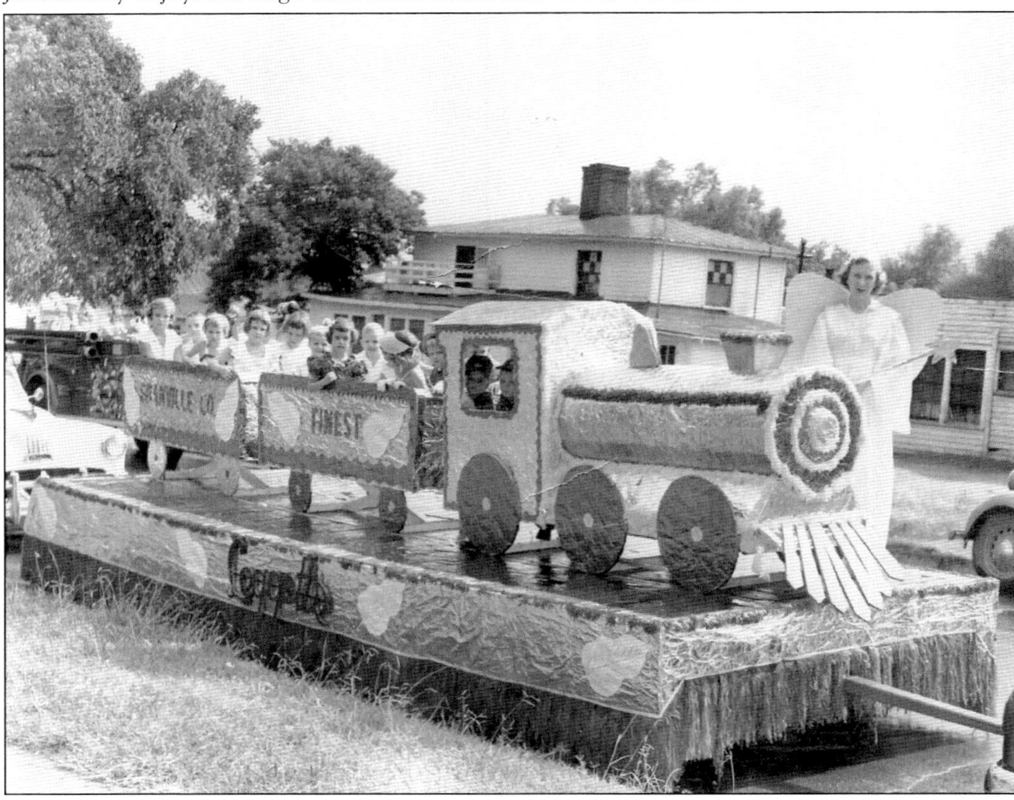

Leggett's Store sponsored this entry in an Oxford Christmas parade in the late 1940s. (Courtesy Jennie O'Brian Schilagi.)

Clessie Thomas is looking very pretty as she smiles for the camera. Many Oxford people know Mrs. Thomas from her long employment at Bowlings' Store.

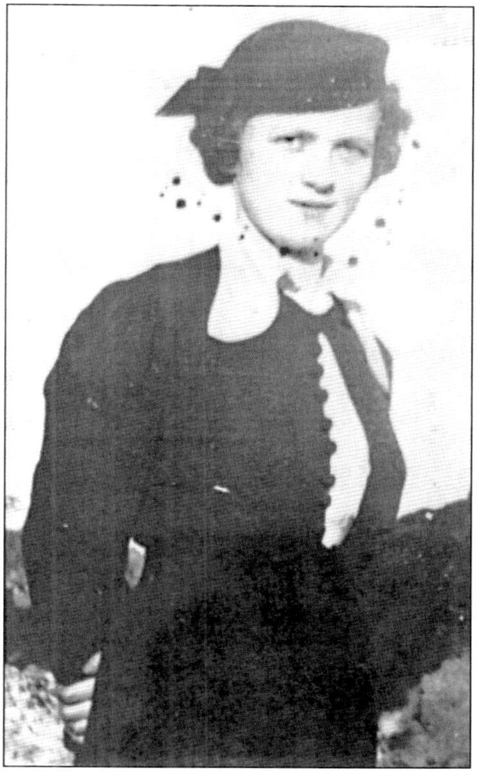

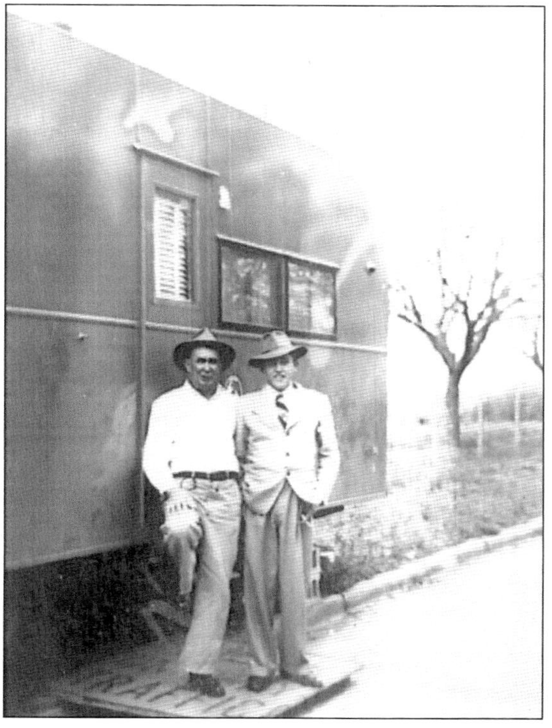

From left to right are Roy Woodlief and Crawford Newton on Forest Street in the 1940s. The trailer behind them was used as the first auto inspection office in Oxford. (Courtesy of Betty King.)

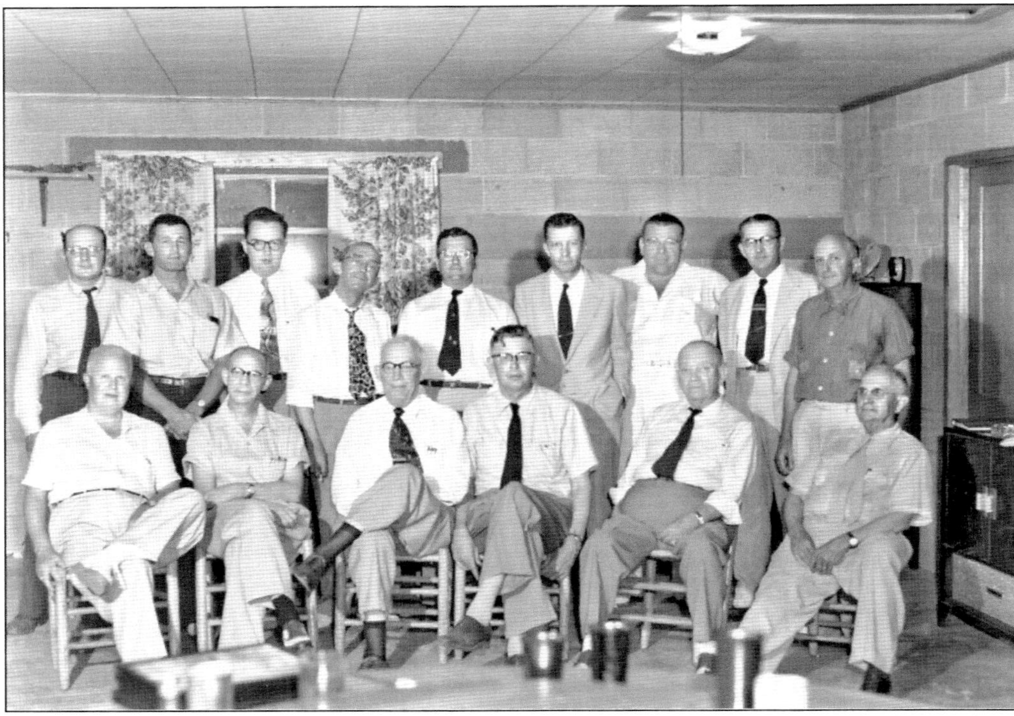

Here is a gathering, which includes many doctors, inside Granville Hospital. The hospital was built in 1938, and there have been many additions made to it since then.

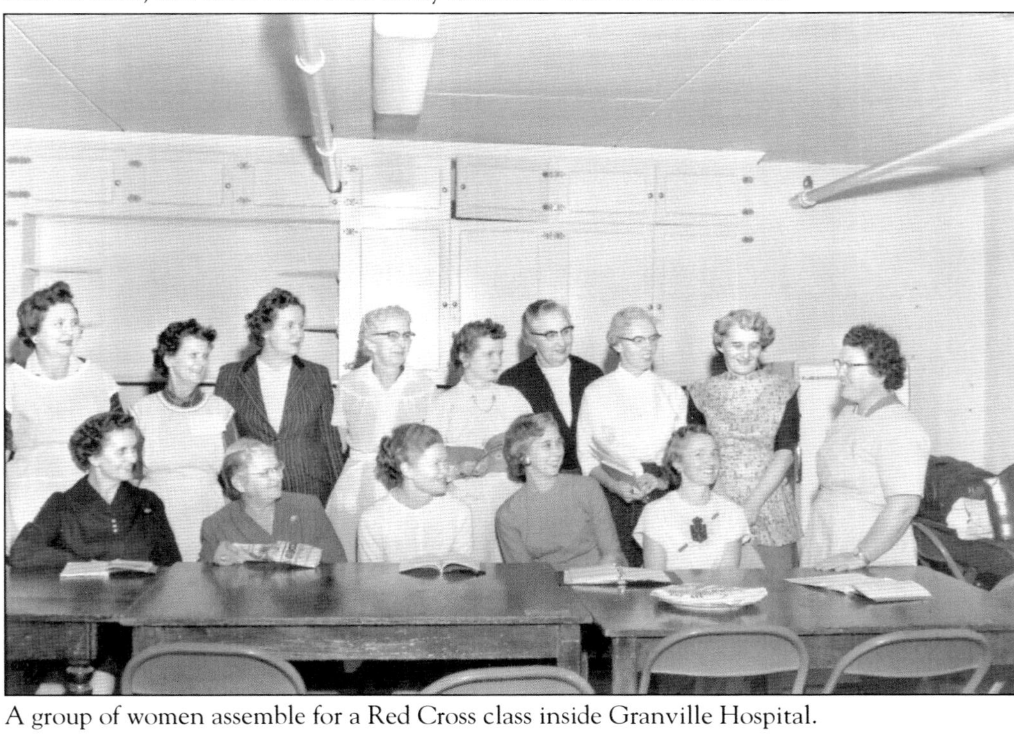

A group of women assemble for a Red Cross class inside Granville Hospital.

Col. John Harris is shown in his Civil War uniform. (Courtesy of Danny Bowling.)

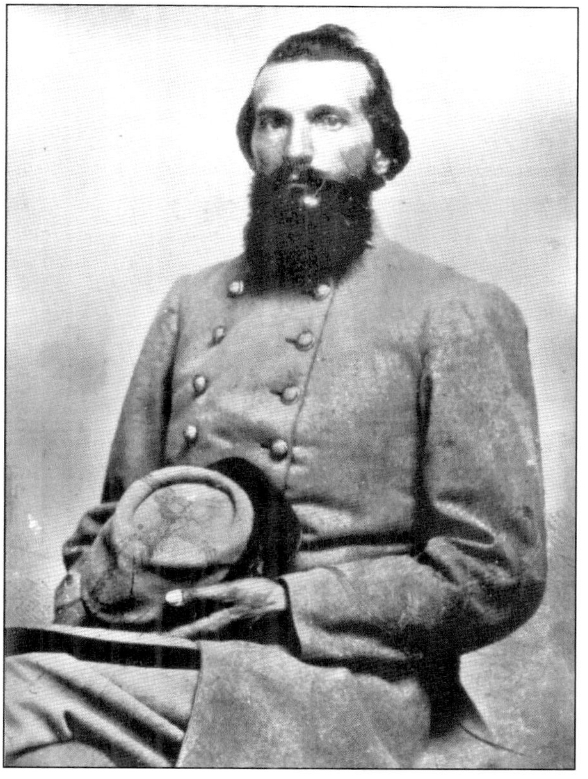

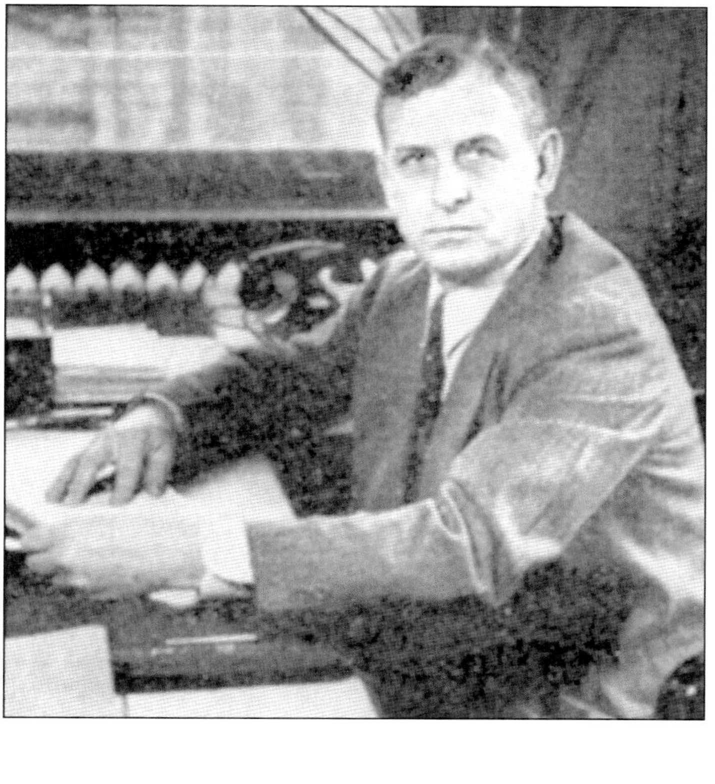

The Richard H. Thornton Library in Oxford was named in honor of a university teacher and book publisher.

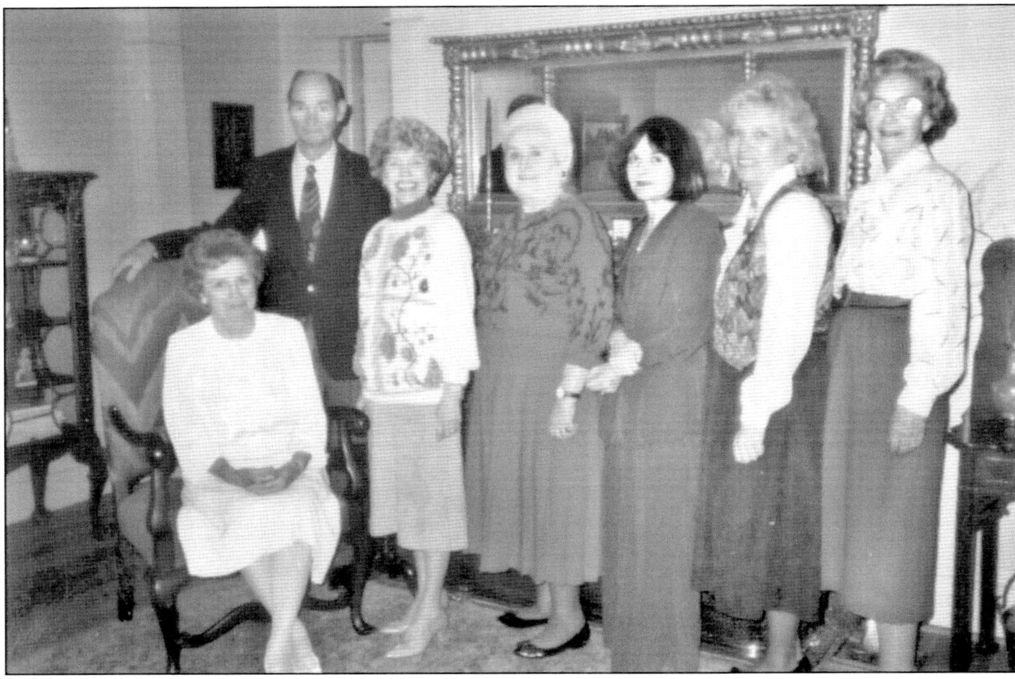

Pictured from left to right are Lib Taylor, Arch Taylor, Sylvia Matthews, Edith Currin, Joann Riley, Pam Thornton, and Lucy Royster in the Taylor house in Oxford.

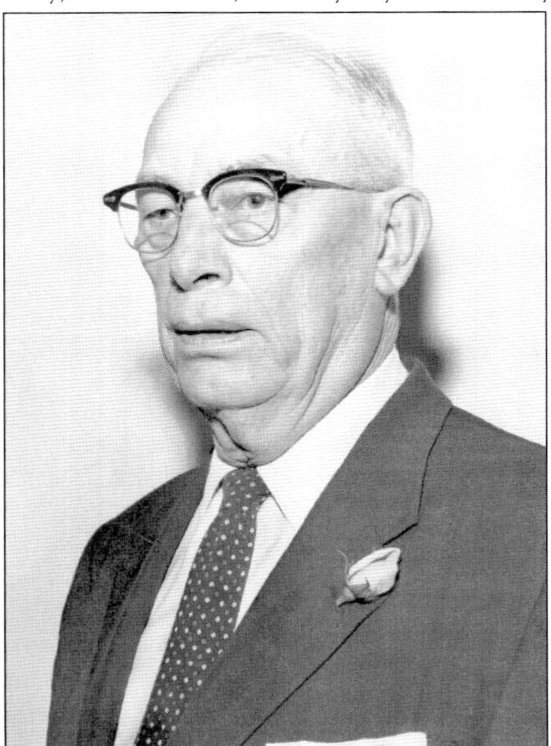

Dr. W.N. Thomas was a founder of Granville Hospital and a very well-known physician. Dr. Thomas also participated in many civic organizations. (Courtesy of Rachel Thomas.)

President Jimmy Carter greets Wilbur Yeargin of Oxford. Yeargin served Oxford in many capacities, including running Yeargin's Warehouse and serving as a Granville County commissioner. (Courtesy of Jean Gill.)

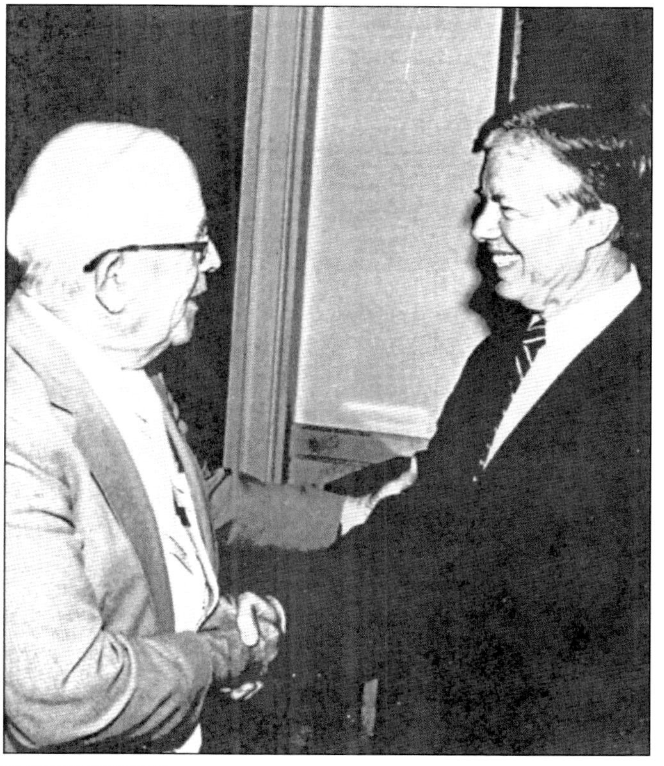

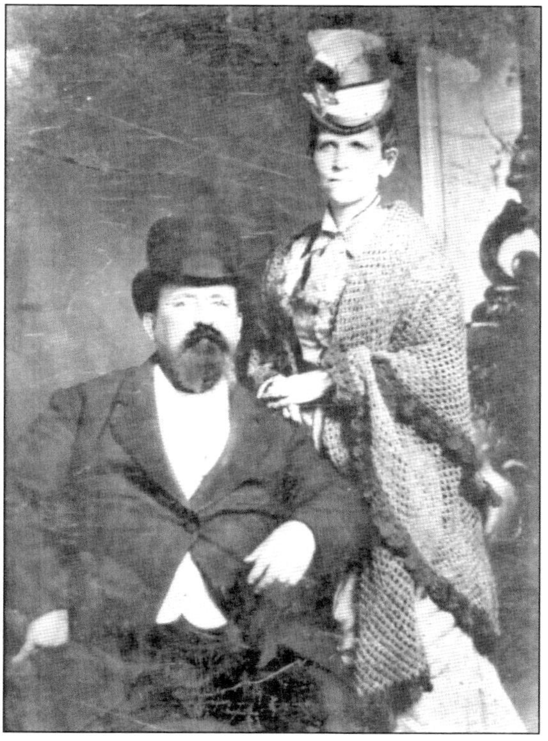

Augustus Landis and his wife pose for a picture in the late 1800s. Landis was a prominent businessman and civic leader in Oxford. (Courtesy of Liz Falkner.)

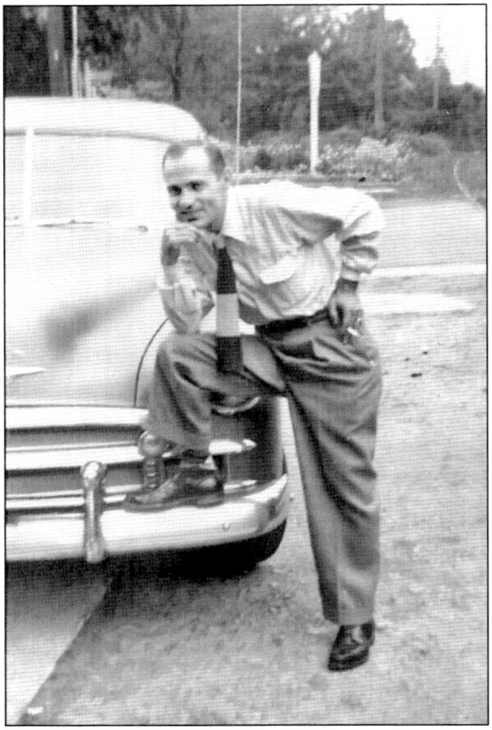

Hart Curl relaxes beside his car. Curl is well known in the area for his "Curl's Corner" column in the *Butner-Creedmoor News* and his former employment as a radio announcer for WOXF in Oxford.

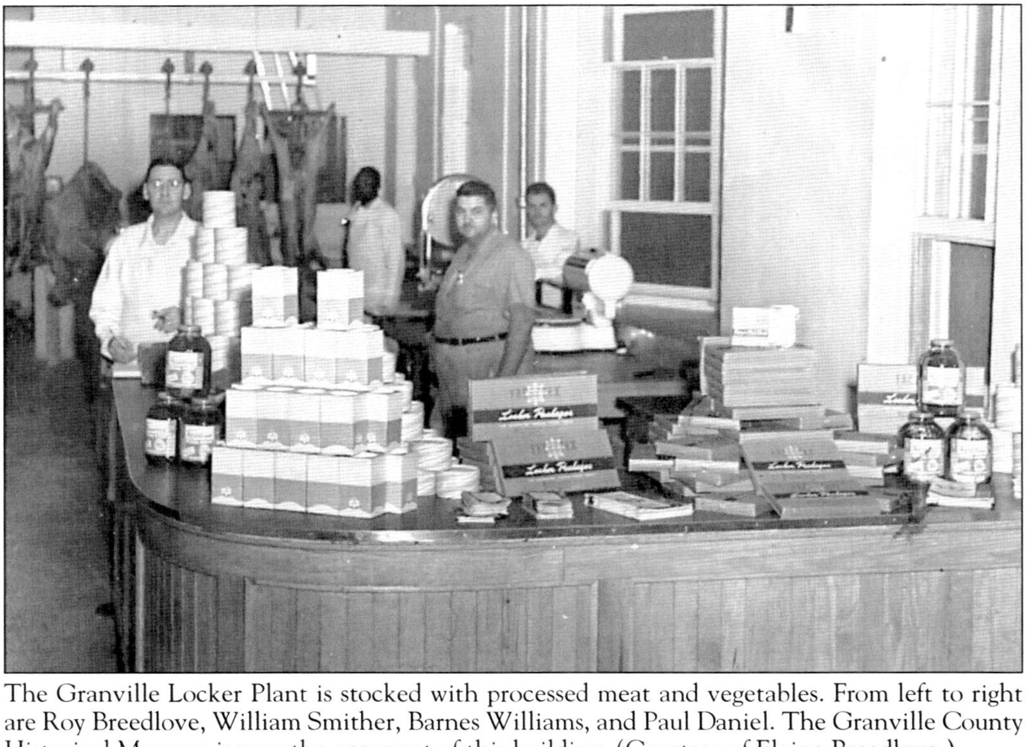

The Granville Locker Plant is stocked with processed meat and vegetables. From left to right are Roy Breedlove, William Smither, Barnes Williams, and Paul Daniel. The Granville County Historical Museum is now the occupant of this building. (Courtesy of Elaine Breedlove.)

Jean and Tommy Gill are shown inside Yeargin's Store in the Salem community in the 1950s.

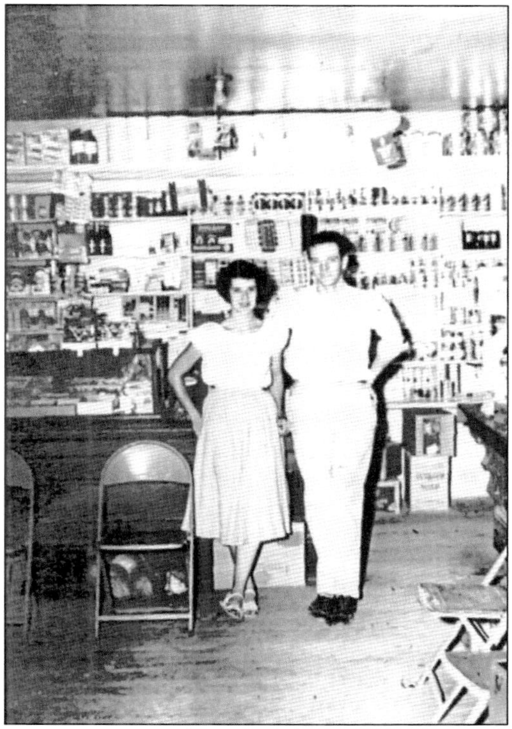

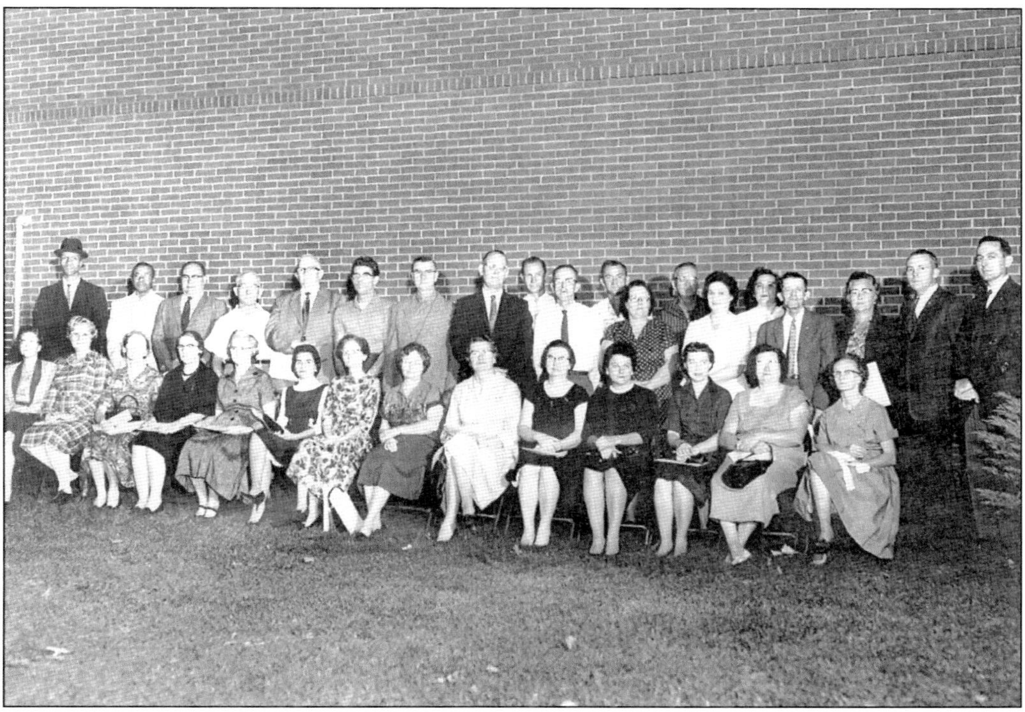

These are employees of Burlington Mills. This clothing and textile enterprise served as the workplace for many Granville County residents. (Courtesy of Barbara Wilkerson.)

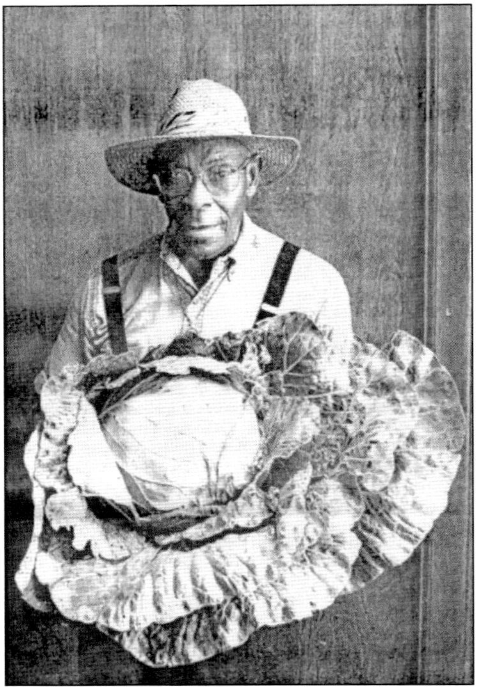

Moses Lyons of Oxford grew this 15-pound cabbage in his garden. (Courtesy of the *Oxford Public Ledger*.)

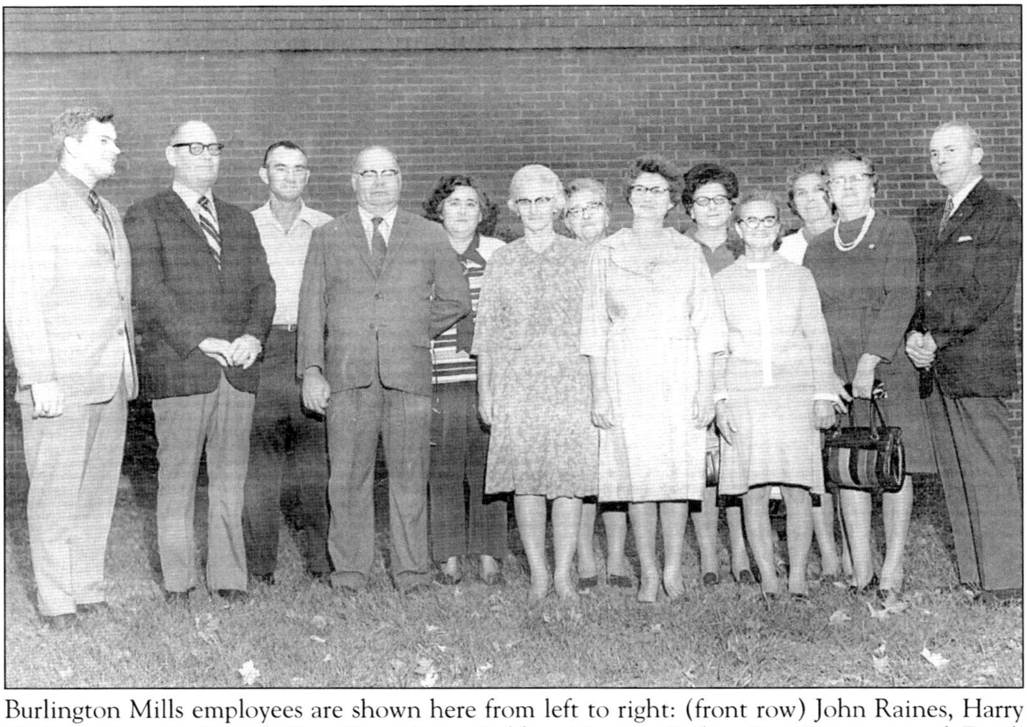

Burlington Mills employees are shown here from left to right: (front row) John Raines, Harry Graham, Lonnie Broyal, Rat Harp, Mag Oakley, Nannie Bailey, Eva Dement, and Frank Bullock; (back row) Turner Cottrell, Margaret Nance, Margaret Madison, Lizzie Moss, and Ruby Moon. (Courtesy of Barbara Wilkerson.)

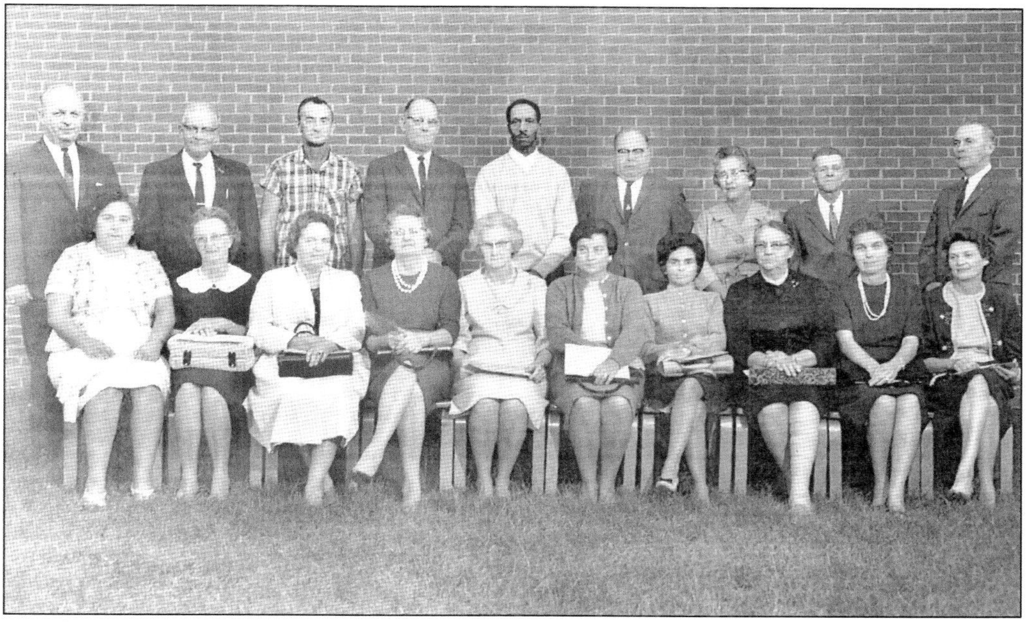

Another group of Burlington Mill's employees, from left to right, are as follows: (front row) Margaret Nance, Nannie Bailey, Mattie Hobgood, Eva Dement, Rat Harp, Lizzie Moss, Ethel Briggs, Minnie Long, Ruby Moon, and Mae Oakley; (back row) Ben Grimes, Harry Allen, Turner Cottrell, Harry Graham, Alvis Slaughter, Lonnie Broyal, Margaret Madison, George Watkins, and Frank Bullock. (Courtesy of Barbara Wilkerson.)

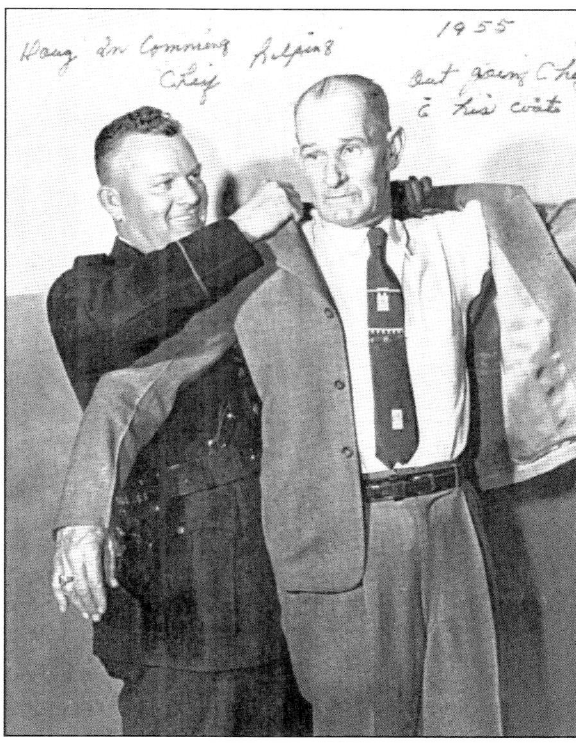

Incoming Oxford Police Chief Doug White, on the left, helps outgoing Chief J.L. Cash with his coat in 1955. (Courtesy of Opal White.)

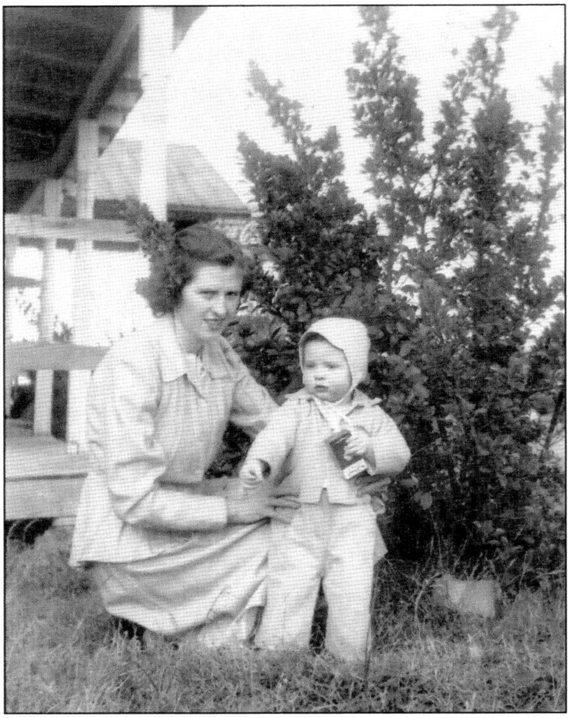

Mozelle Milton Woodlief holds son Al Woodlief in 1951 in front of Davis Averette Country Store in Providence. This store burned down in 1972. Al Woodlief is now mayor of Oxford.

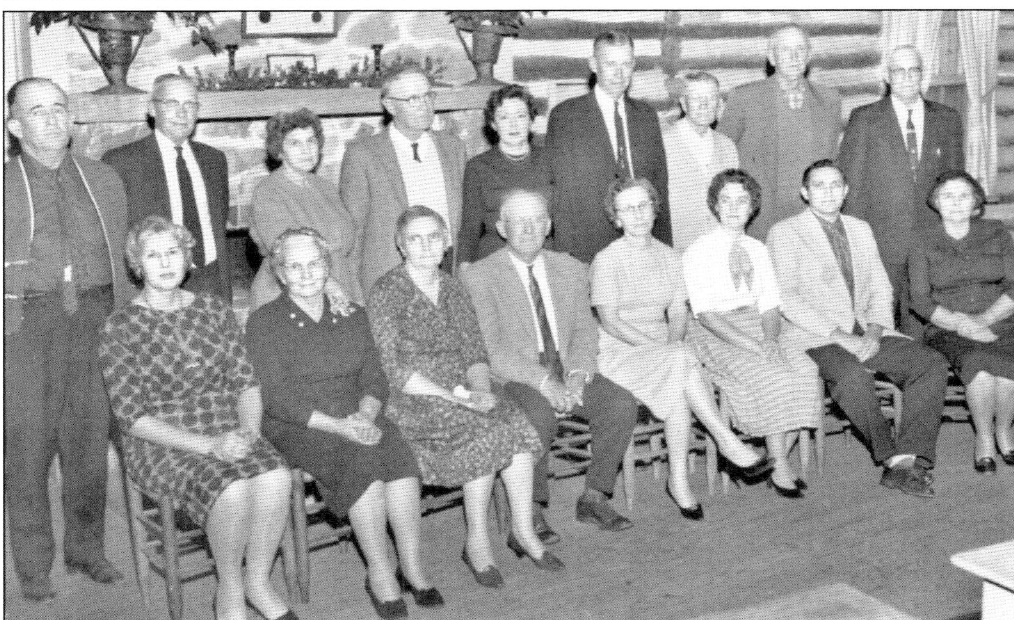

A Sunday school class from Salem United Methodist Church is shown in the Grange Hall in Oxford in 1961. From left to right are (front row) Virginia Yeargin, Ruby Crews, Katherine Crews, Daniels Crews, Essie Riggan, Shirley Ossman, ? Ossman, and Bessie Mangum; (back row) Wilbur Yeargin, Jim Hart, Rosalyn Crews, Norfleet Crews Jr., Nadine Parham, ? Riggan, Lonnie Mangum, Roy Crews Sr., and George Parham. (Courtesy of Jean Gill.)

Three

School Days

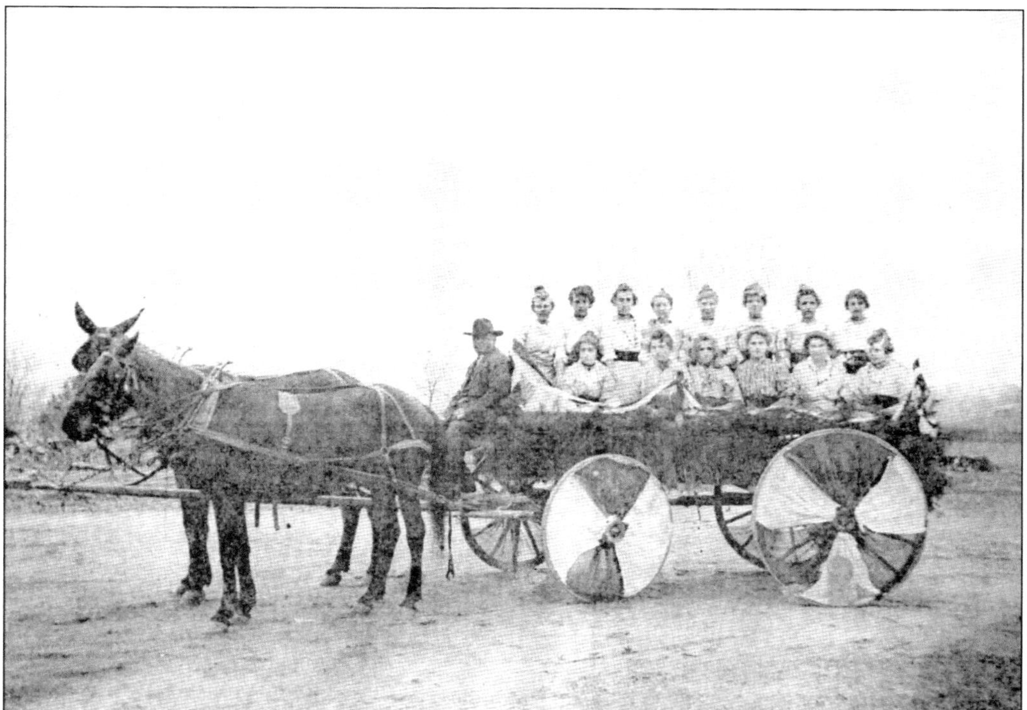

Fred Currin and his mules drive a wagonload of Oxford College students in a parade in 1918. (Courtesy of Edythe Day.)

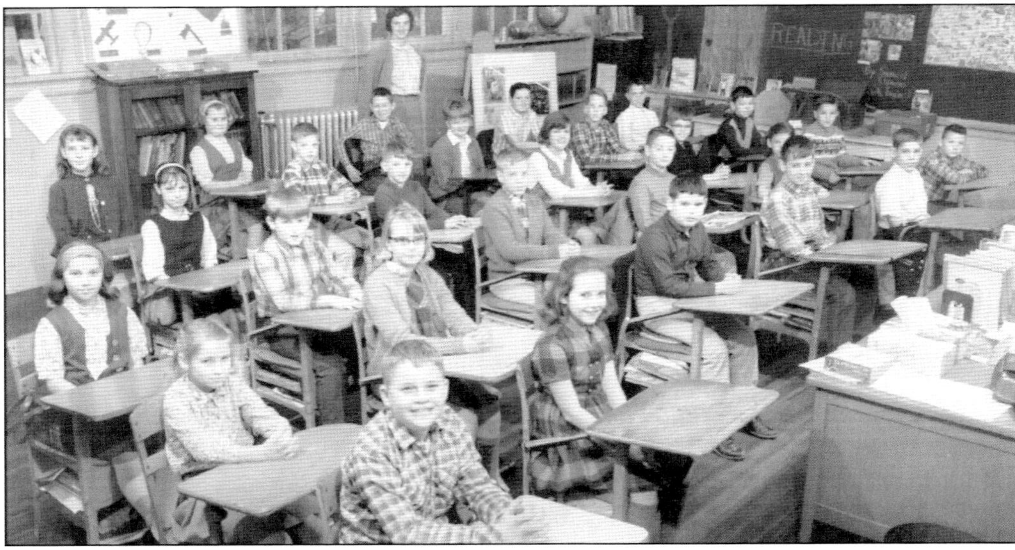

Fifth-grade students at Oxford Elementary School in 1965 turn to the camera. From left to right are (first row) Cathy Collins, Becky Currin, and Lee Corbitt; (second row) unidentified, Rhonda Hayes, Gary King, Mittie Wilkins, and Sheila Shearin; (third row) Roxanne Moore, Ronald Franklin, Ricky Blevins, Donald Franklin, and Claude Allen; (fourth row) Bobby Ross, Dale Pittard, Cora Currin Beasley, Steve Pruitt, and Woody Gill; (fifth row) Ricky Newcomb, Kennon Jones, Wordie Huff, Wanda Garrett, and unidentified; (sixth row) Wade Boyd, William Day, Eddie Benson, and Danny Henley. Martha Jackson is the teacher standing. (Courtesy of Becky Currin.)

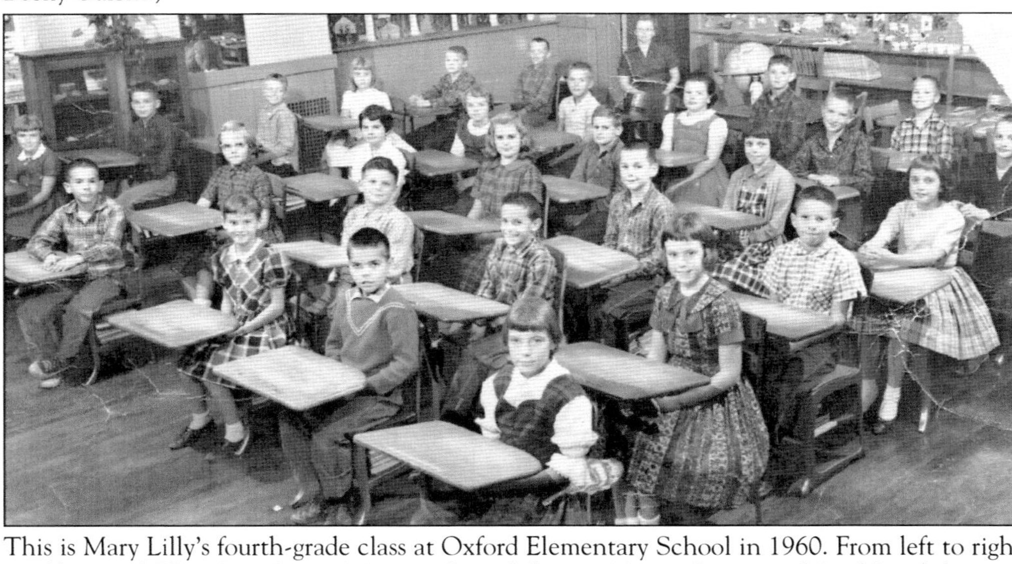

This is Mary Lilly's fourth-grade class at Oxford Elementary School in 1960. From left to right are (first row) Elise Cox, Sanne Magnan, Barry Johnson, Nancy Swain, and Reid Boyd; (second row) Leslie Saunders, Al Barnes, Russell Murray, Joyce Ollis, Drew Morgan, and Steve Wright; (third row) Teresa Kutteh, Sears Day, Patricia Hayes, Peter Floyd, Darlene Currin, and Bruce Currin; (fourth row) Sam White, Melinda Brooks, Ruth Hubler, Glenda Williams, and William Adcock; (fifth row) unidentified, Robbie Clark, Clifton Beal, Lucy Bode, Nicky Evans, and David Hicks. (Courtesy of Becky Currin.)

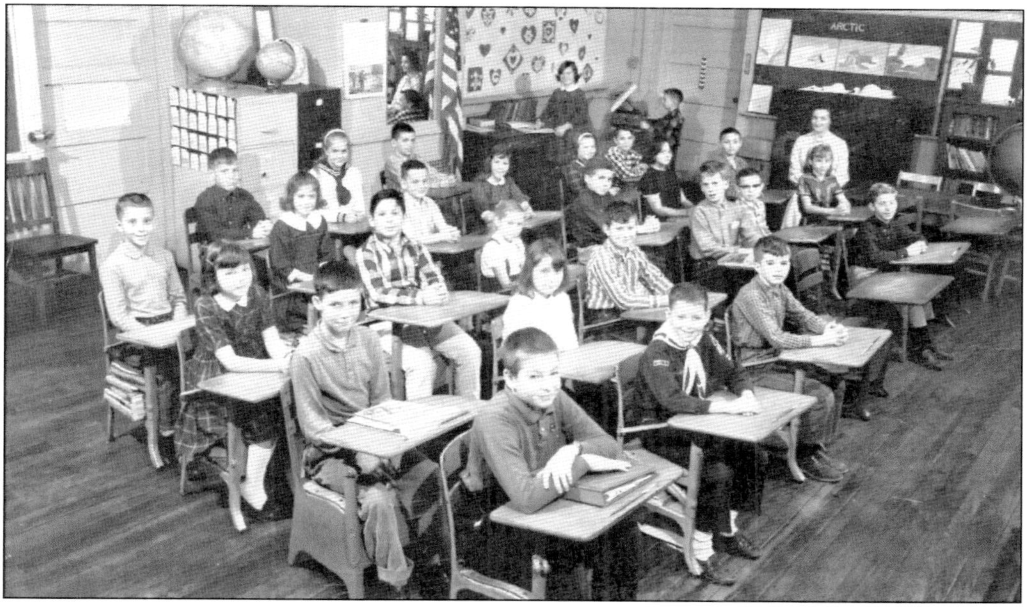

Billie Allen's fourth-grade class at C.G. Credle Elementary School takes a break in 1964. From left to right are (first row) Danny Thomerson, Nancy Keras, Danny Miller, and Burton Gibbs; (second row) Lynwood Sizemore, Donna Spears, Phillip Sorrentino, Bonnie Hobgood, and Butch Reinitz; (third row) Rebecca Ison, Tim Partin, Becky Currin, Andy Hielema, and Wordie Huff; (fourth row) Johnny Webb, Lorene Currin, Gary Parrott, and Kennon Jones; (fifth row) Bonnie Bromberg, Gail Longmire, Ronnie Boyd, and unidentified; (sixth row) Wade Boyd, Robert Oliver, and Kay Caulder. Standing in the back are Marsha Currin and Bobby Ross. (Courtesy of Becky Currin.)

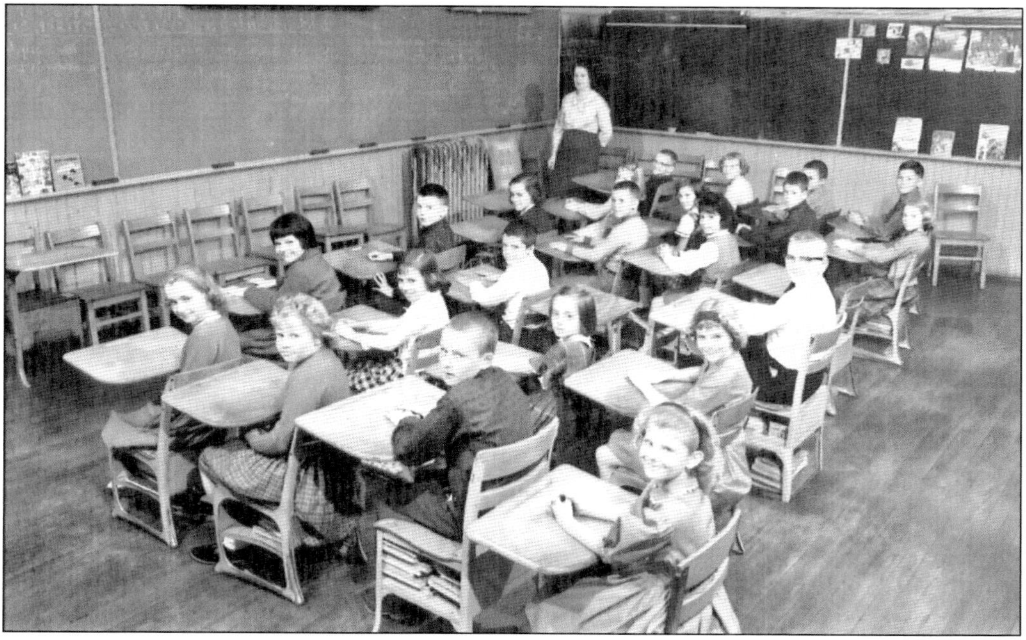

This is Sue Bryan's fourth-grade class at C.G. Credle Elementary School in 1962.

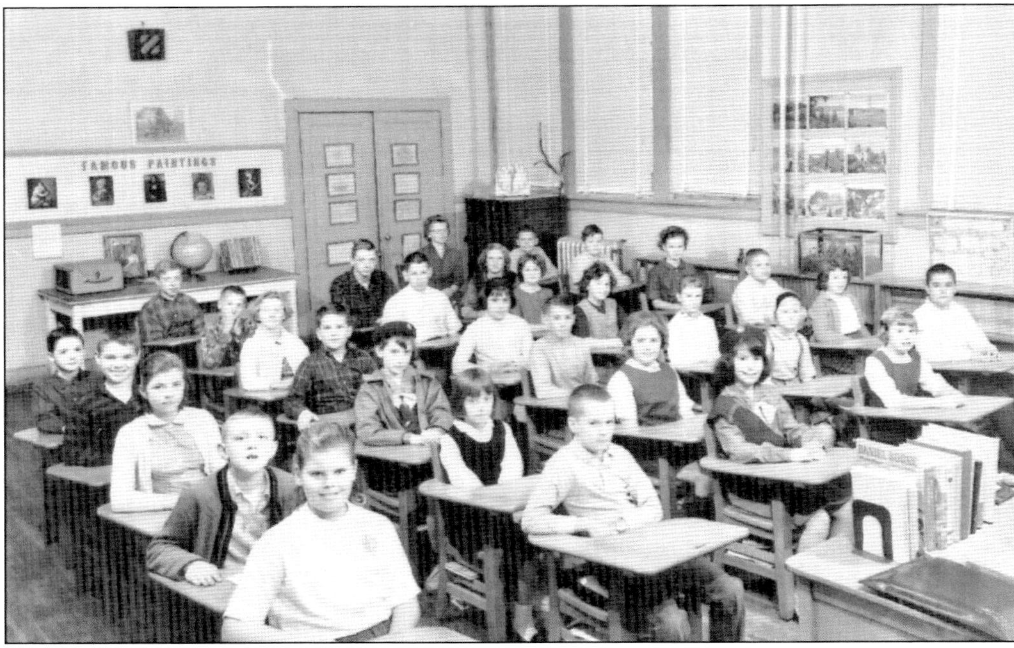

Students in Mary Lilly's fifth-grade class at Oxford Elementary School in 1963 pause from their studies for a moment.

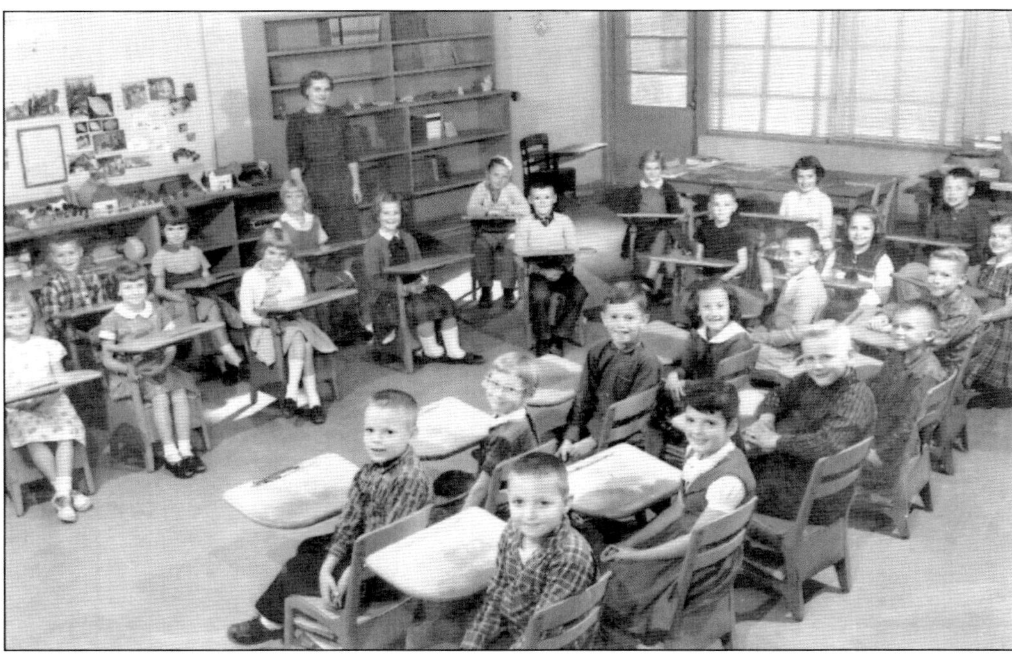

Eager young minds await instruction in Mildred Wood's second-grade class at C.G. Credle. This picture was taken in 1960.

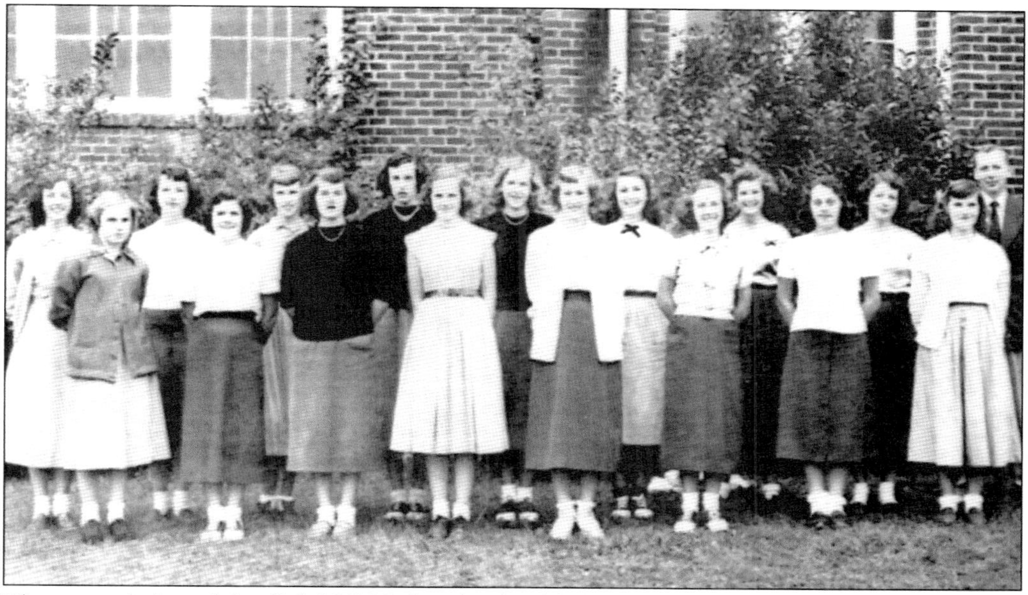

The young ladies of the Oak Hill High School softball team stand outside the school in 1953. (Courtesy of Rowena Wheeler.)

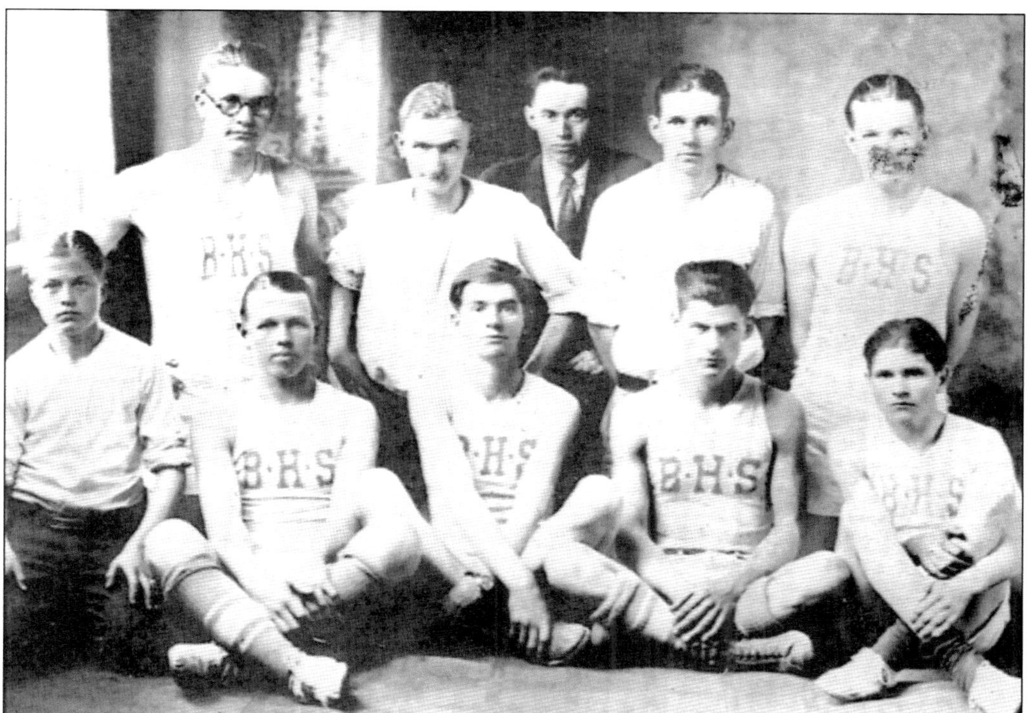

This is the Berea High School boys' basketball team of 1927.

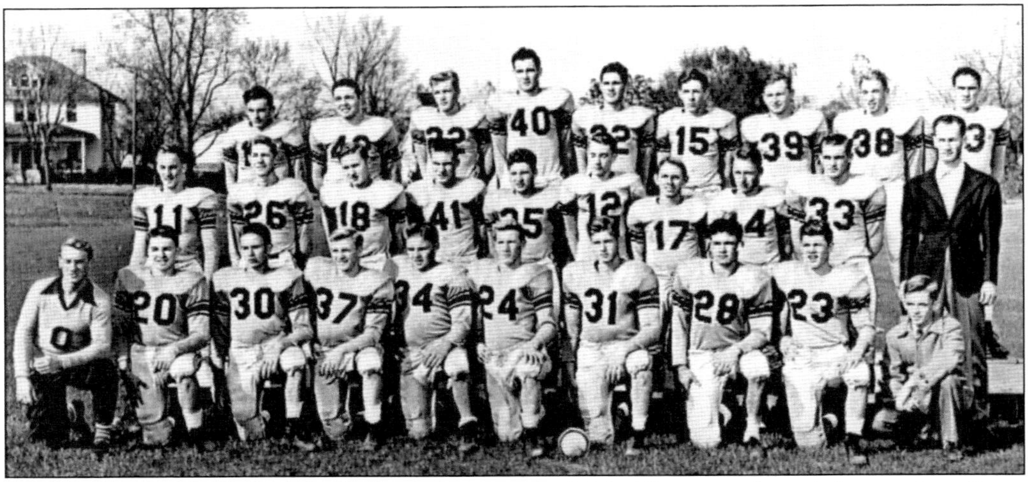

The Oxford High School football team poses in 1948. They are, from left to right, (front row) William Burwell, Sid Cutts, Ralph Blackwell, unidentified, Harold Currin, Nat Burwell, Maurice Blackwell, John Parham, Genen Seabolt, and Jimmy Stegall; (middle row) Pete Strother, George Moore, Joe Bryan, Hinnant Suitt, Norris Cole, Arch Fort, Dick Young, John Boyd, James Smith, and Coach Bob Culton; (third row) Waverly Barnes, Tom Jordan, Sam Finch, Thomas Chappell, Luther Daniel, Howard Critcher, Nathaniel Burwell, Robert Carr, and Doug Currin.

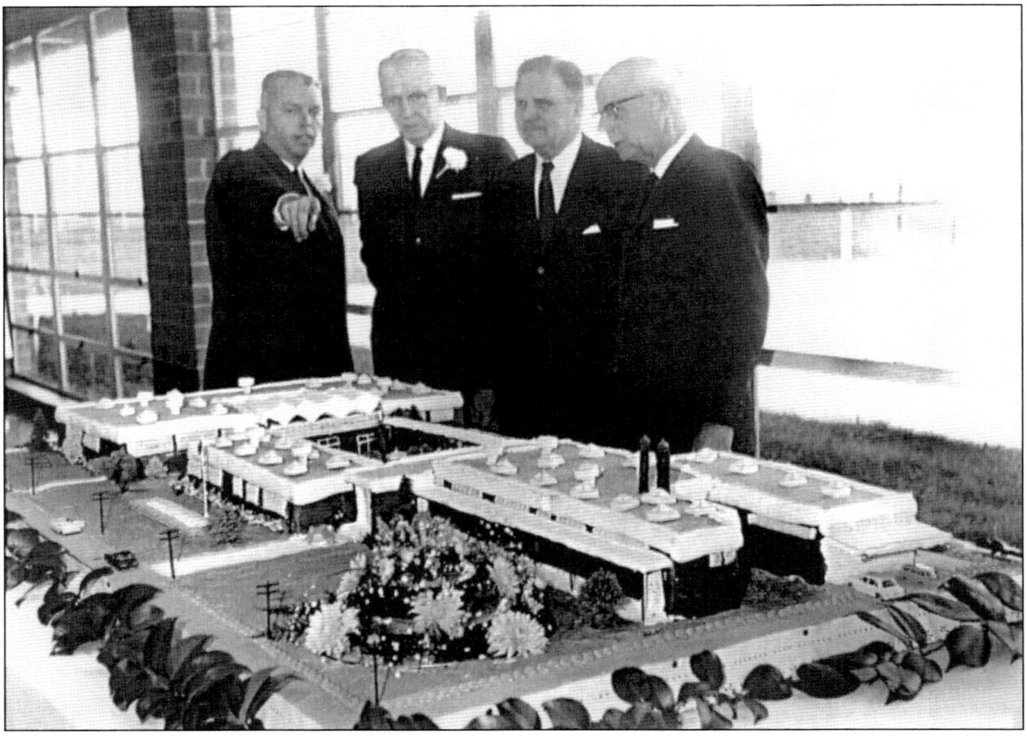

Dignitaries look at a model cake of the new J.F. Webb High School. James Webb, second from right, is the son of John Frederick Webb, for whom the school is named. James served as NASA administrator from 1961 until 1968. This picture is from 1963, when J.F. Webb opened.

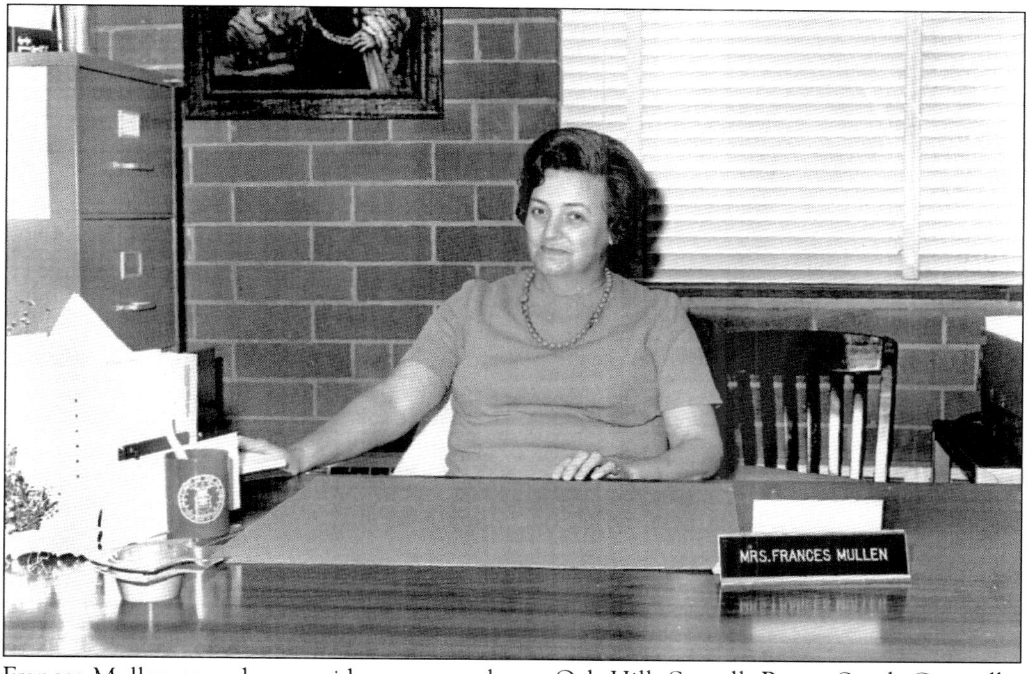

Frances Mullen served as a guidance counselor at Oak Hill, Stovall, Berea, South Granville, and J.F. Webb High Schools from 1962 to 1984. She is shown here in her office at J.F. Webb. (Courtesy of Sharon Mullen Watts.)

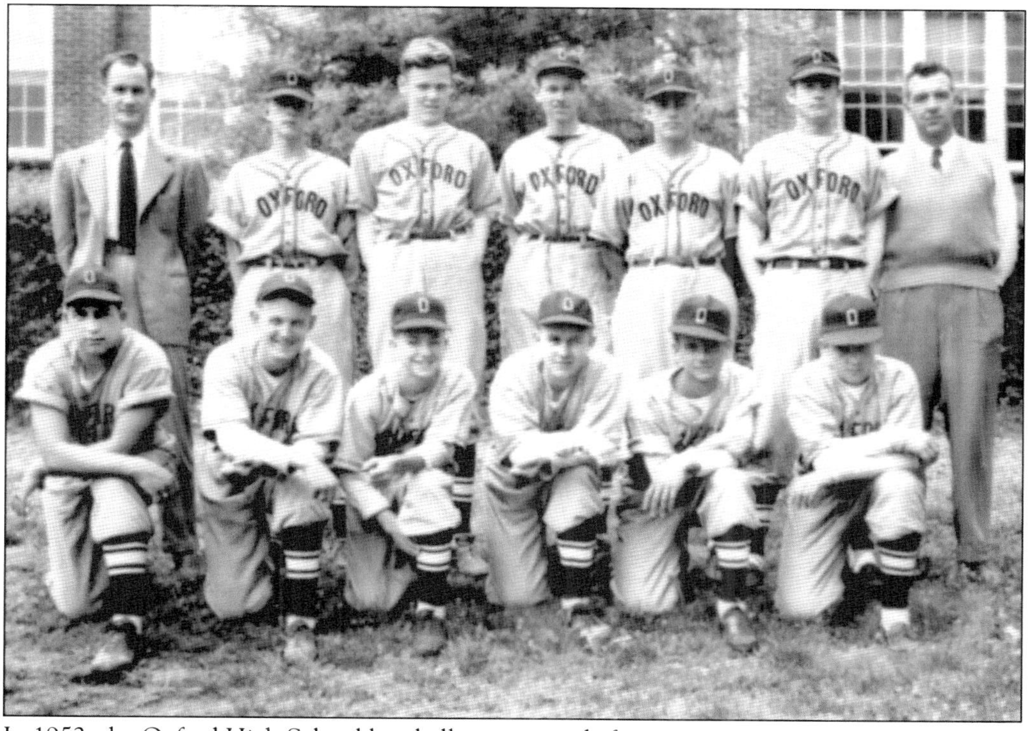

In 1952, the Oxford High School baseball team is ready for action.

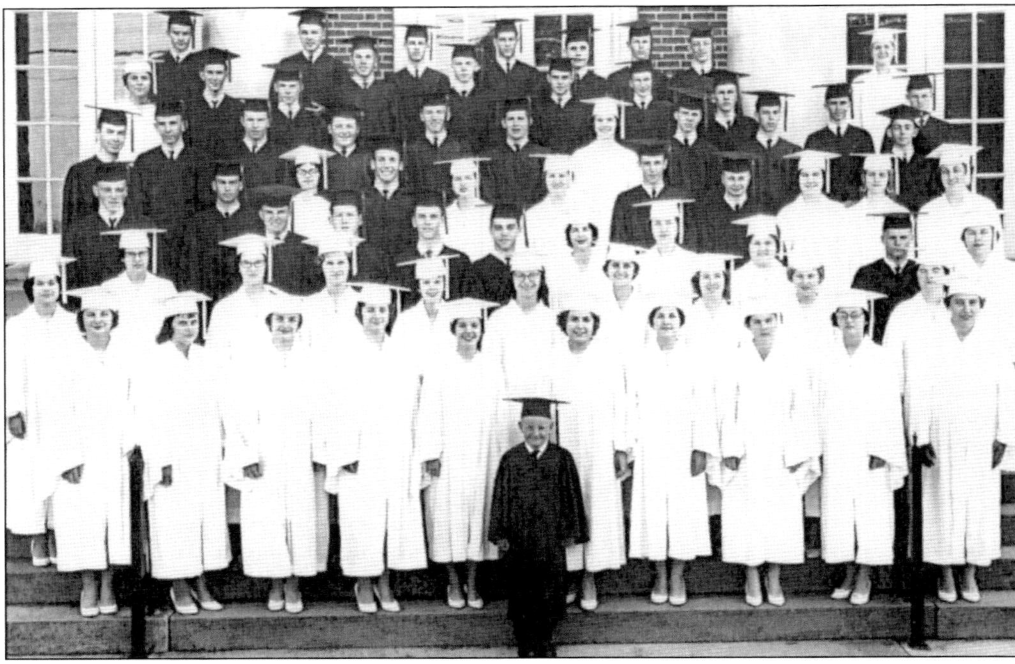

Here is the graduating class of Oxford High School of 1962.

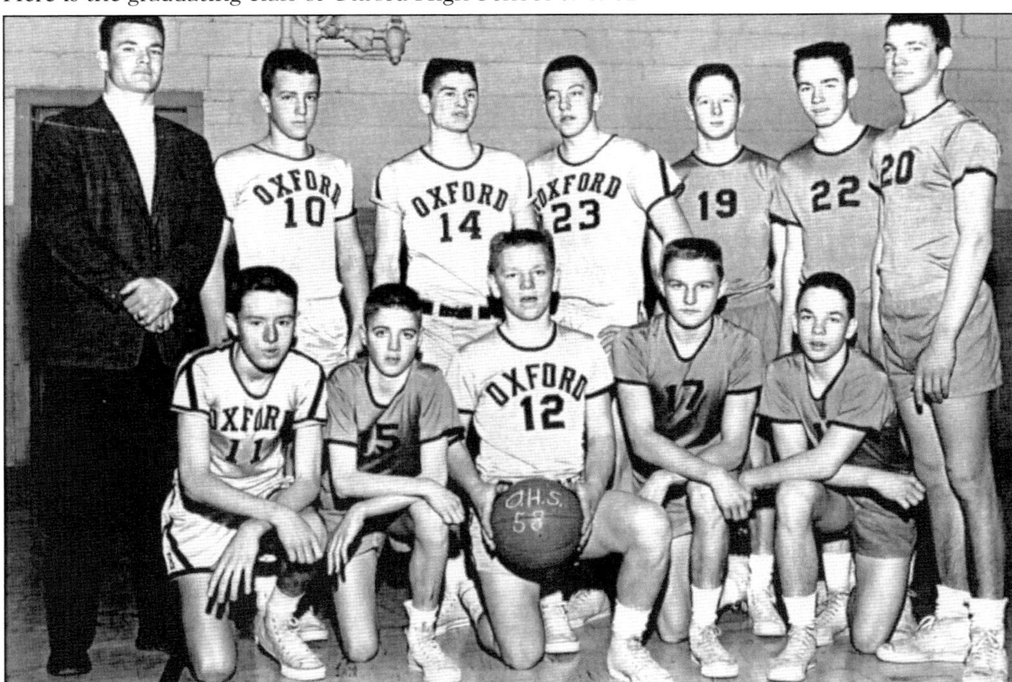

Coach John Parham stands with his team from Oxford High School in 1958. From left to right are (front row) Billy Daniel, Donnie Parrott, Cas Spencer (with ball), Roy Dean, and Tommy Adams; (back row) Bobby Finch, Ray Williford, Billy Elliott, Bobby Finch, Donnie Hawks, and David Norris.

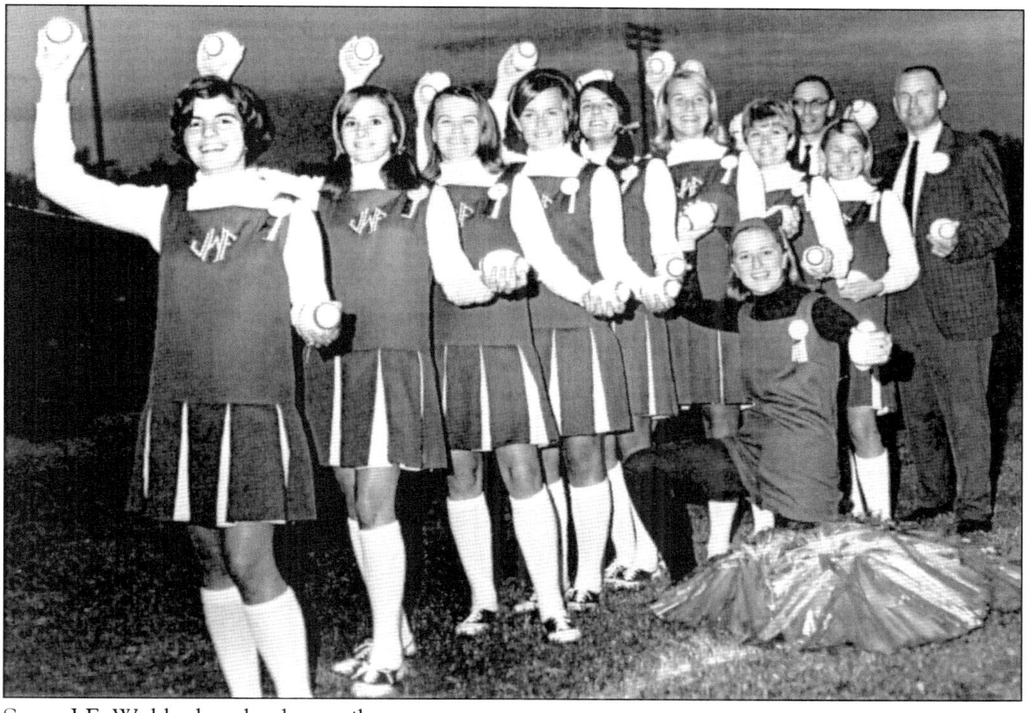

Some J.F. Webb cheerleaders strike a pose.

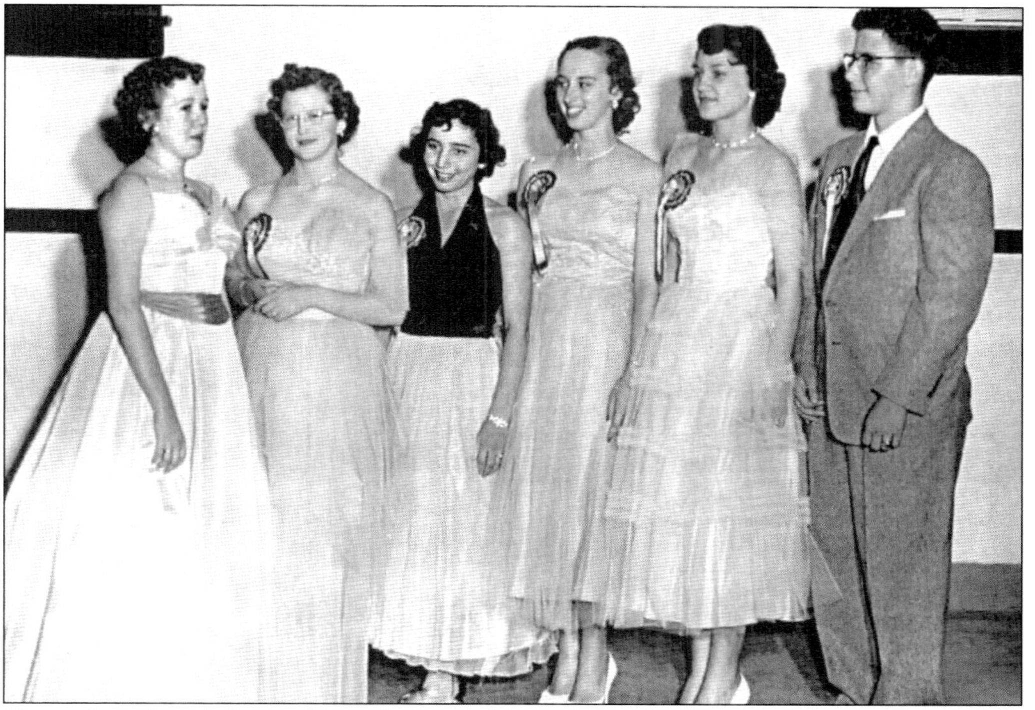

Shown here from left to right, Roberta Rucker, Nancy Finch, Jan Park, Ann Chappell, Sue Green, and Harvey Horowitz served as Oxford High School marshalls in 1954.

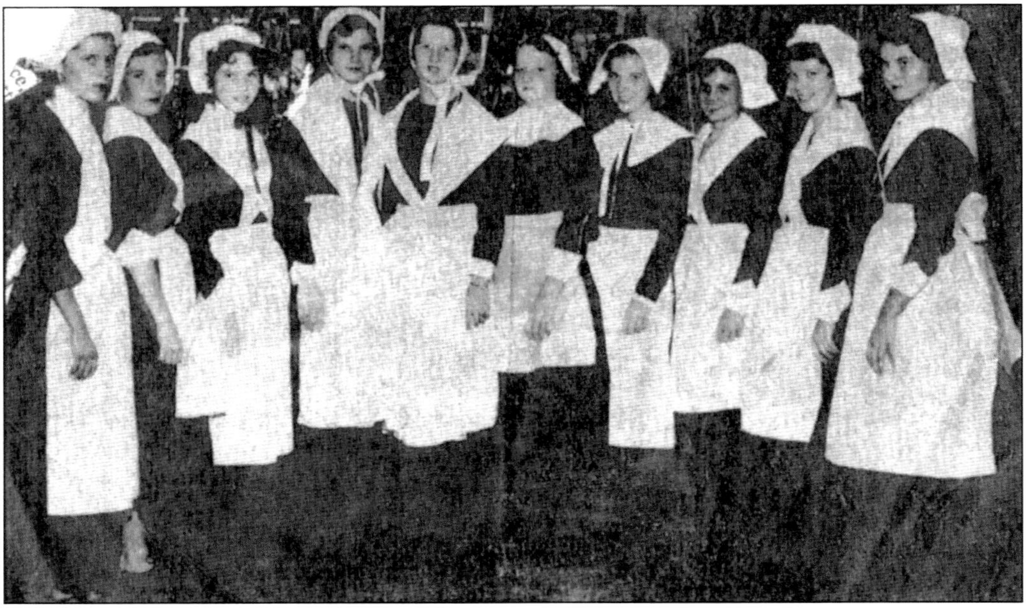

These lovely school girls donned Puritan attire to suggest Thanksgiving days of old at Oxford High School in 1959. From left to right are Betty Whitehurst, Daisy Hall, Ann Gholson, Linda Day, Judy Hart, Faye Hicks, Bobbie Rawls, Mary Campbell, Claudia Currin, and Peggie Averett. (Courtesy of Danny and Linda Bowling.)

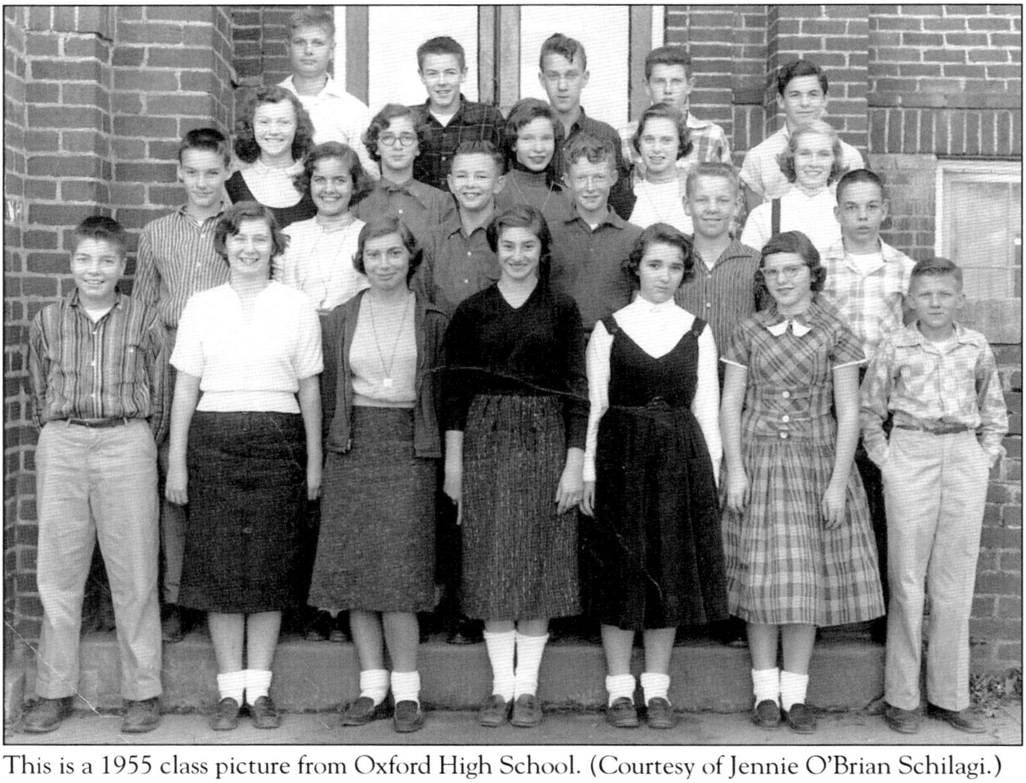

This is a 1955 class picture from Oxford High School. (Courtesy of Jennie O'Brian Schilagi.)

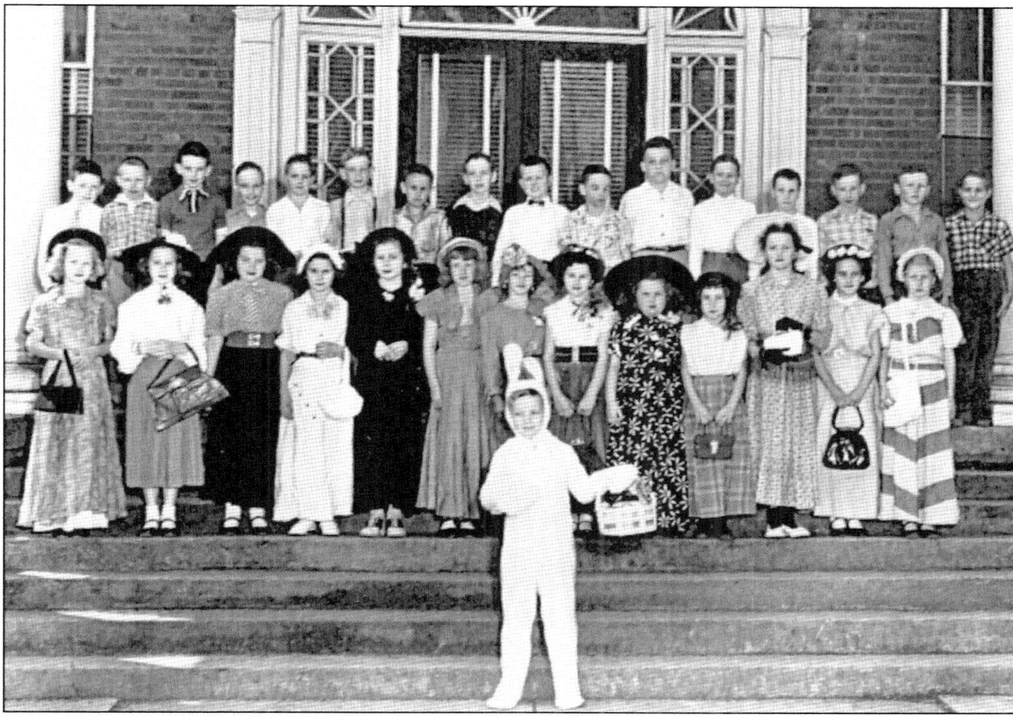

School-age children are all dressed up for an Easter celebration.

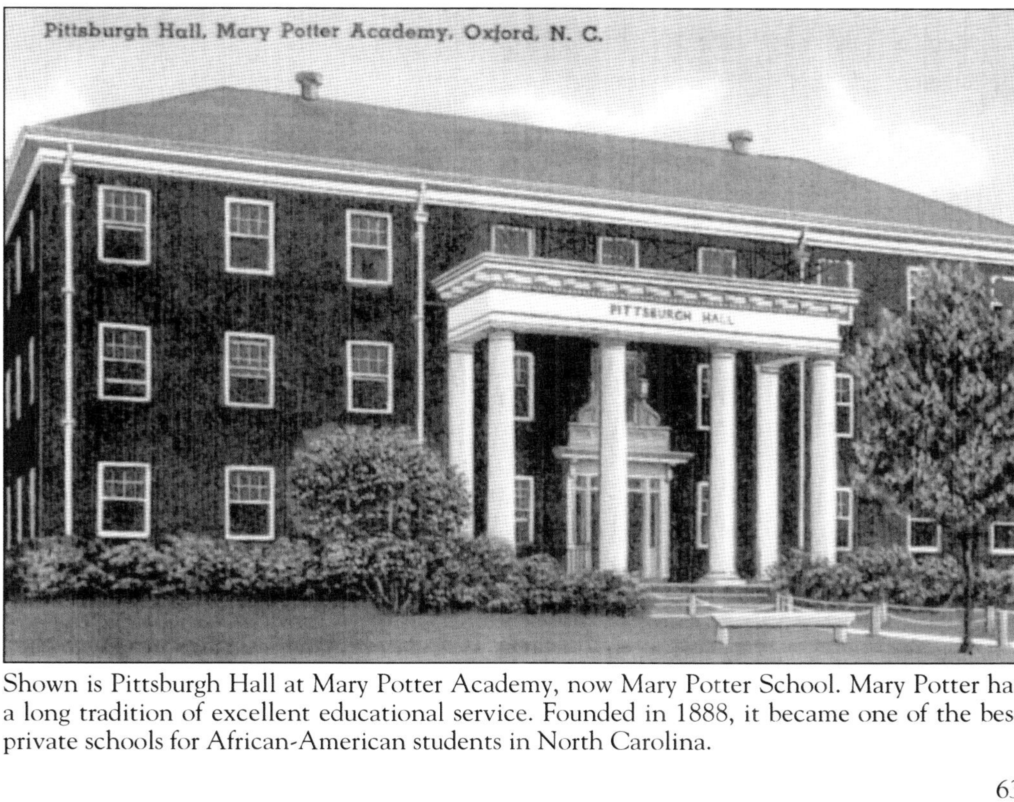

Shown is Pittsburgh Hall at Mary Potter Academy, now Mary Potter School. Mary Potter has a long tradition of excellent educational service. Founded in 1888, it became one of the best private schools for African-American students in North Carolina.

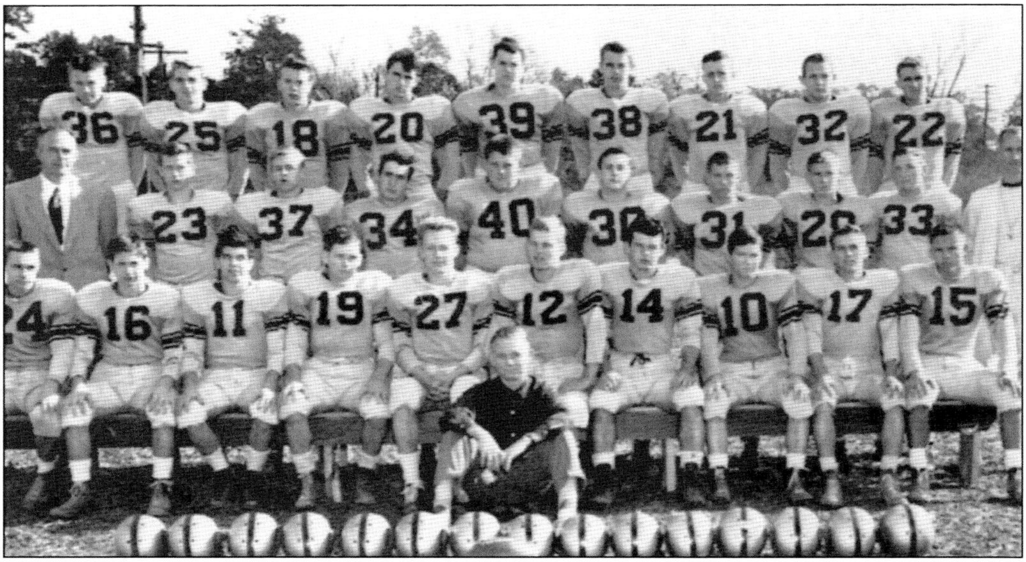

This is the 1952 Oxford High School football team. They are, from left to right, (front row) Jessie Holmes, manager; (second row) Doogie Peele, Billy Blackwell, Jimmy O'Brien, John Crumpler, Dick Dickerson, Henry Saye, Lindsey Currin, John Norris, Ben Brummitt, and Mike Powell; (third row) Coach Huss, Bobby Blackwell, Leonard Dean, Taylor Wilson, Taylor Jackson, J.P. Jones, Charles Wildman, Norman Arrington, Donald Hedgepeth, and Coach Culton; (fourth row) Ronald Sneed, Beeny Currin, Billy Ellis, Bobby Bradsher, Charles Easton, Cam Easton, Ronald Ragland, James Watkins, and Joe Daniel.

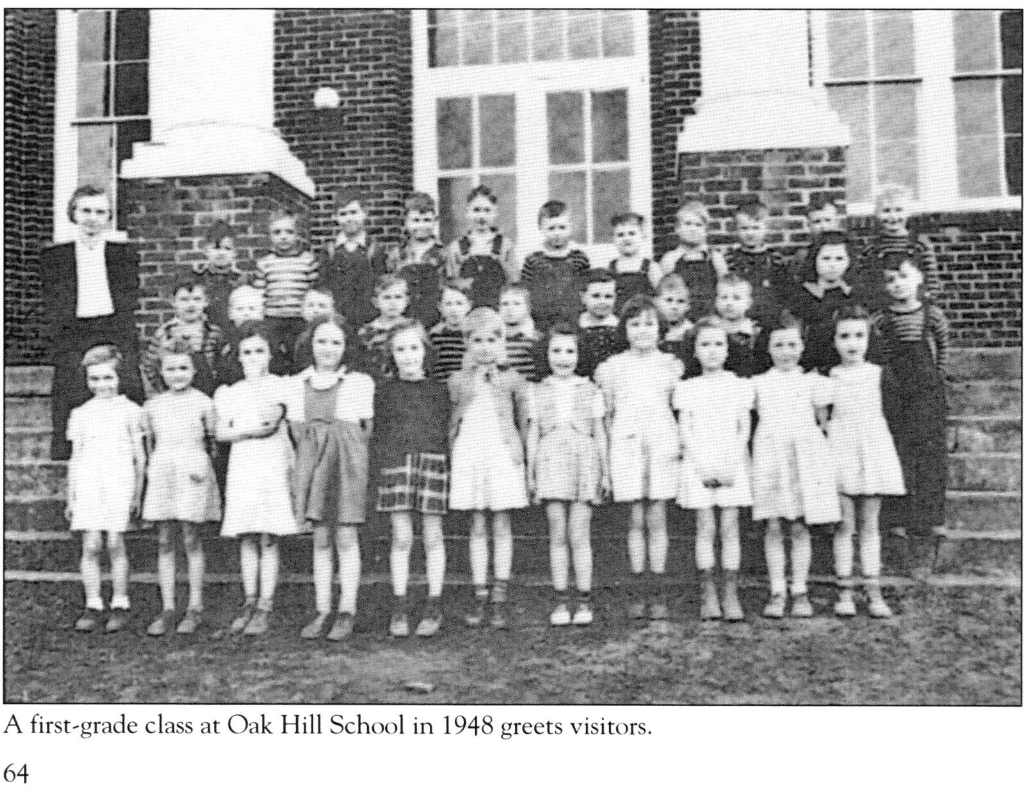

A first-grade class at Oak Hill School in 1948 greets visitors.

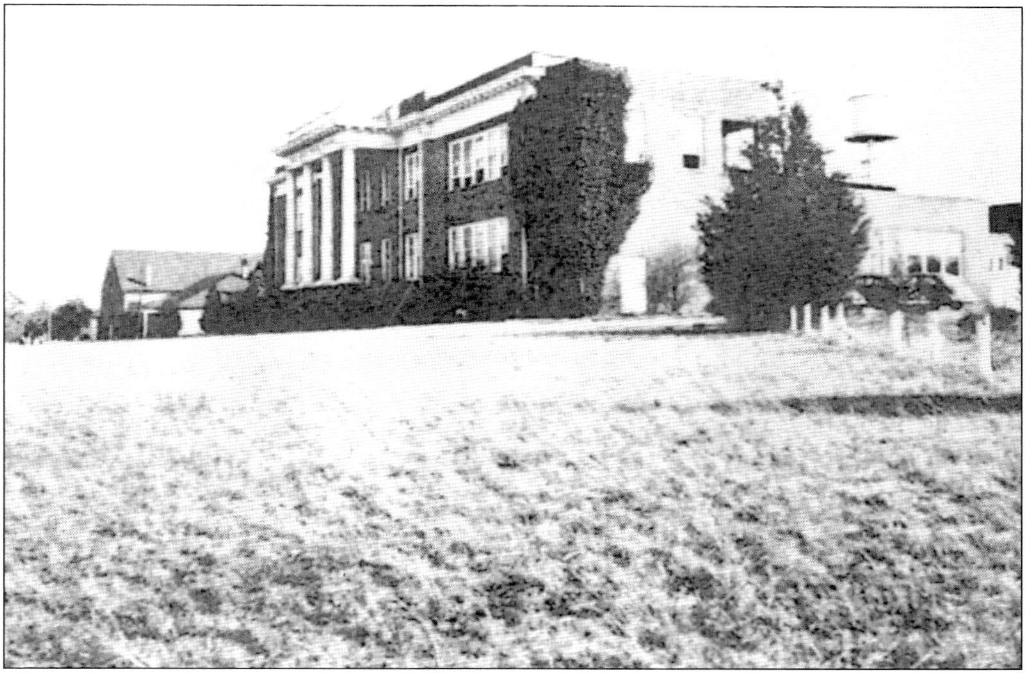

This is Oak Hill School as it looked in 1948.

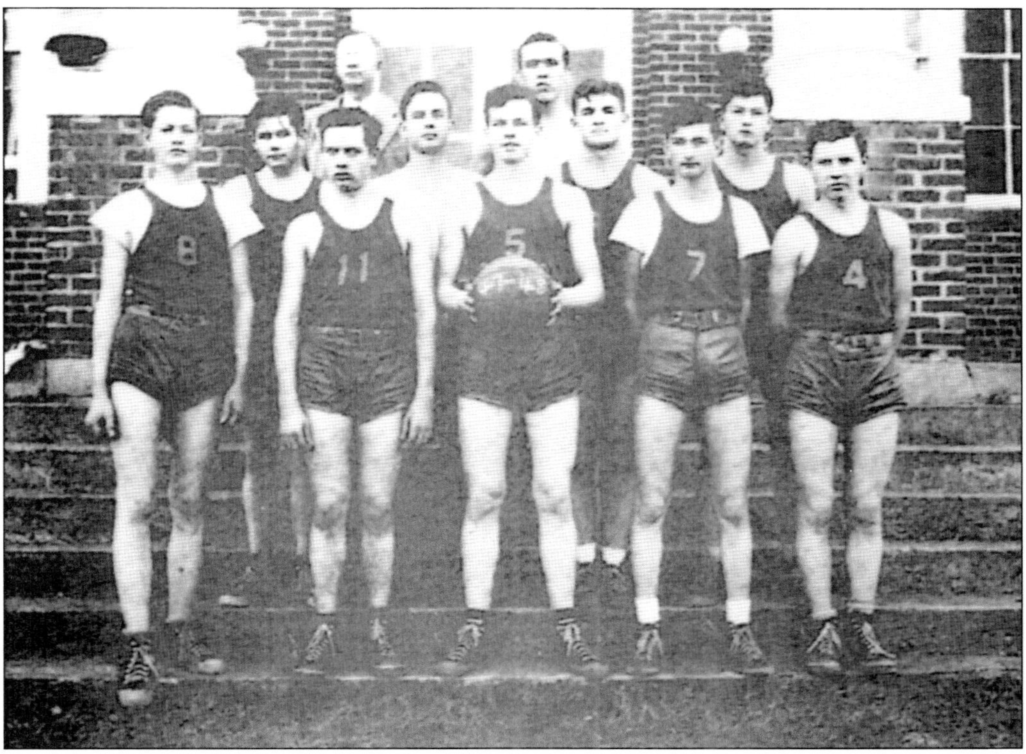

The boys' basketball team of Oak Hill High School is ready for a game in 1947.

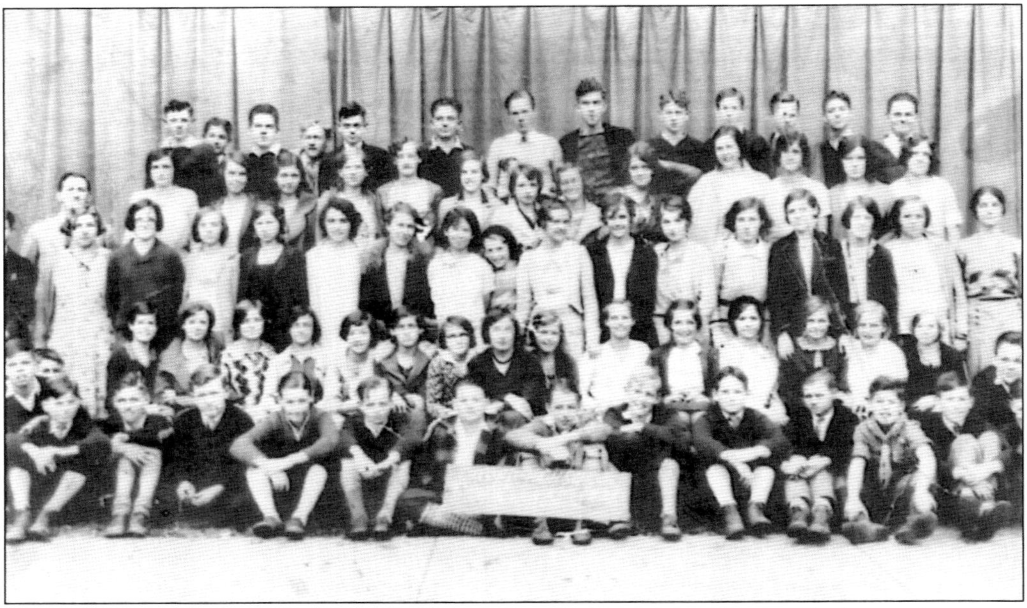

These are the Oxford High School freshmen of 1930. (Courtesy of Nettie Dickerson.)

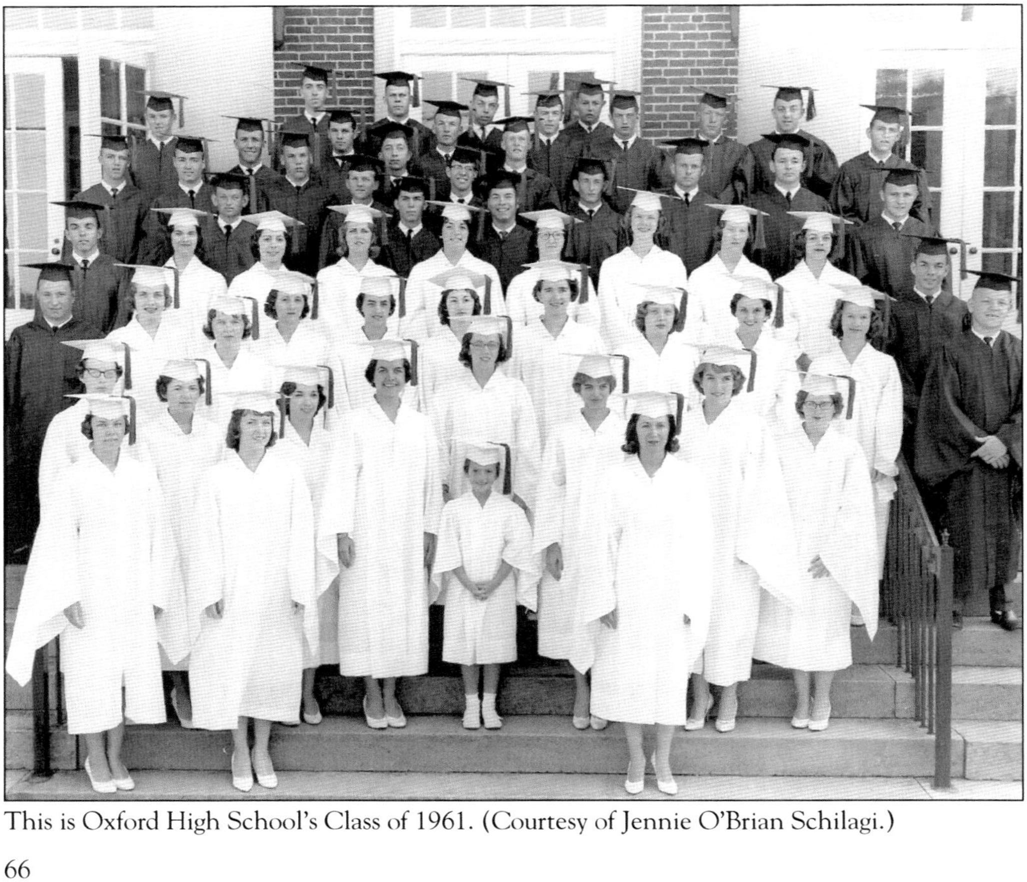

This is Oxford High School's Class of 1961. (Courtesy of Jennie O'Brian Schilagi.)

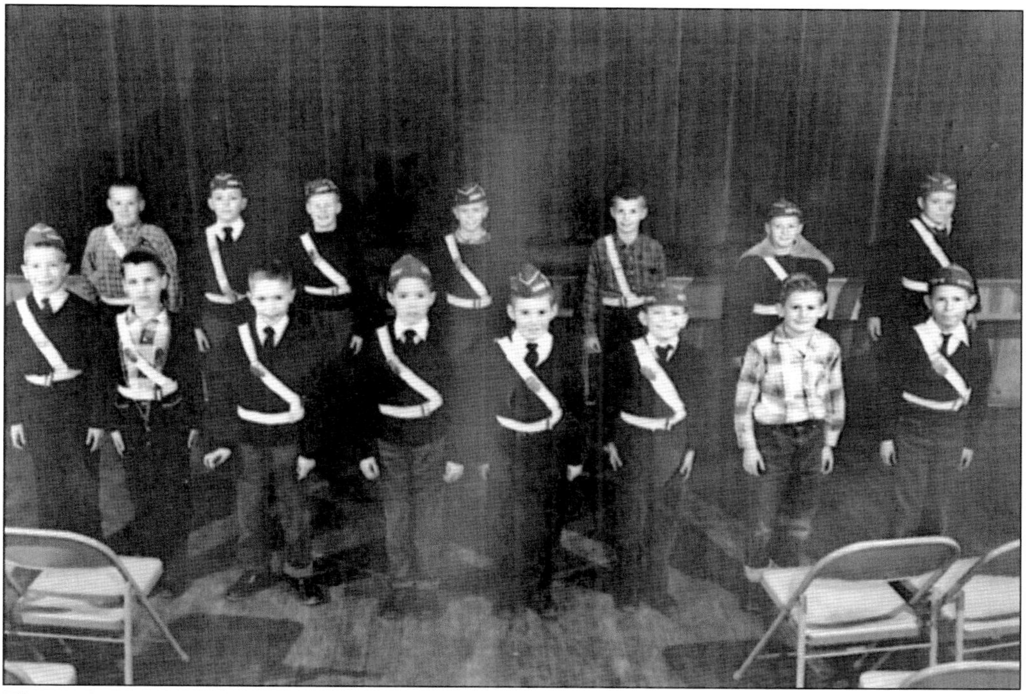

The 1959 C.G. Credle School Patrol is ready for duty.

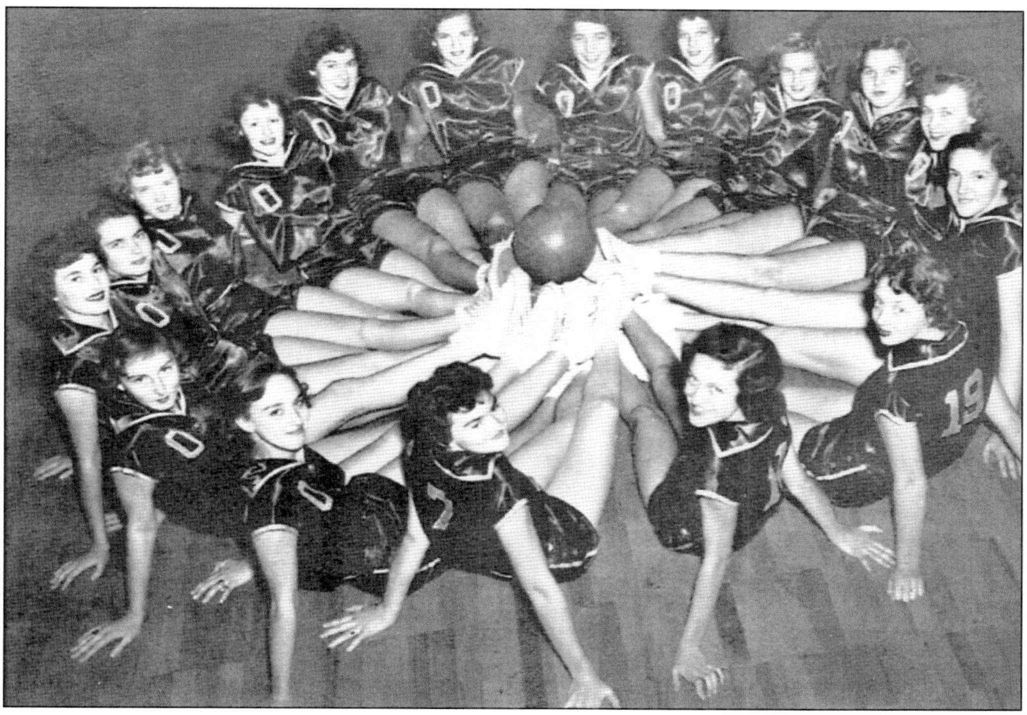

Balancing the ball with their toes is the 1952 Oxford High School girls' basketball team.

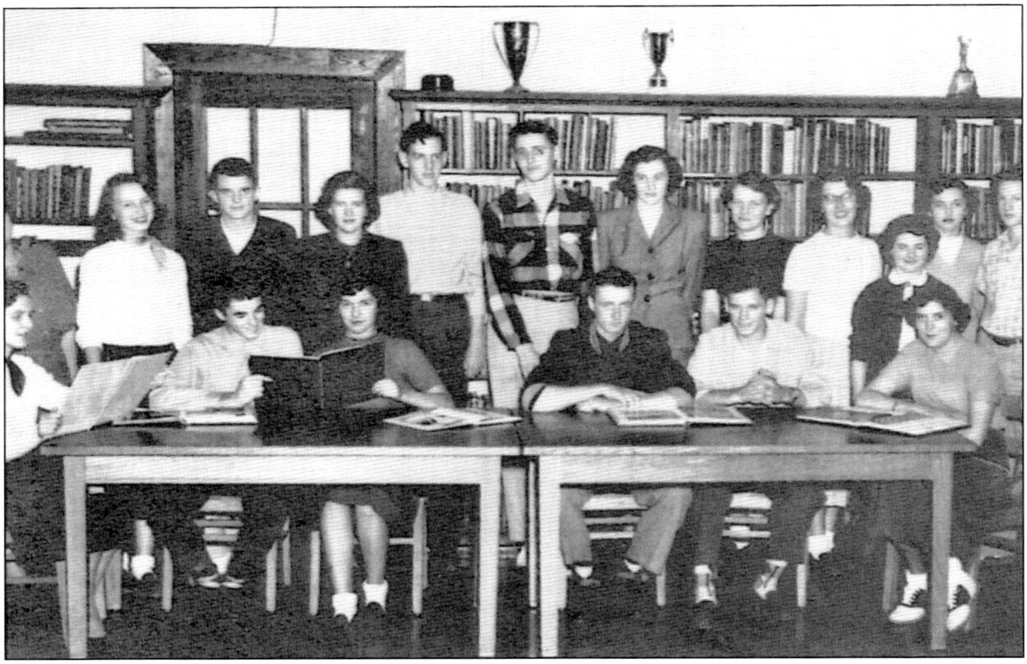
The Library Club of Oxford High School in 1952 looks very studious.

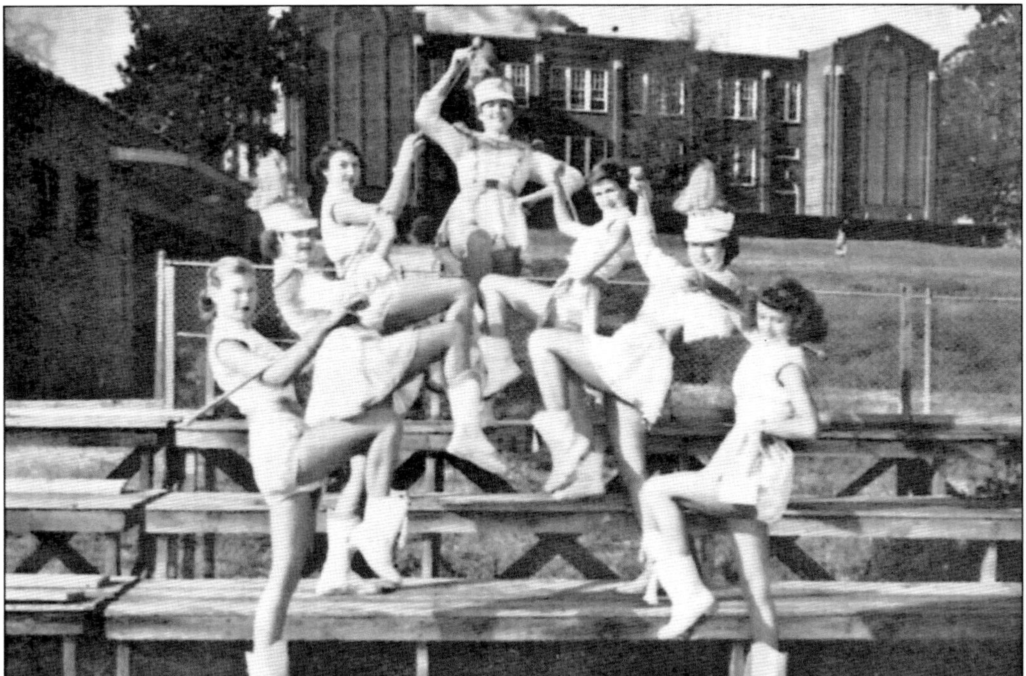
These girls are the Oxford High School Majorettes of 1952.

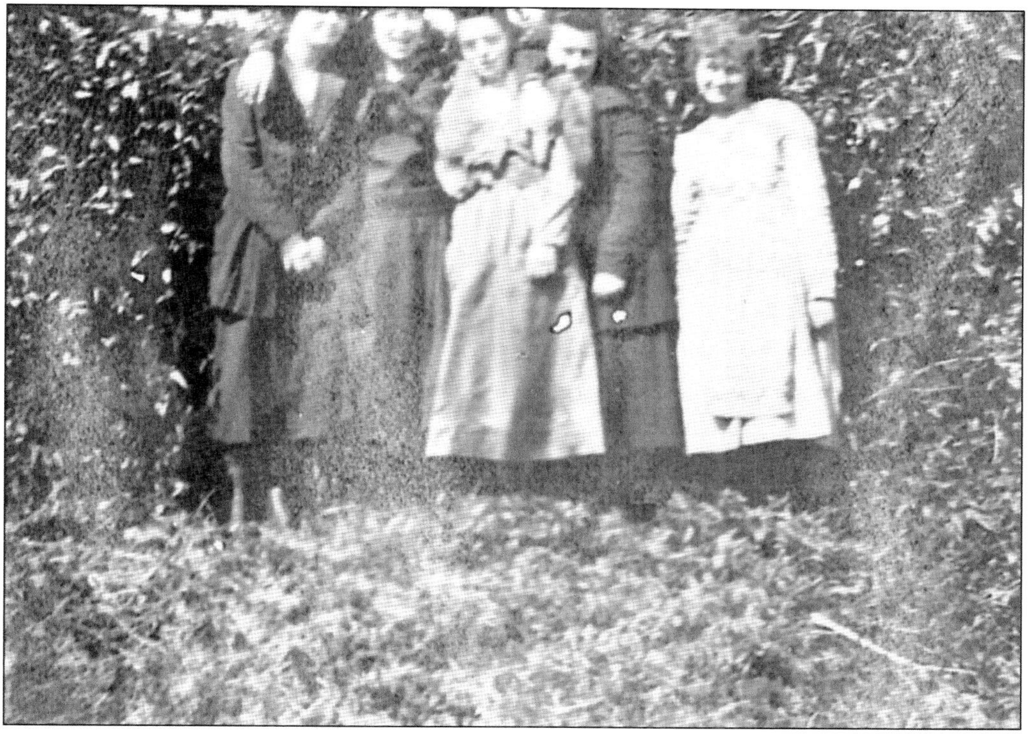

Ladies from Oxford Female College look to the camera in the early 1900s.

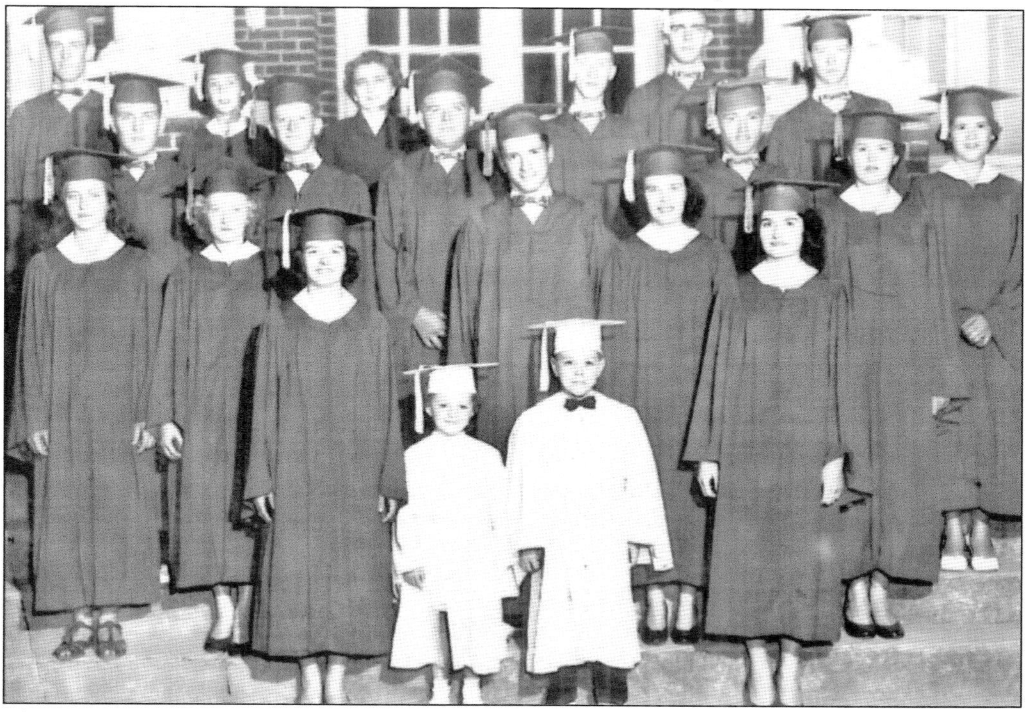

This is the 1955 Berea High School graduating class. (Courtesy of Birk Lunsford.)

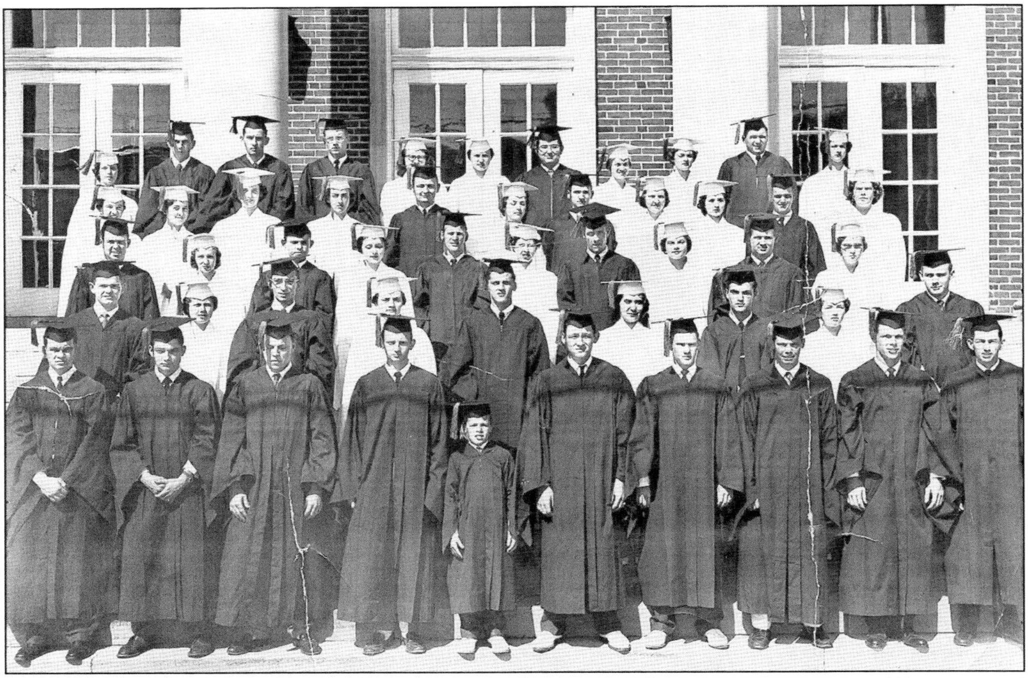

The 1956 Oxford High School graduating class poses for a group picture. (Courtesy of Josephine Currin.)

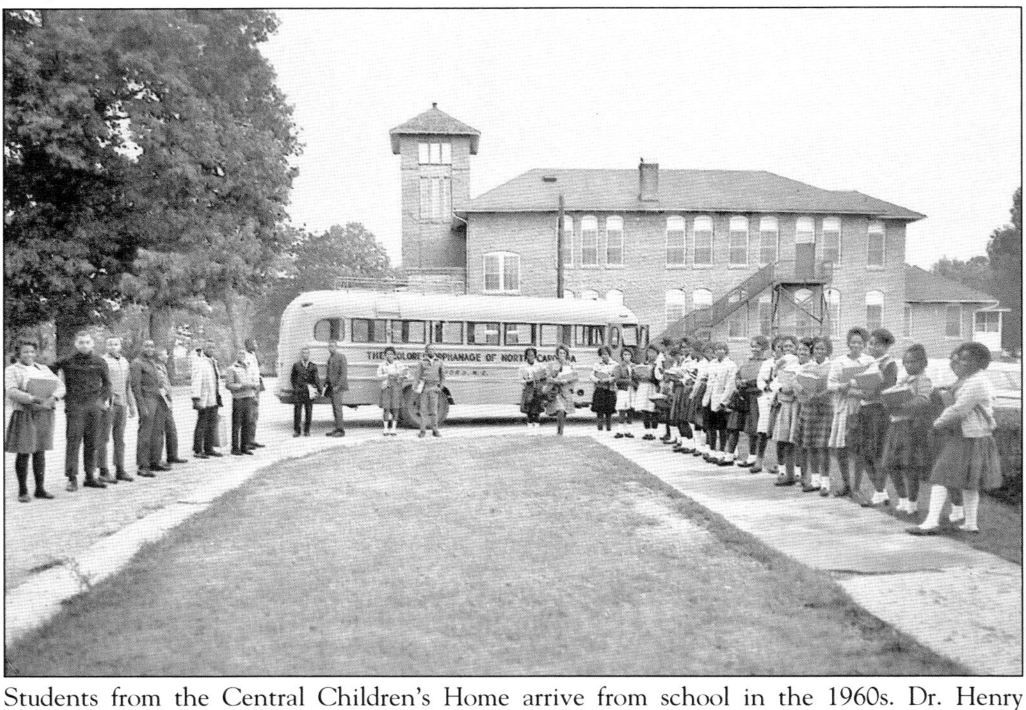

Students from the Central Children's Home arrive from school in the 1960s. Dr. Henry Cheatham, at one time a United States congressman, served as superintendent from 1907 to 1935. (Courtesy of Mike Alston.)

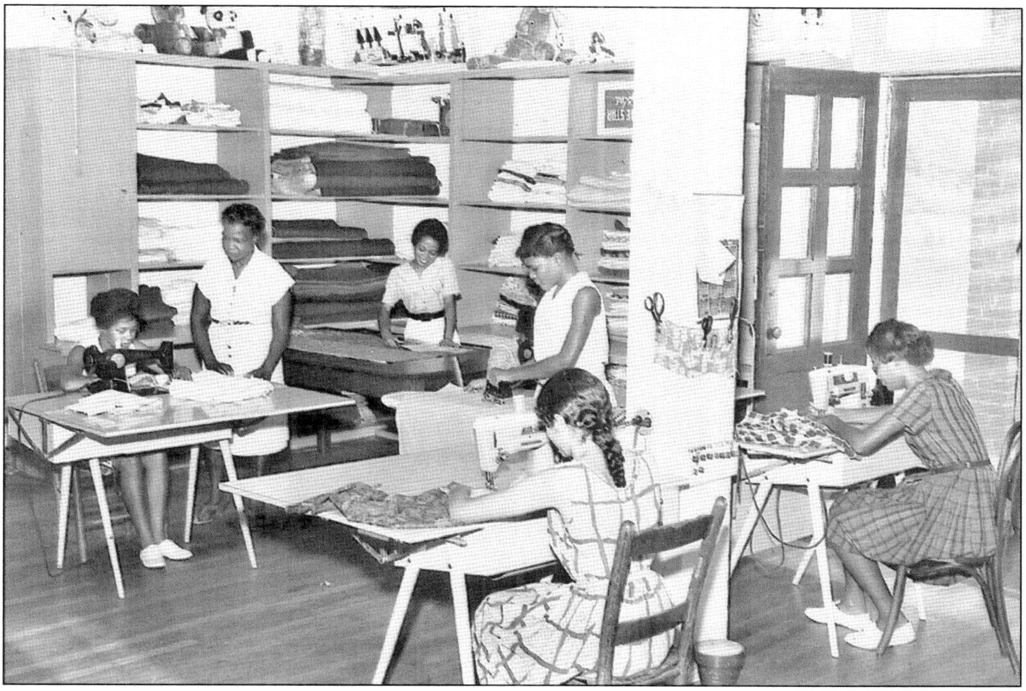

Vocational training is taking place in 1955 at the Central Children's Home in Oxford. (Courtesy of Mike Alston.)

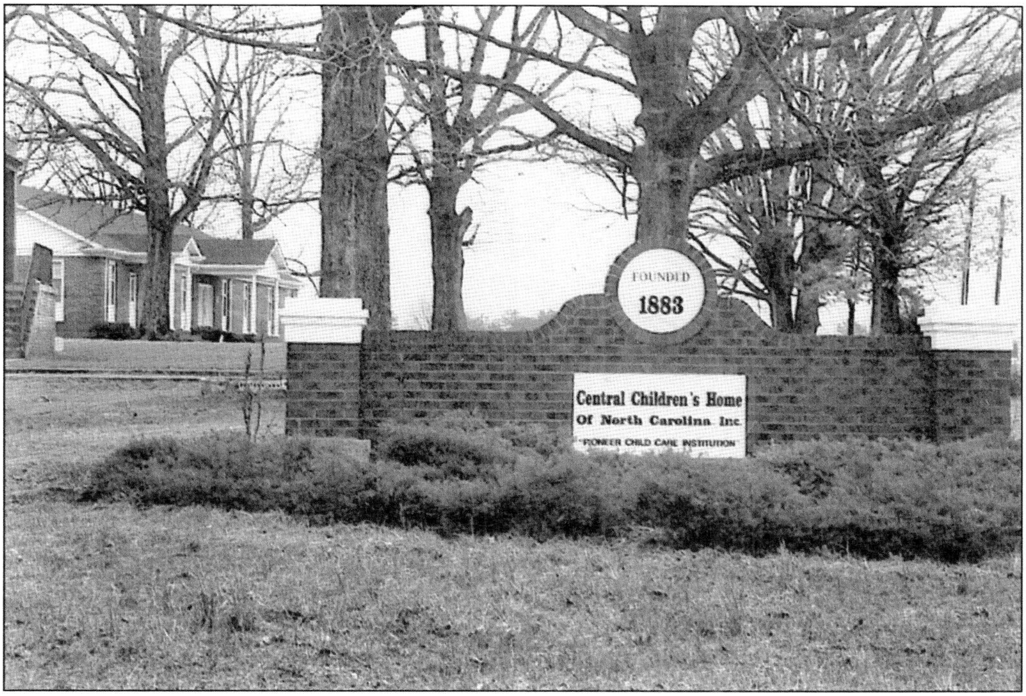

Part of the campus of the Central Children's Home is shown. This orphanage was founded in 1883. (Courtesy of Mike Alston.)

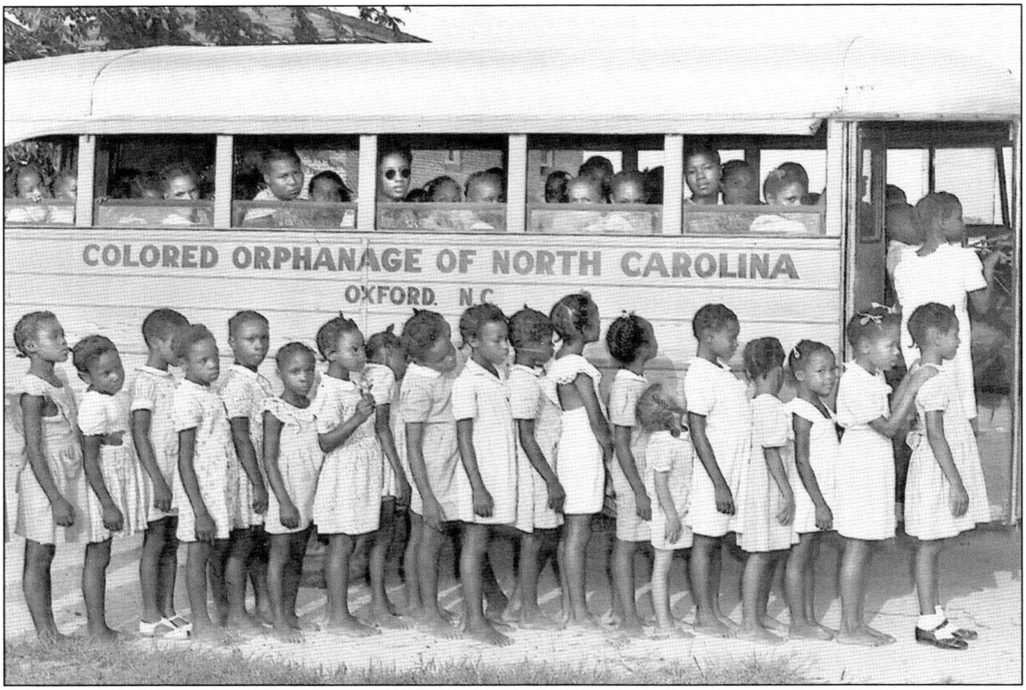

Students of the Colored Orphanage of North Carolina are in line in the 1950s to board a bus.

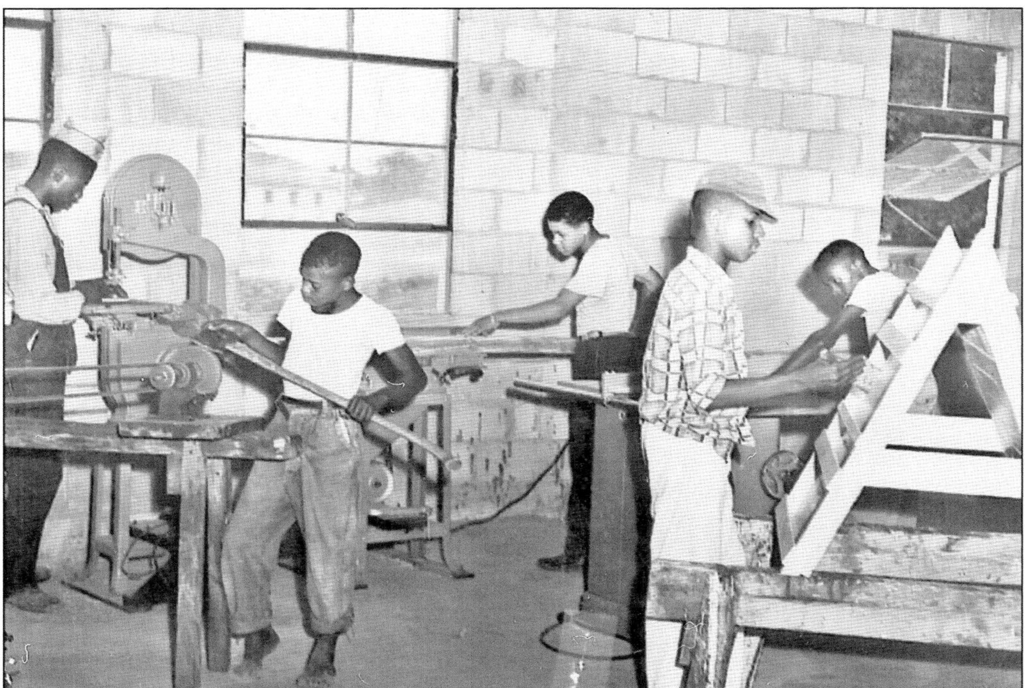

Another vocational training class is being conducted at the Central Children's Home. (Courtesy of Mike Alston.)

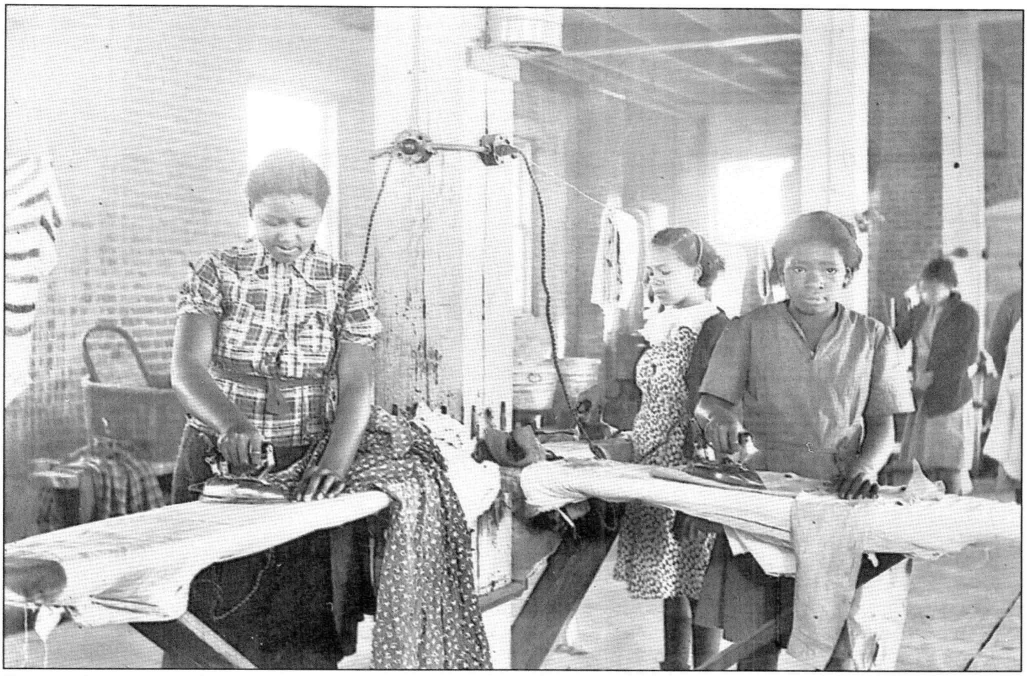

Young ladies are busy in the laundry room of the Central Children's Home in the 1950s. (Courtesy of Mike Alston.)

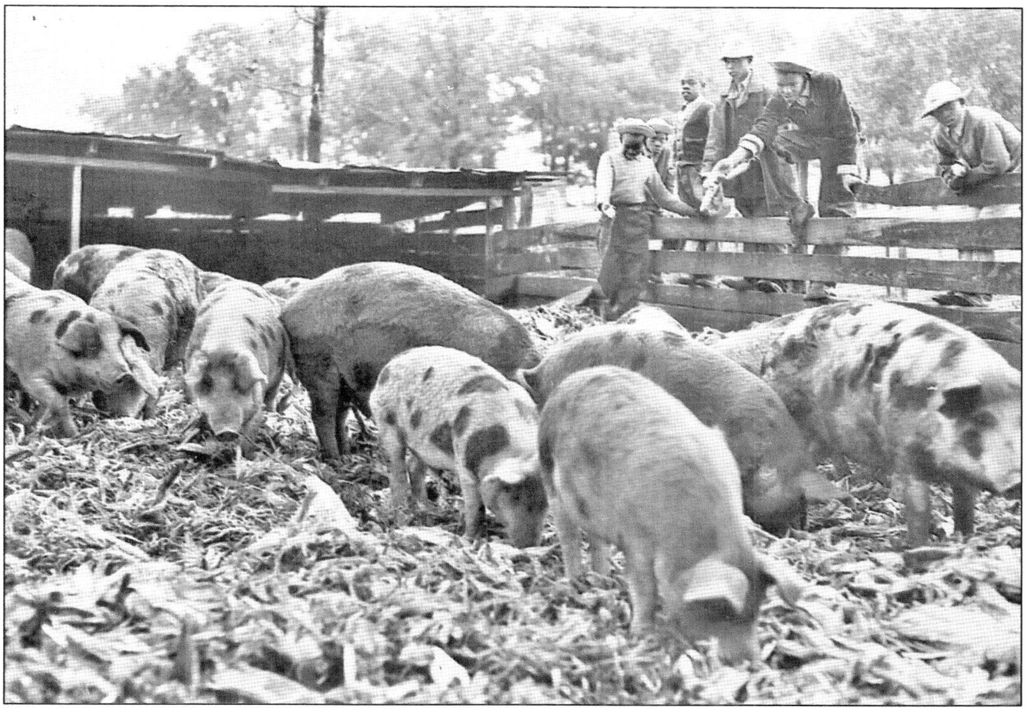

Pigs are doing their job—eating—at the Central Children's Home farm in 1949. (Courtesy of Mike Alston.)

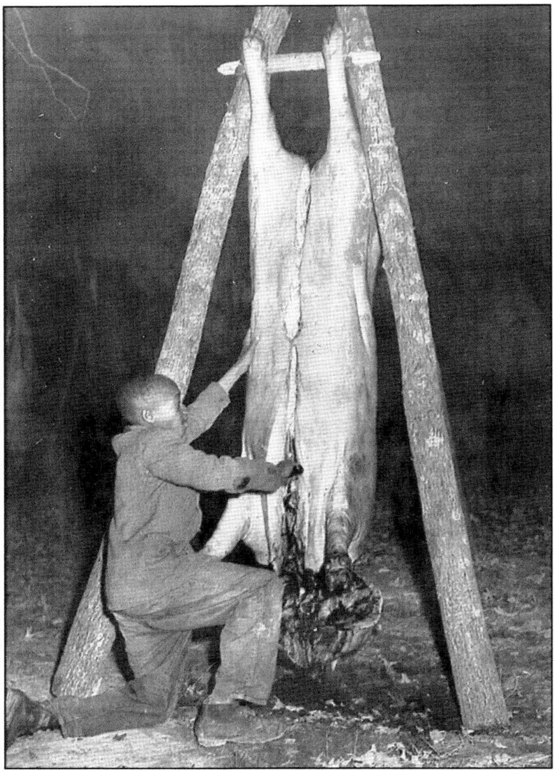

A young man prepares a pig at the Central Children's Home in 1950. (Courtesy of Mike Alston.)

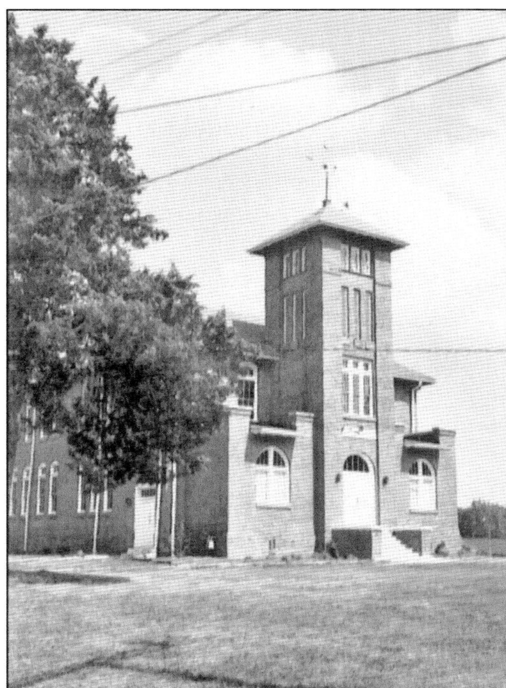

Cheatham Hall is listed on the National Register of Historic Places. Henry Cheatham was a longtime superintendent of the Central Children's Home and at one time a United States congressman. (Courtesy of Mike Alston.)

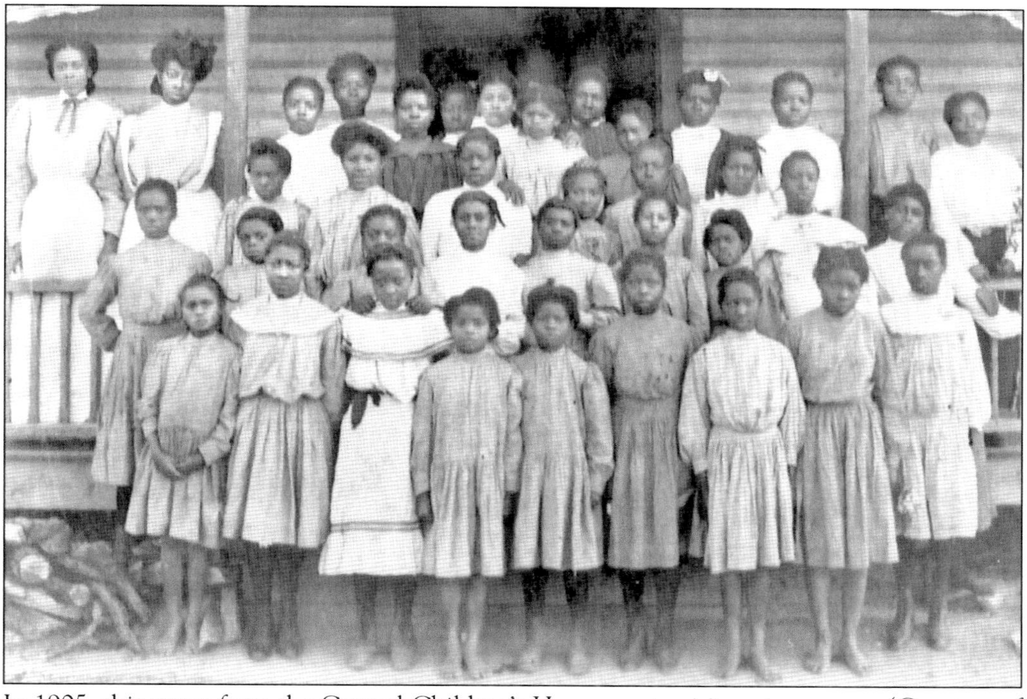

In 1905, this group from the Central Children's Home greets visitors to campus. (Courtesy of Mike Alston.)

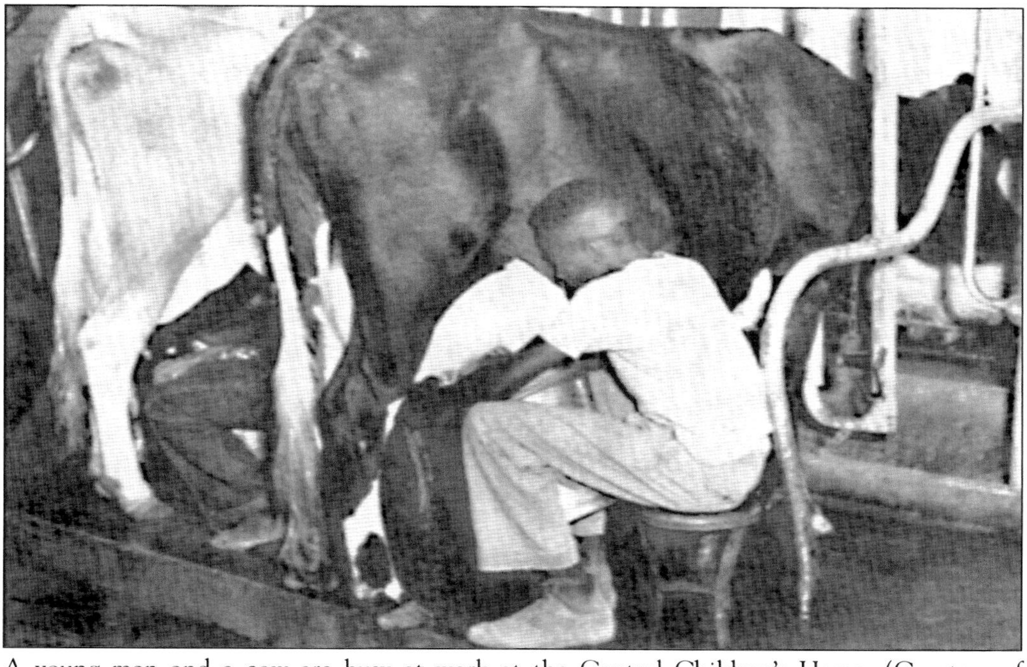

A young man and a cow are busy at work at the Central Children's Home. (Courtesy of Mike Alston.)

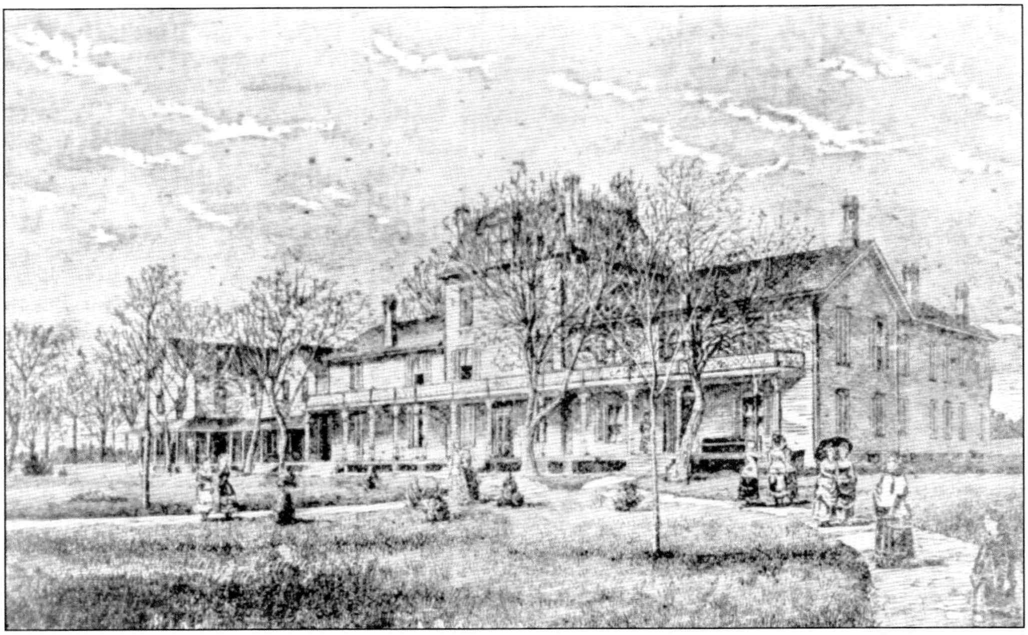

This drawing depicts how Oxford Female College looked in the 1800s. This college operated from 1850 to 1925, educating over 5,000 women from around the state and beyond.

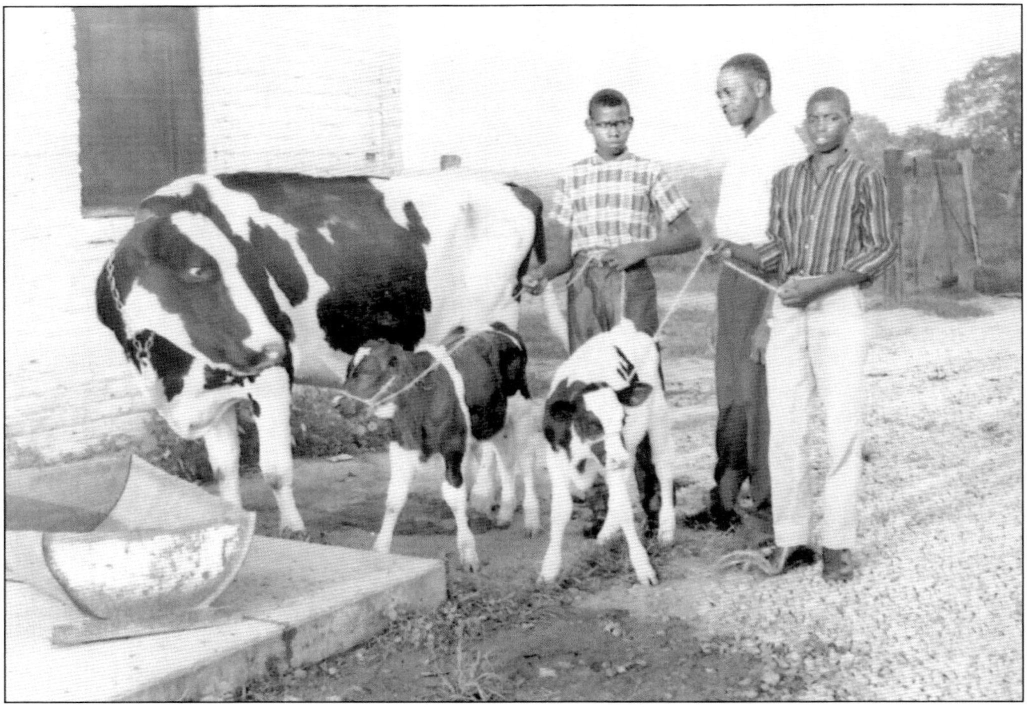

Central Children's Home staff and students are watching a cow and her calves in the 1950s. (Courtesy of Mike Alston.)

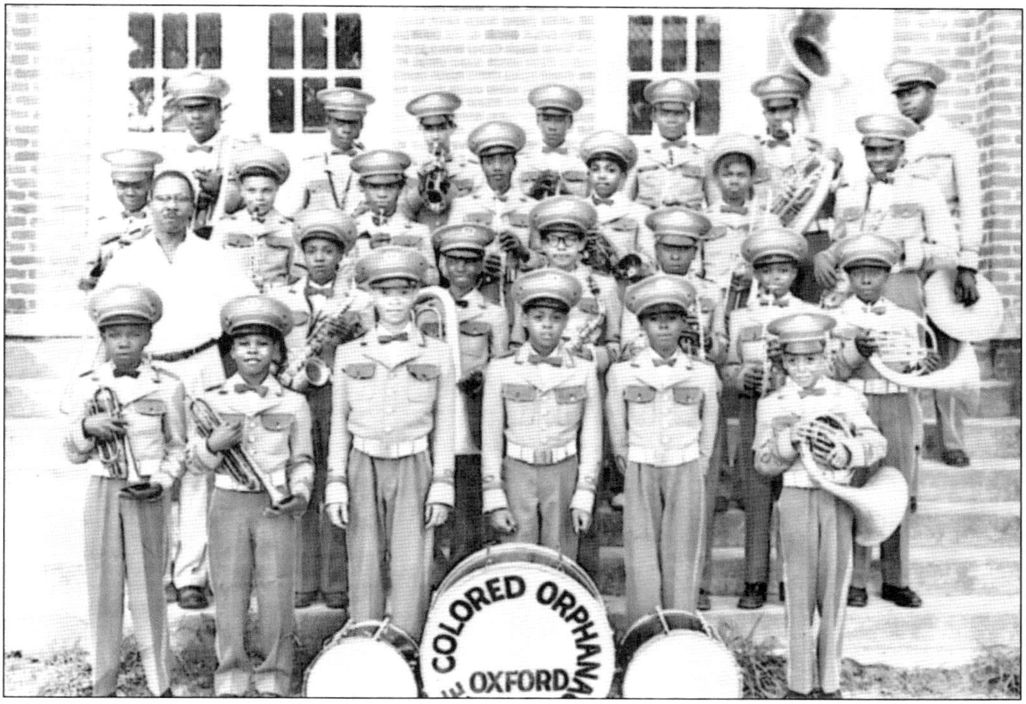

This is the Oxford Colored Orphanage band as it looked in the 1950s. Claude Taylor is the director. (Courtesy of Mike Alston.)

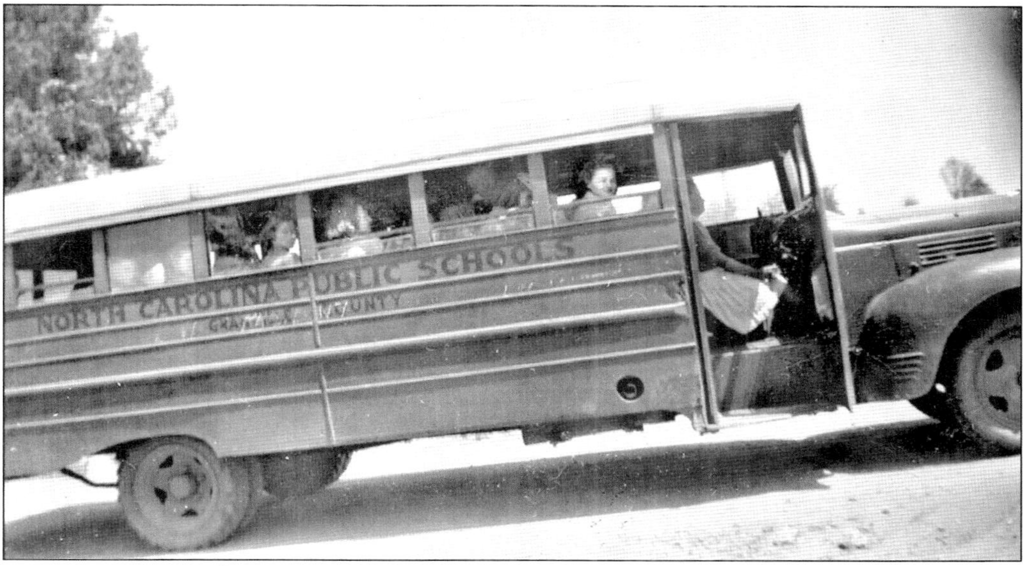

Hop on! A Granville County school bus is waiting for students in the 1940s. (Courtesy of Mildred Harris.)

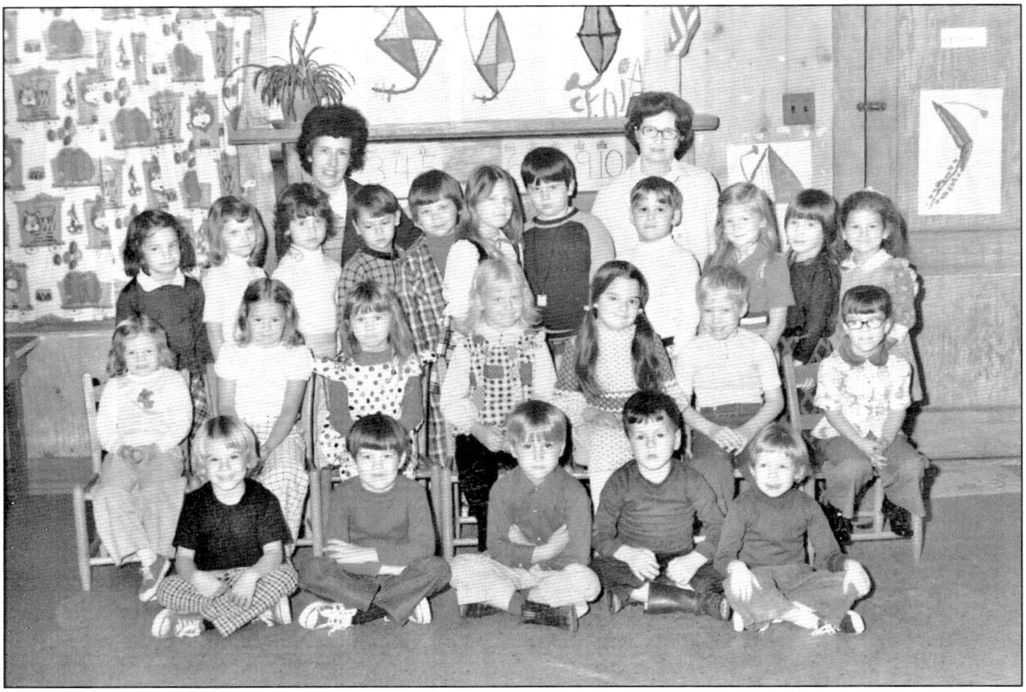

An Oxford pre-school class looks on in the early 1970s. Their school was located on Kingsbury Street. (Courtesy of Jean Gill.)

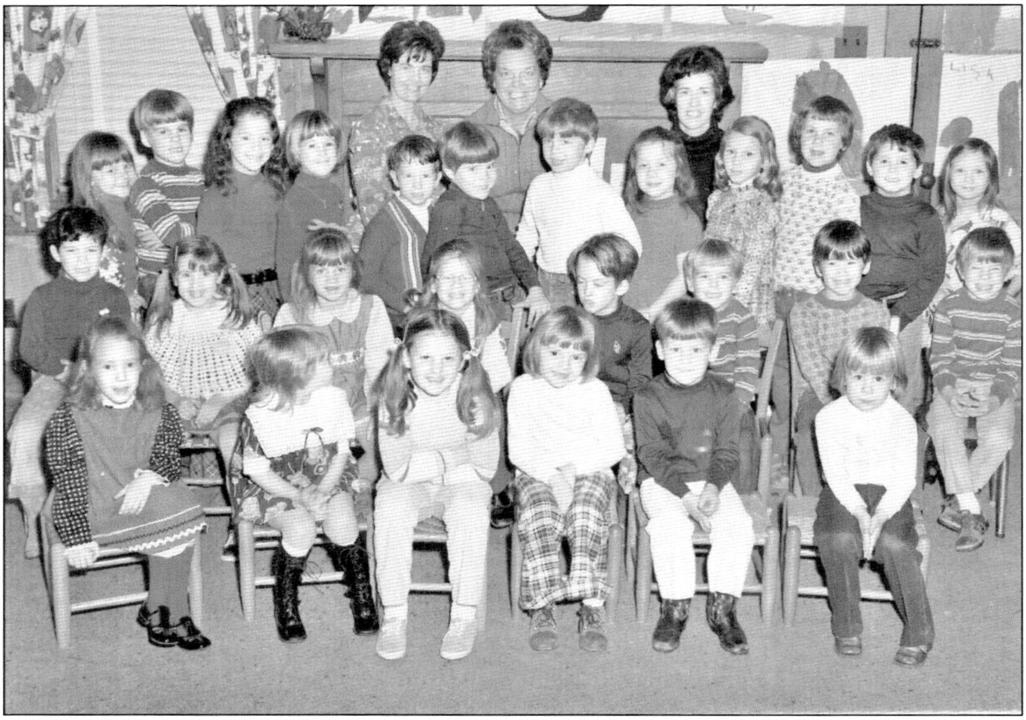

This is a 1973 Oxford pre-school class. (Courtesy of Jean Gill.)

THE OXONIAN

Vol. 2 December, 1917 No. 1

TO OUR SOLDIER BOYS

—Earle Hunt, '19

Go forth! go forth 'cross the ocean deep,
Or the desert far and wide!
Though loved ones you leave behind may weep,
Just think of your country's pride.
Go fight for the right of the U. S. A.!
May our country forever live!
Each fight like a man as brave as you can,
If even your life you must give.

Come back, come back to the U. S. A.!
When the fierce war times are o'er.
You'll be welcomed again to your old home town
As you've never been welcomed before.
Come back with your lives to your children and wives,
To your sisters and brothers return.
Your fathers will cheer, when your brave deeds they hear,
And dear mothers' love will still burn.

This poem was written by Earle Hunt of Oxford High School. It was published in *The Oxonian* school paper in 1917. (Courtesy of Bob and Judy Hunt.)

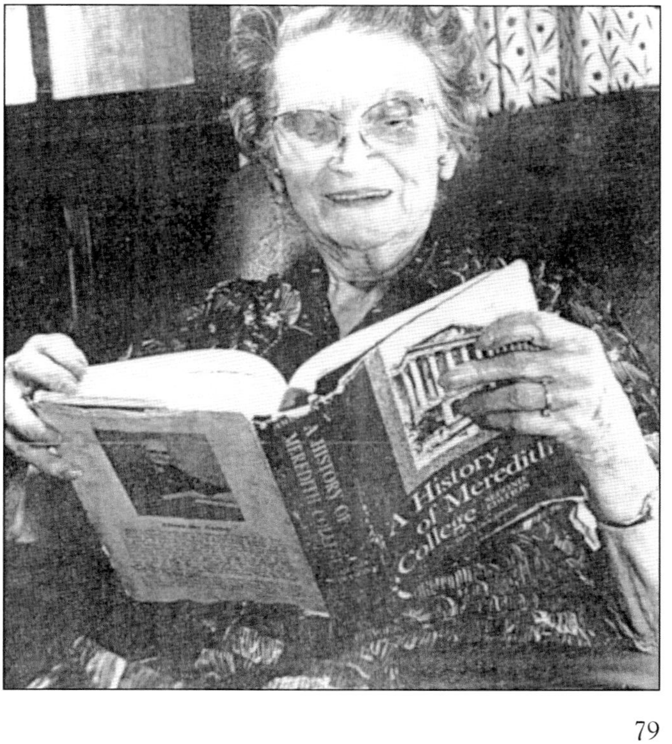

Gladys Strickland Satterwhite was a longtime teacher at Oxford High School. Shown here reading a history of Meredith College, she was a 1924 graduate of the college.

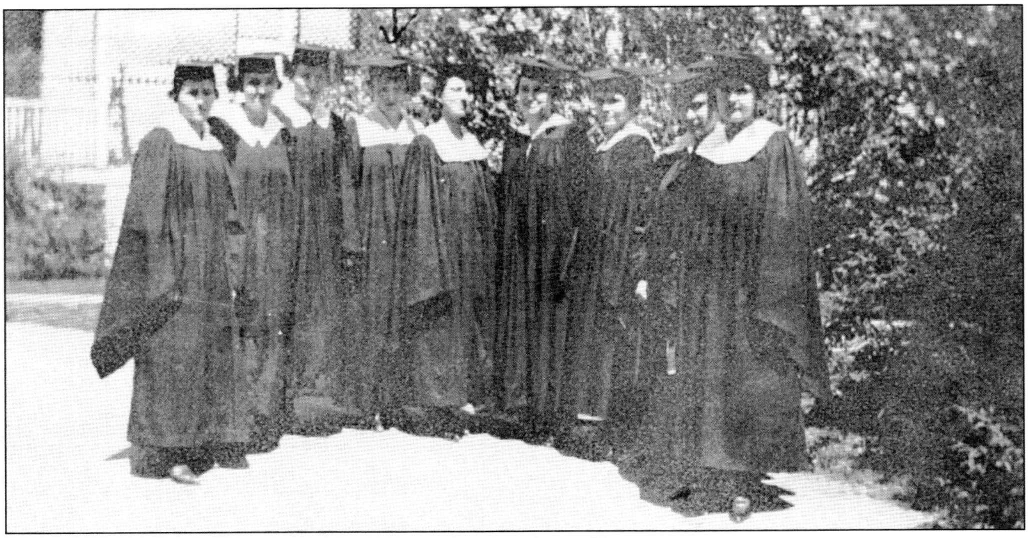

These young ladies are graduates of Oxford Female College in 1918.

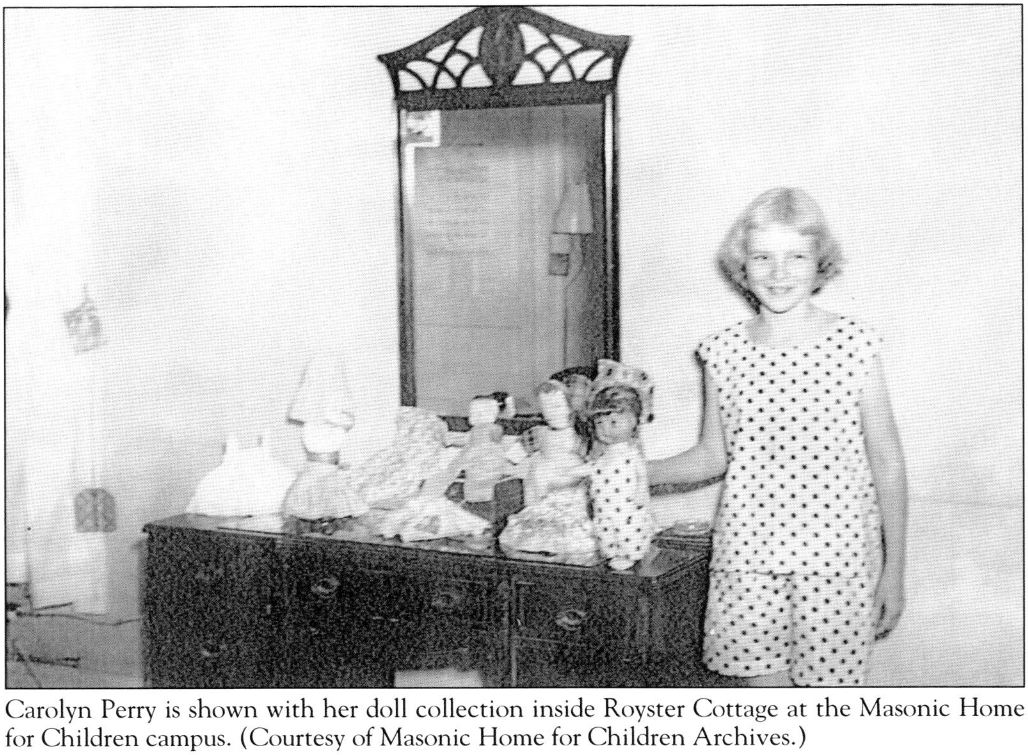

Carolyn Perry is shown with her doll collection inside Royster Cottage at the Masonic Home for Children campus. (Courtesy of Masonic Home for Children Archives.)

Shown here from left to right are Mary Louise Wheeler, Peggy Orthella Wheeler, and Shirley Ann Wheeler Currin at Stem School in 1952. (Courtesy of Shirley Currin.)

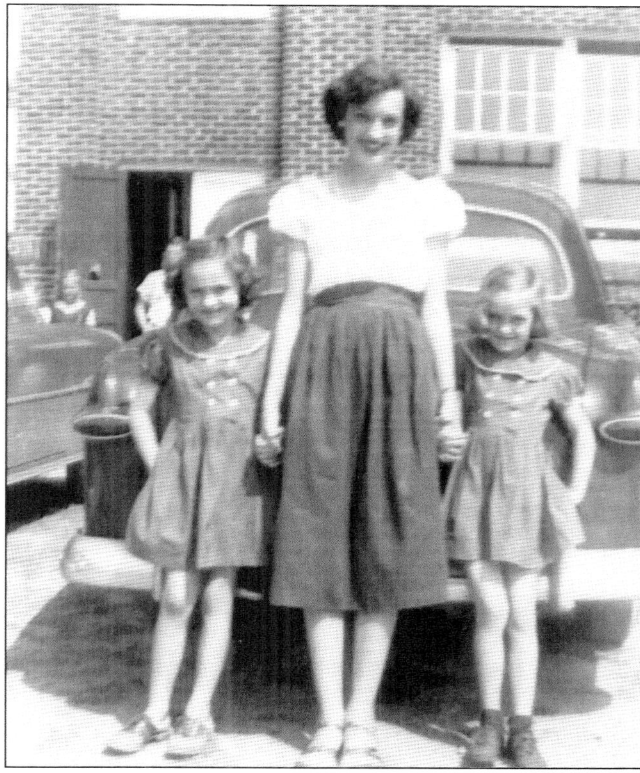

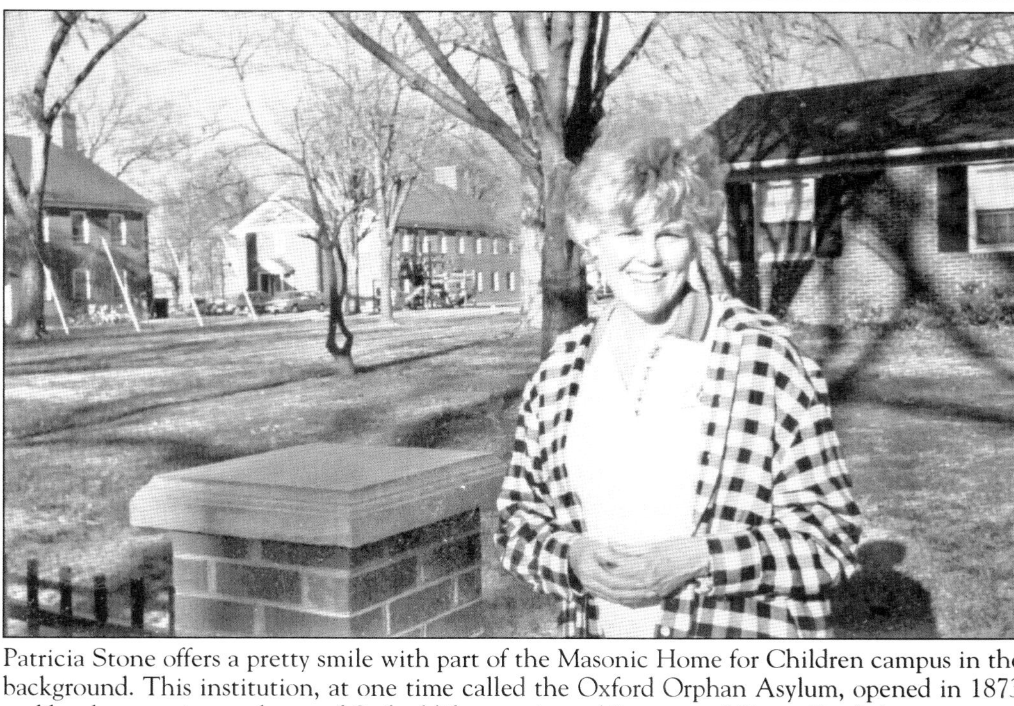

Patricia Stone offers a pretty smile with part of the Masonic Home for Children campus in the background. This institution, at one time called the Oxford Orphan Asylum, opened in 1873 and has been an integral part of Oxford life ever since. (Courtesy of Sigma Finch.)

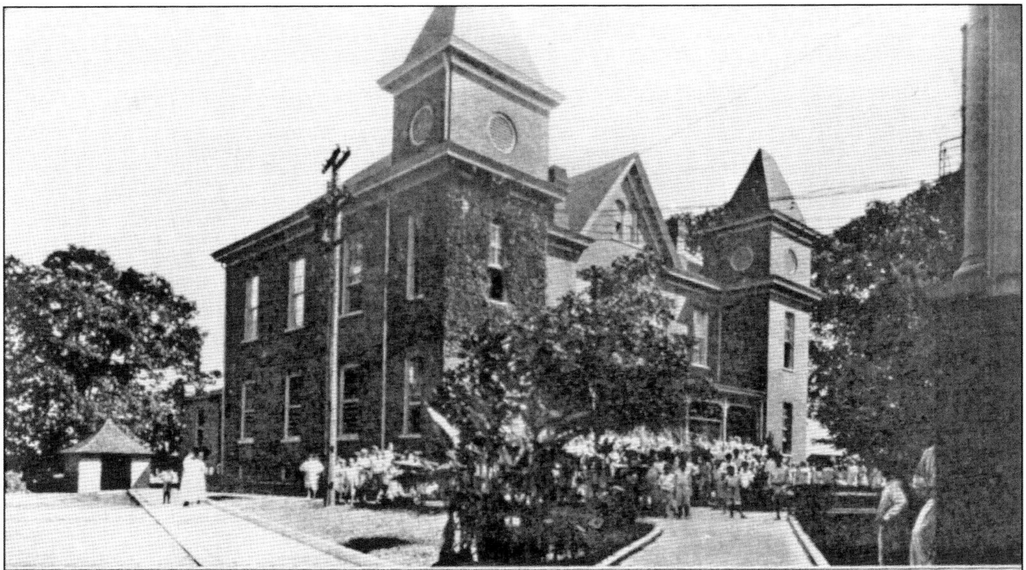

GRAND LODGE HALL UPSTAIRS, DINING HALL FIRST FLOOR—SOME OF THE 380 CHILDREN

Some of the children of the Oxford Orphanage congregate outside the Grand Lodge Hall. (Courtesy of Masonic Home for Children.)

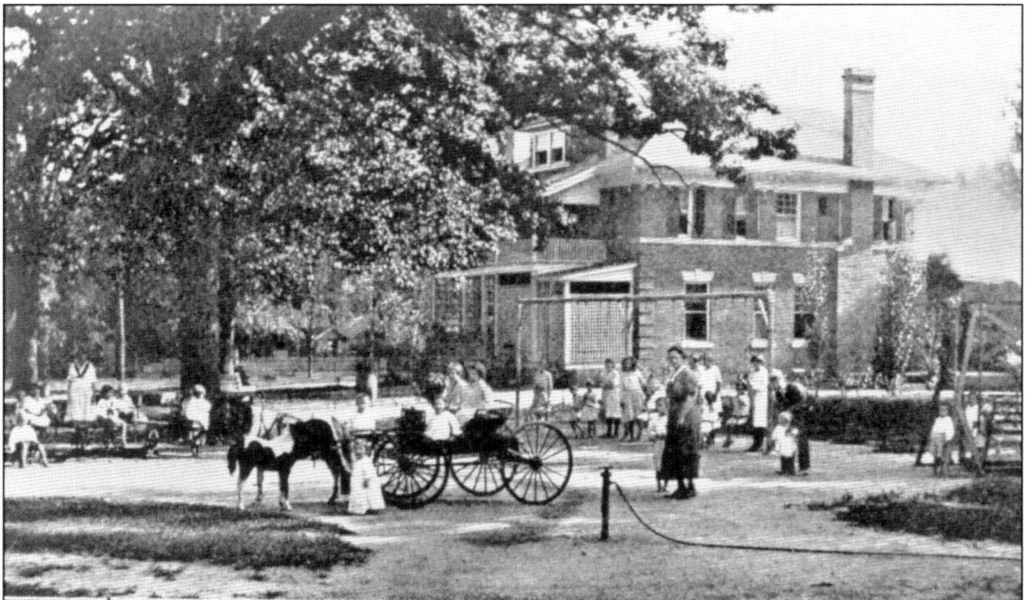

CHILDREN FROM BABY COTTAGE ON THEIR PLAYGROUND

Outside the Baby Cottage at the Oxford Orphanage, children are at play. (Courtesy of Masonic Home for Children.)

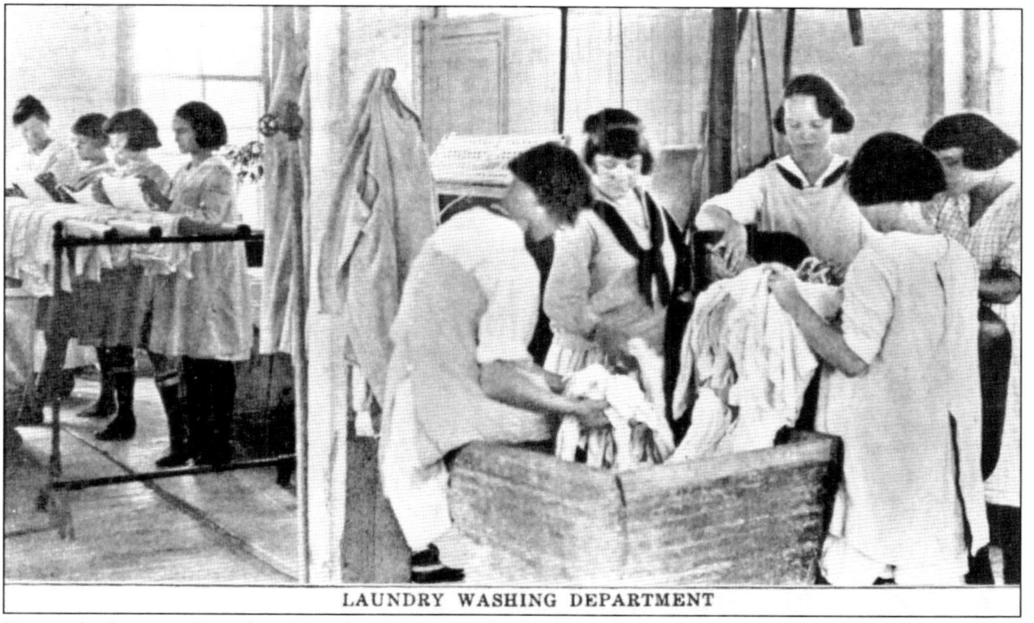

Dirty clothes need washing, and girls at the Oxford Orphanage are hard at work. (Courtesy of Masonic Home for Children.)

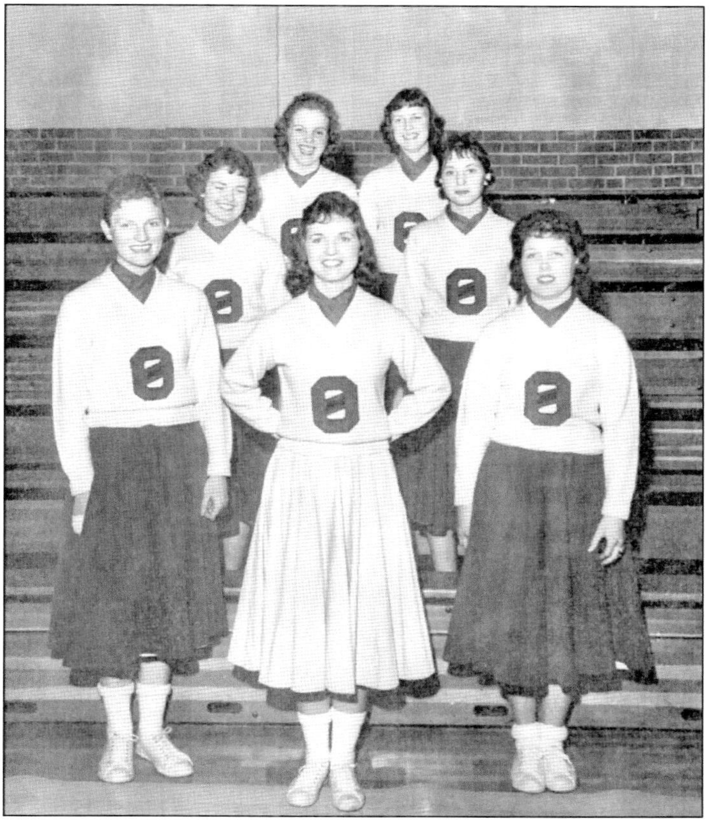

Ready for a basketball game, the Oxford Orphanage cheerleaders are ready to support their team. This picture was taken in the 1950s. (Courtesy of Masonic Home for Children.)

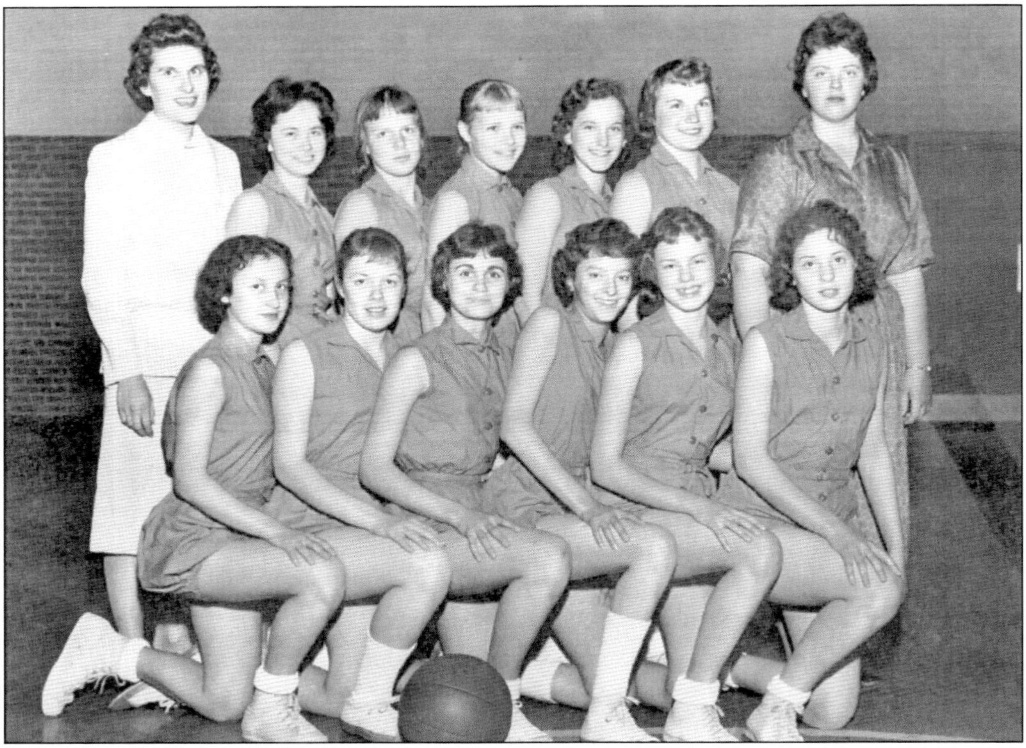

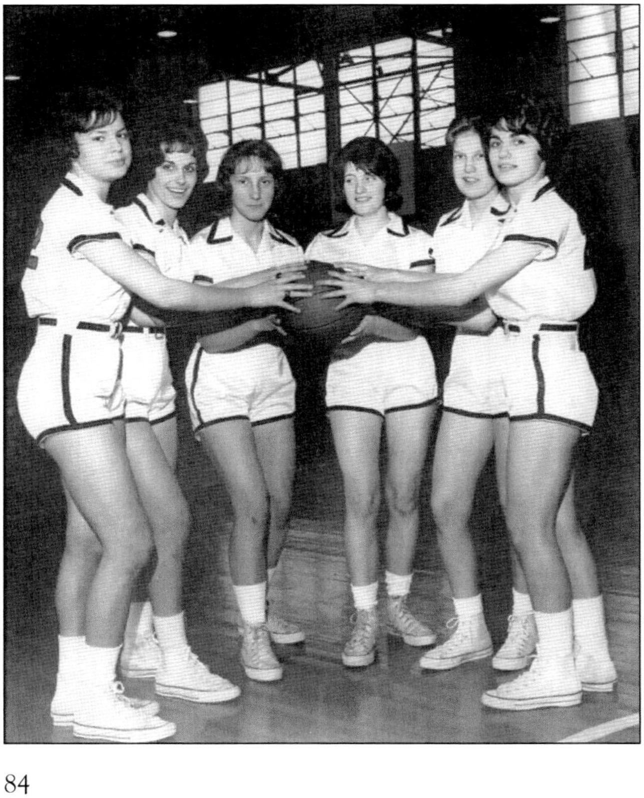

The Oxford Orphanage girls' basketball team is shown in the early 1960s. (Courtesy of Masonic Home for Children.)

This group of girls played for Oxford Orphanage in the mid-1960s. (Courtesy of Masonic Home for Children.)

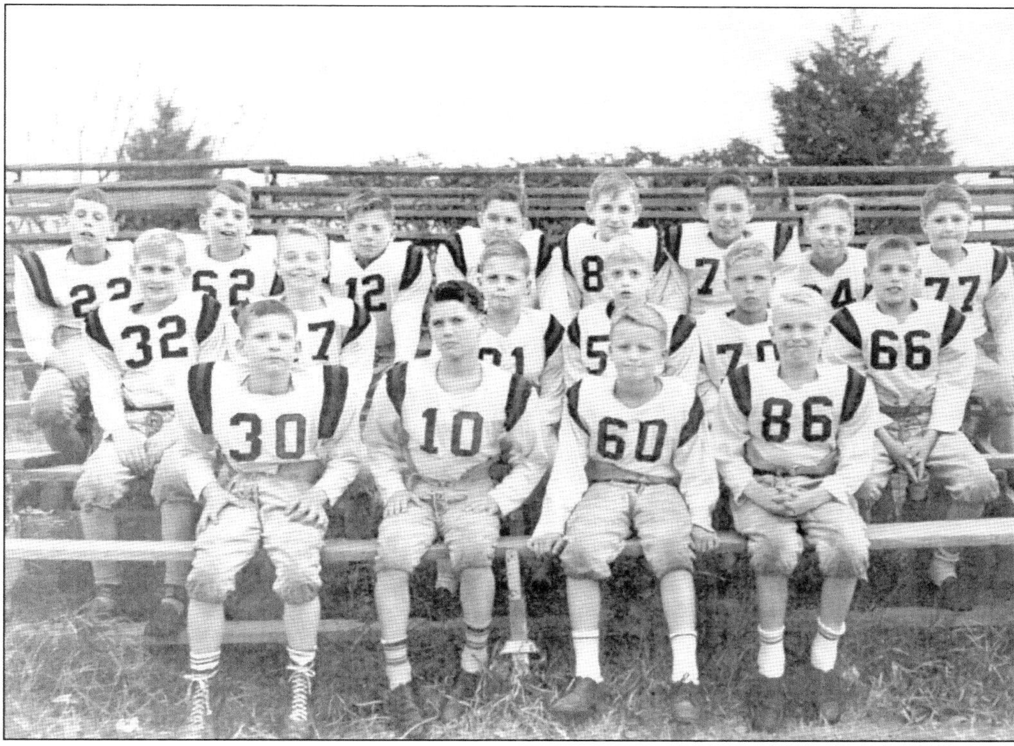

Some with their game faces on, the Oxford Orphanage Midget football team in the 1960s looks ready to go. (Courtesy of the Masonic Home for Children.)

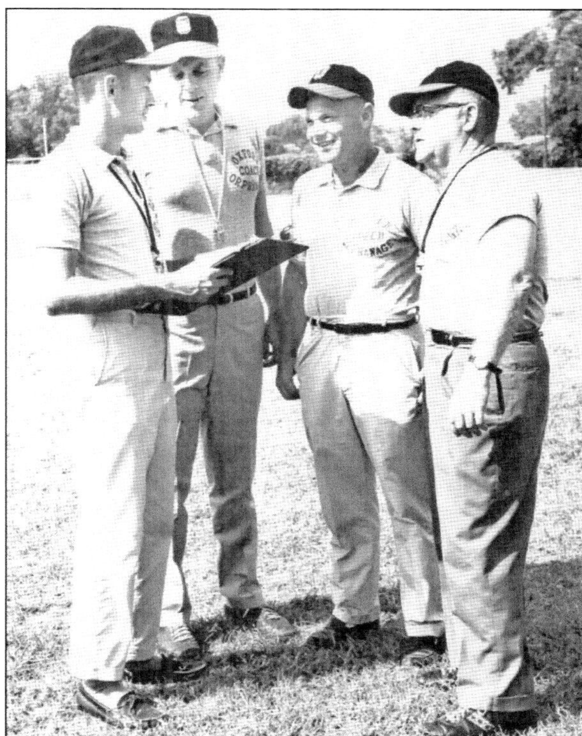

In the early 1960s, coaches at Oxford Orphanage included Jimmie Burnett, Jimmy Fleming, Bev Hester, and Garland Talton. (Courtesy of Masonic Home for Children.)

GOOD GIRLS WANTED.

During February the demand has been urgent for neat, industrious, intelligent and truthful girls, without any near relations. All our girls have inherited their share of original sin, and most of them have the usual allowance of poor kin. We generally find them ignorant of learning and religion, sensual and selfish—having never been taught to be any thing else. We use our best efforts to improve them; but the improvement comes slowly. Success often crowns patient labor. Yet we are afraid to endorse them highly. Those who want girls, should not require flattering recommendations nor expect a girl, endowed with all the cardinal virtues, to nurse, cook, wash and keep house ten years for her victuals and clothes.

This advertisement, which appeared in the Oxford Orphan Asylum paper in 1879, targets the public for possible adoption of the orphanage's girls. Attitudes about the children have changed for the better over the years. (Courtesy of Masonic Home for Children.)

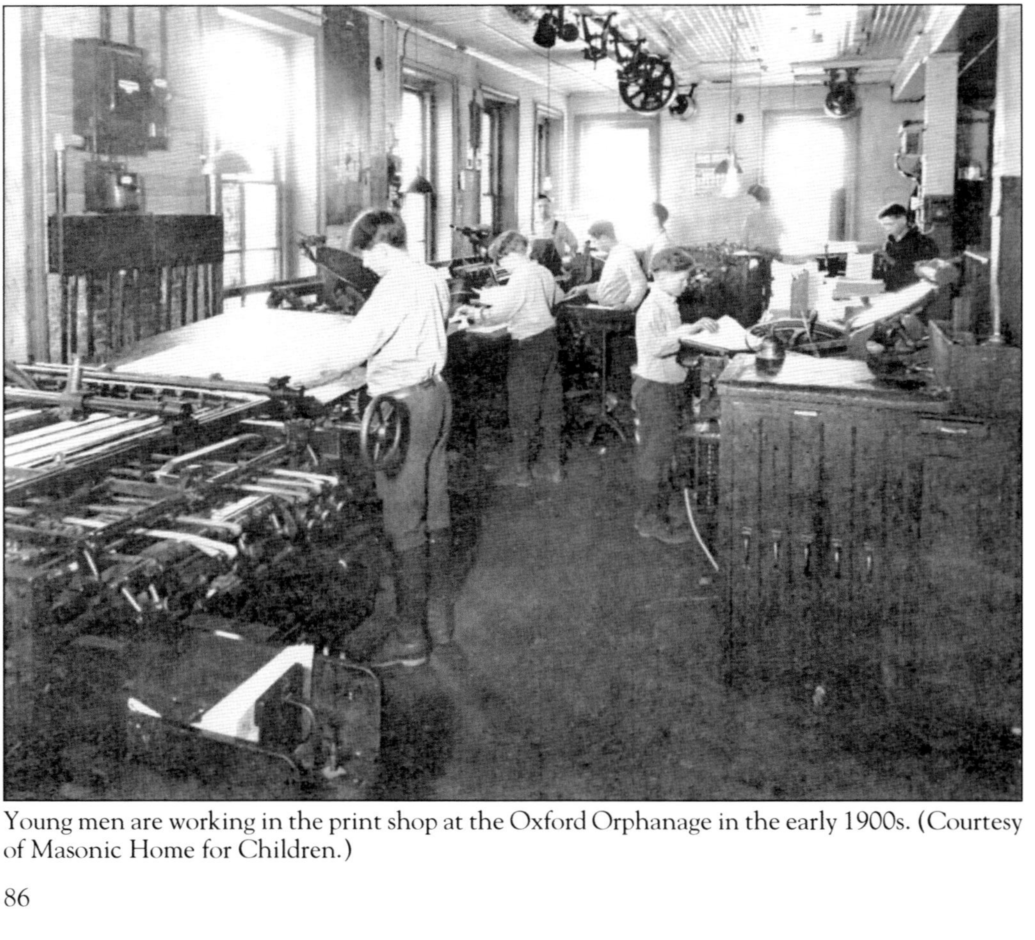

Young men are working in the print shop at the Oxford Orphanage in the early 1900s. (Courtesy of Masonic Home for Children.)

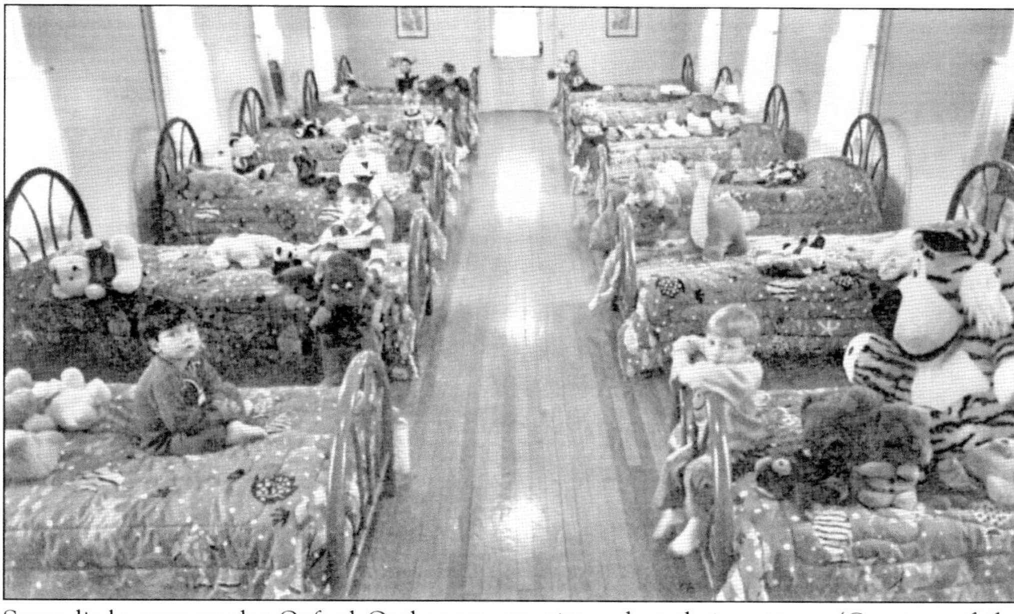

Some little ones at the Oxford Orphanage are pictured at their cottage. (Courtesy of the Masonic Home for Children.)

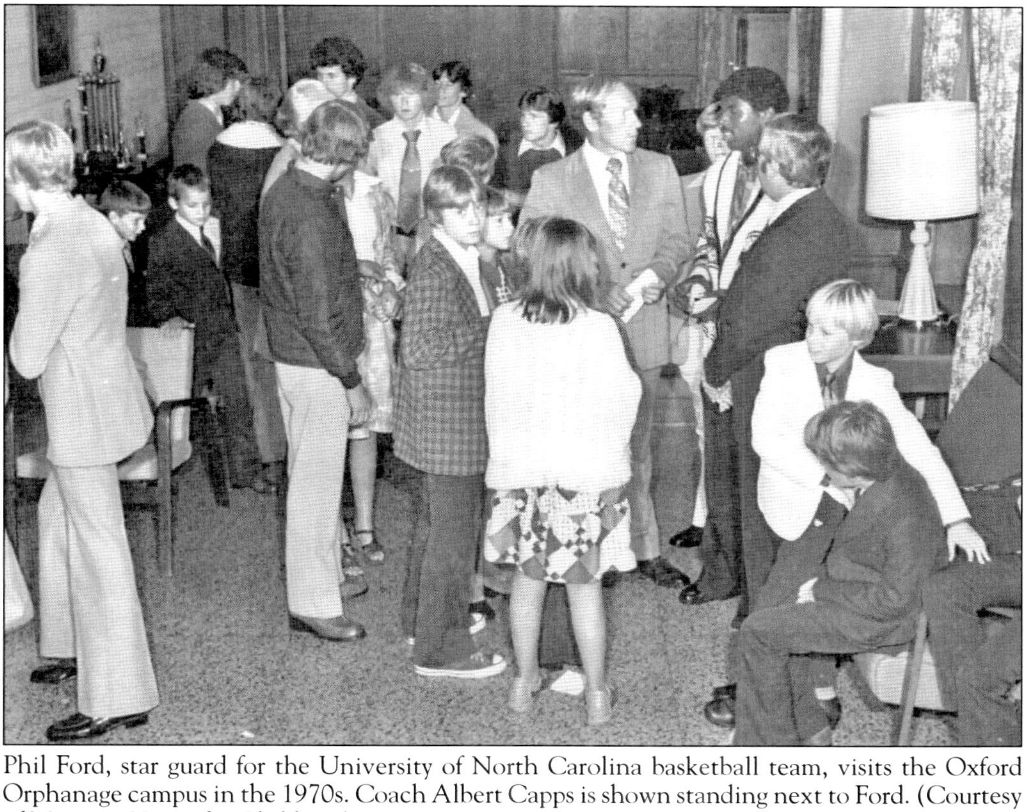

Phil Ford, star guard for the University of North Carolina basketball team, visits the Oxford Orphanage campus in the 1970s. Coach Albert Capps is shown standing next to Ford. (Courtesy of Masonic Home for Children.)

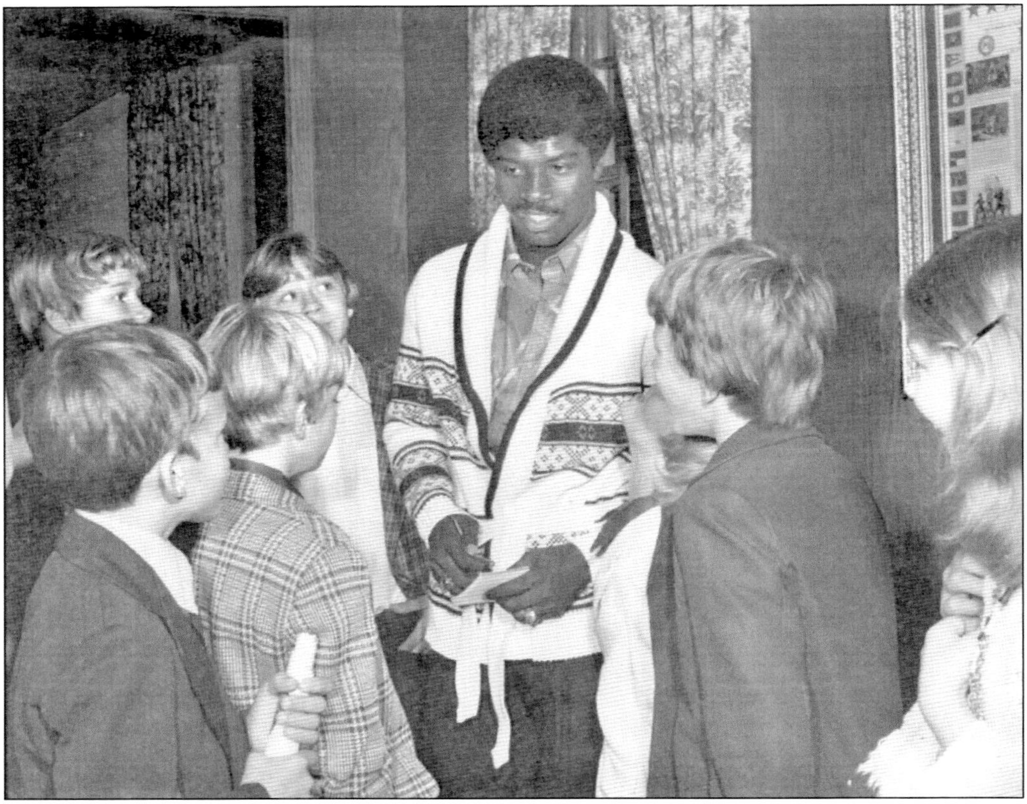

Wide-eyed youngsters line up to get Phil Ford's autograph at the Oxford Orphanage. (Courtesy of Masonic Home for Children.)

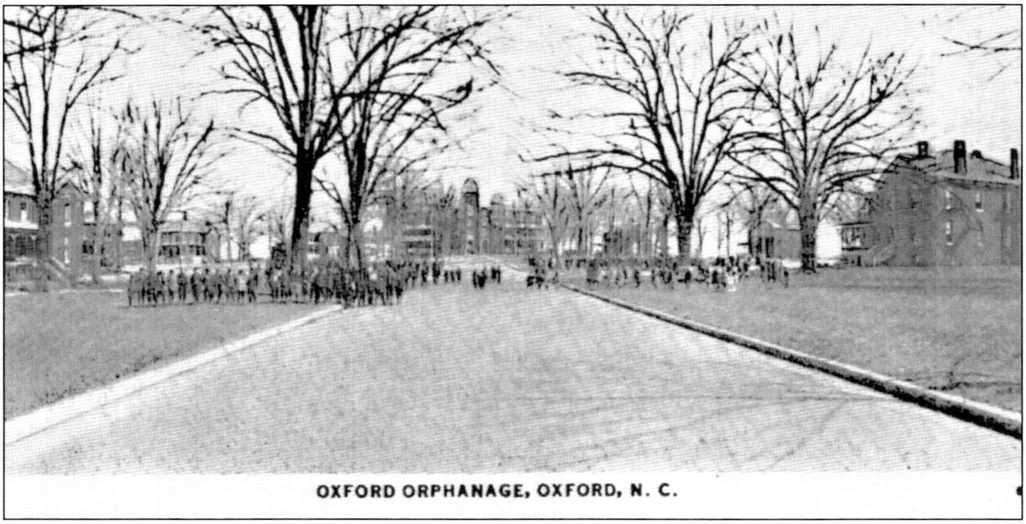

This view shows the main entrance to the Oxford Orphanage in the very early 1900s. Many of the children are waiting to say hello. (Courtesy of Masonic Home for Children.)

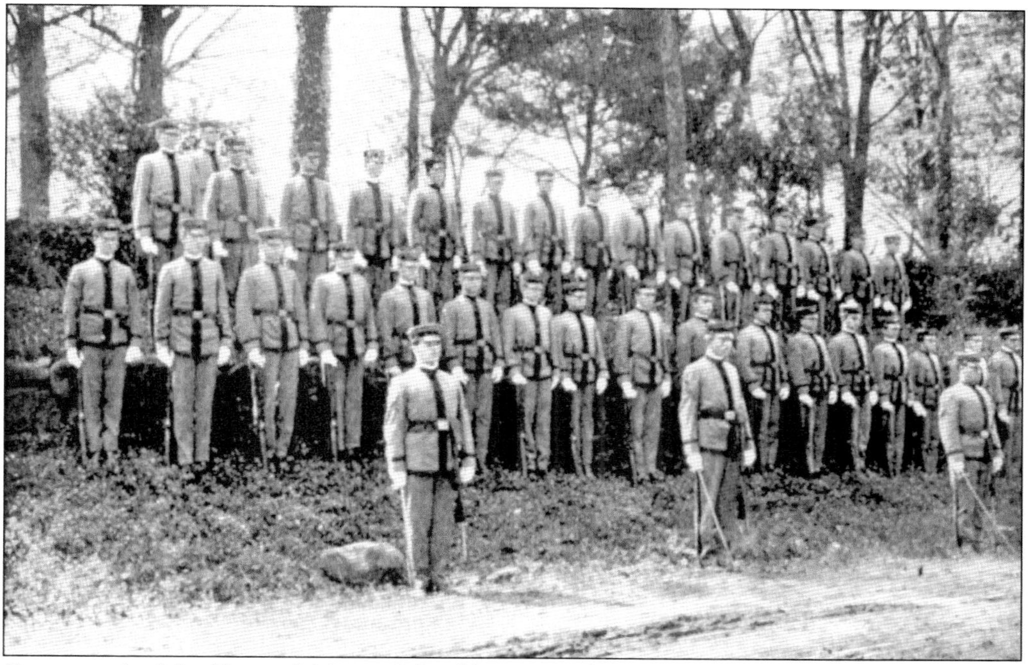

Company A of the Horner Military School line up in formation in the early 1900s.

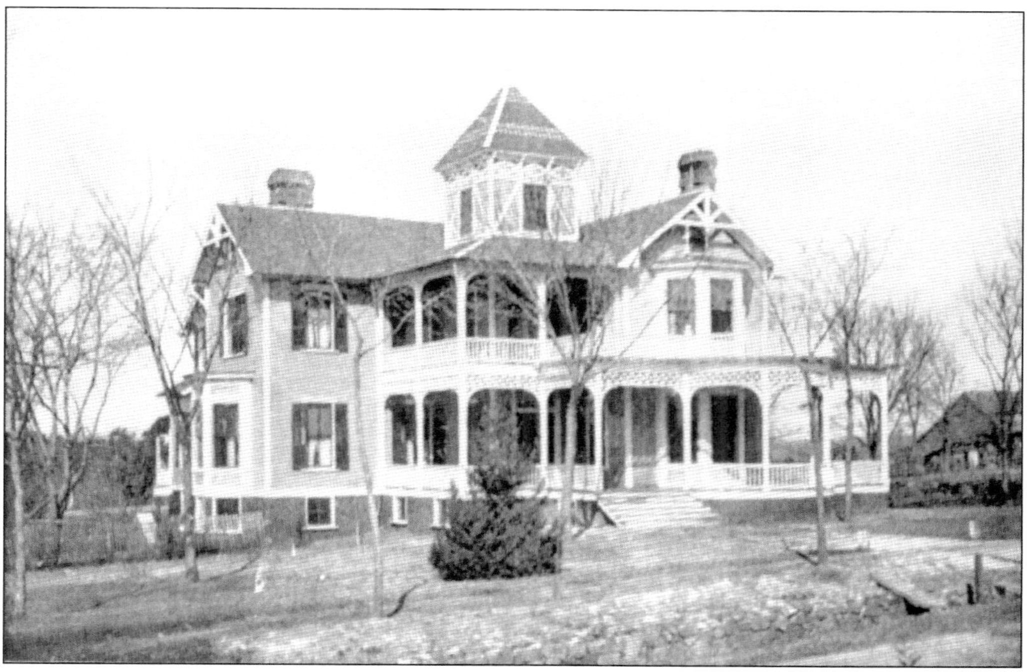

Principal J.C. Horner of Horner Military School lived here, and the school library was also housed here. This school operated on Military Street in Oxford from 1851 to 1914 under the leader ship of James and Jerome Horner. Military training was offered for its boarding of students.

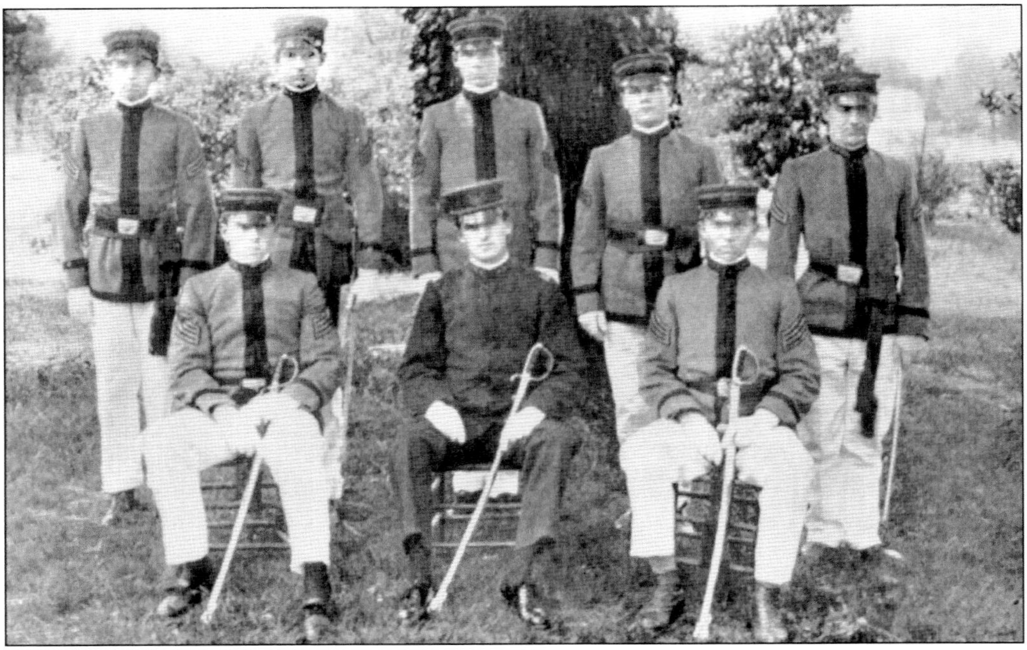

Here are the commissioned officers at Horner Military School in 1910.

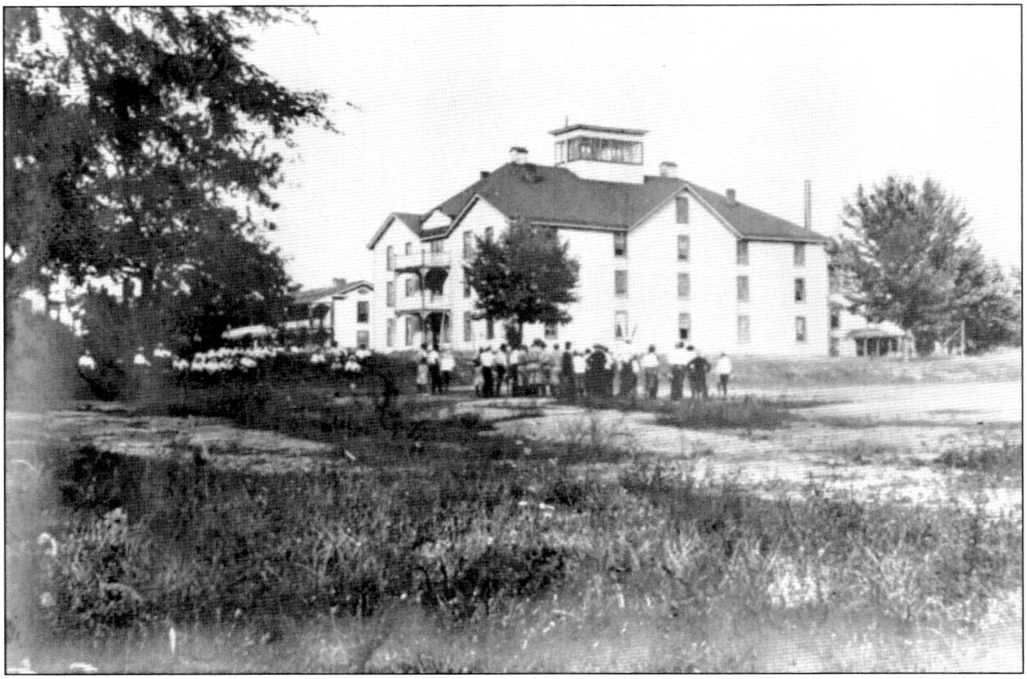

Part of the campus can be seen of the Horner Military School.

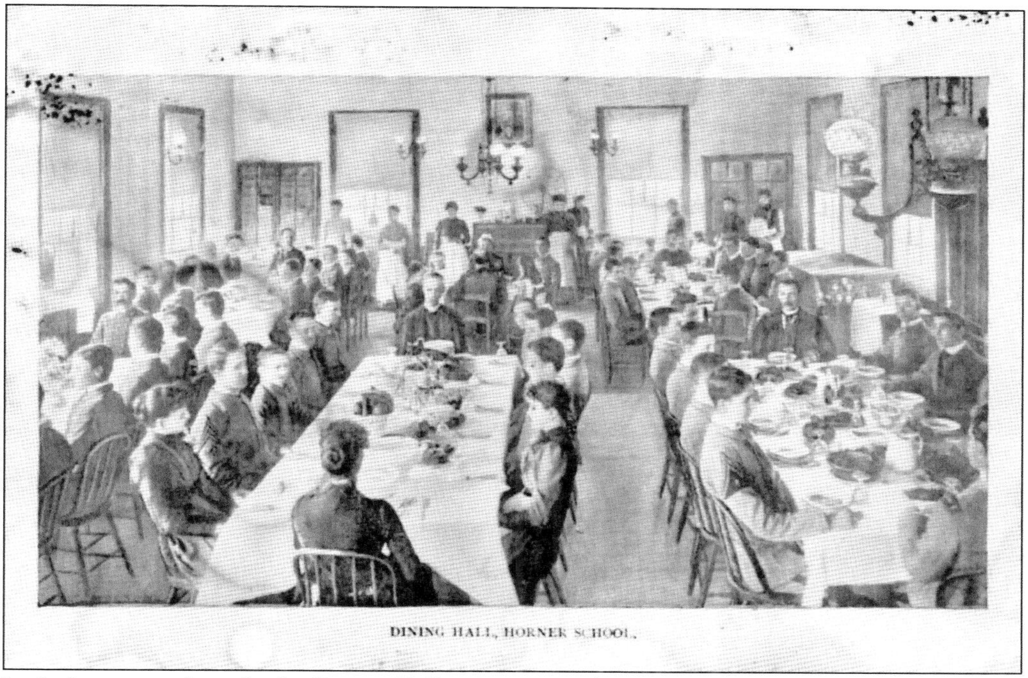

Let's share a meal inside the Dining Hall at Horner Military School in 1892.

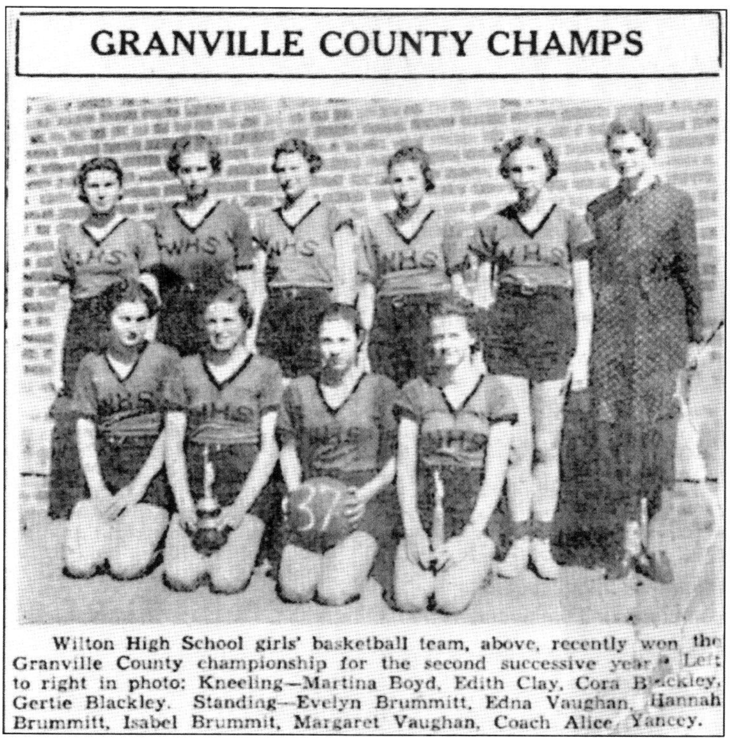

GRANVILLE COUNTY CHAMPS

Wilton High School girls' basketball team, above, recently won the Granville County championship for the second successive year. Left to right in photo: Kneeling—Martina Boyd, Edith Clay, Cora Blackley, Gertie Blackley. Standing—Evelyn Brummitt, Edna Vaughan, Hannah Brummitt, Isabel Brummit, Margaret Vaughan, Coach Alice Yancey.

In 1937, the Wilton High School girls' basketball team won the Granville County championship. From left to right are (kneeling) Martina Boyd, Edith Clay, Cora Blackley, and Gertie Blackley; (standing) Evelyn Brummitt, Edna Vaughn, Hannah Brummitt, Isabel Brummitt, Margaret Vaughn, and Coach Alice Yancey. (Courtesy of Isabel Brummitt.)

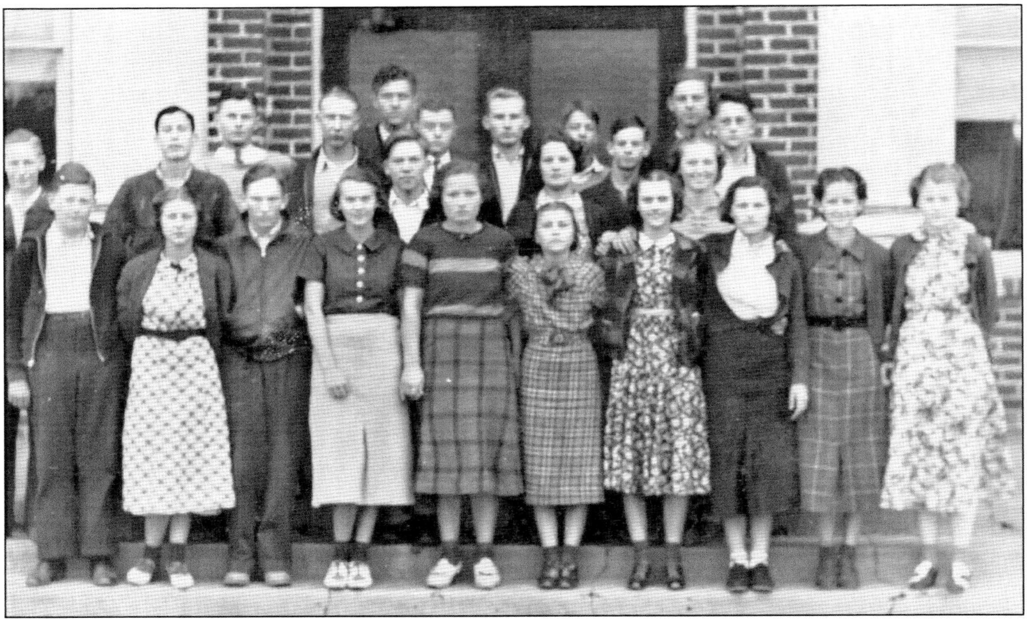

These young people were the seniors of Stovall High School in 1937. (Courtesy of Lisa Oakes.)

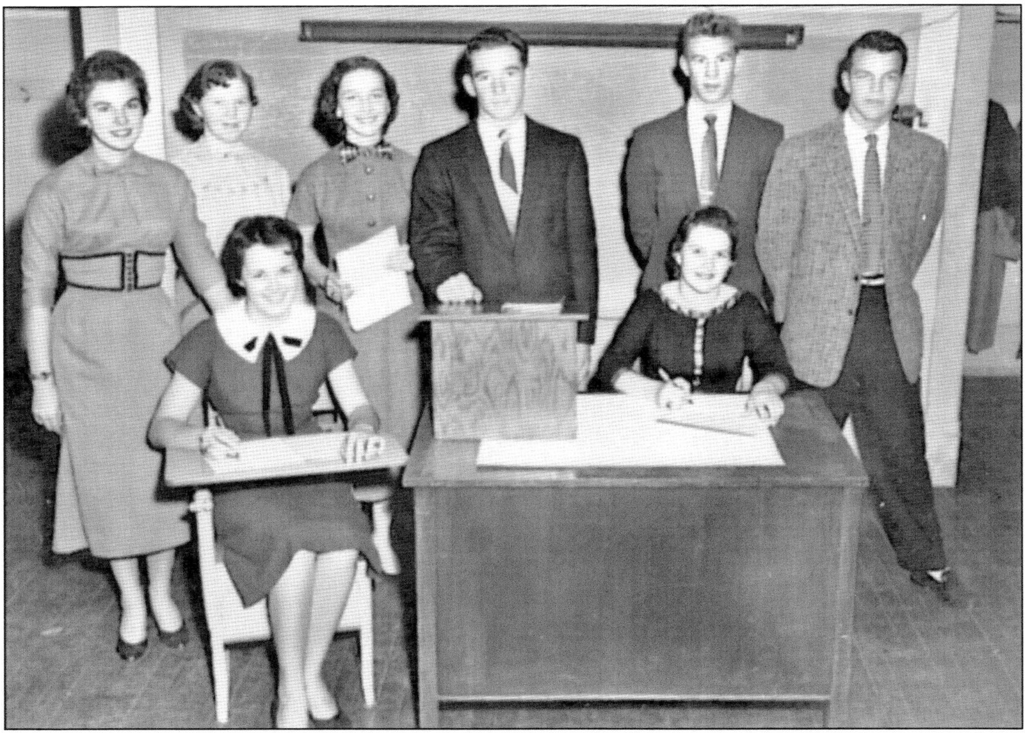

These are the senior class officers of Stovall High School in 1957. Shown from left to right are (seated) Betty Currin (treasurer) and Judith Bigger (secretary); (standing) Ruth Allgood (testator), Goldie Clack (class poet), Annette Young (reporter), Gerald Stovall (class president), Leroy Beam (prophet), and Horace Gill (giftorian). (Courtesy of Lisa Oakes.)

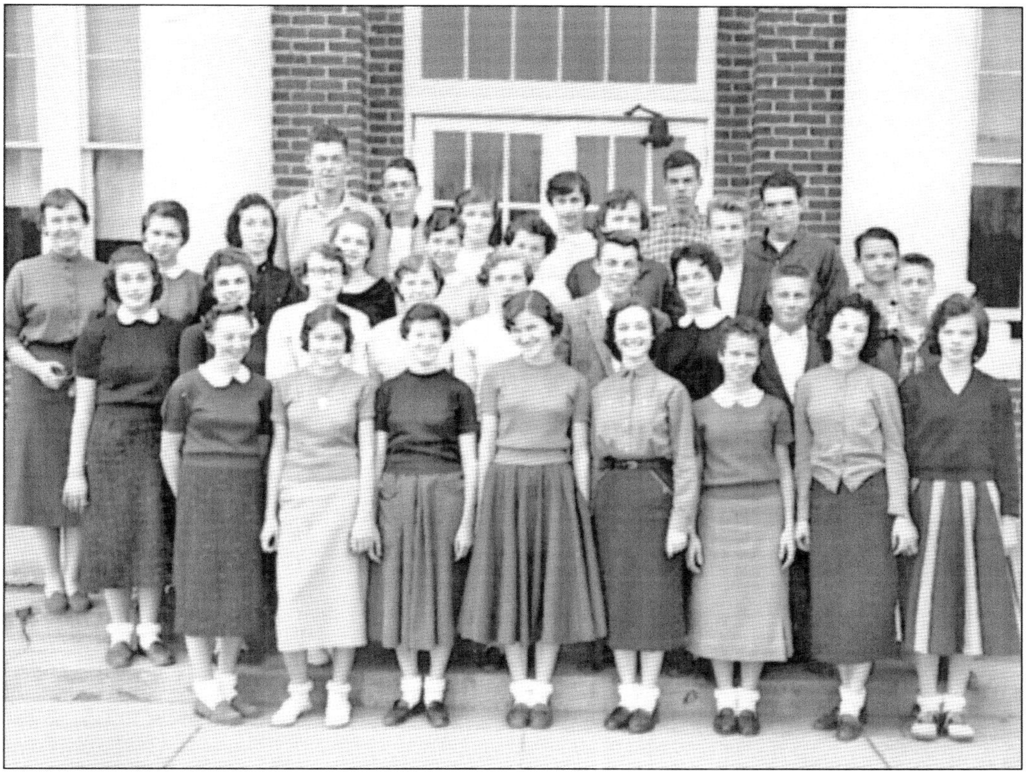

This is the senior class of 1957 at Stovall High School. (Courtesy of Lisa Oakes.)

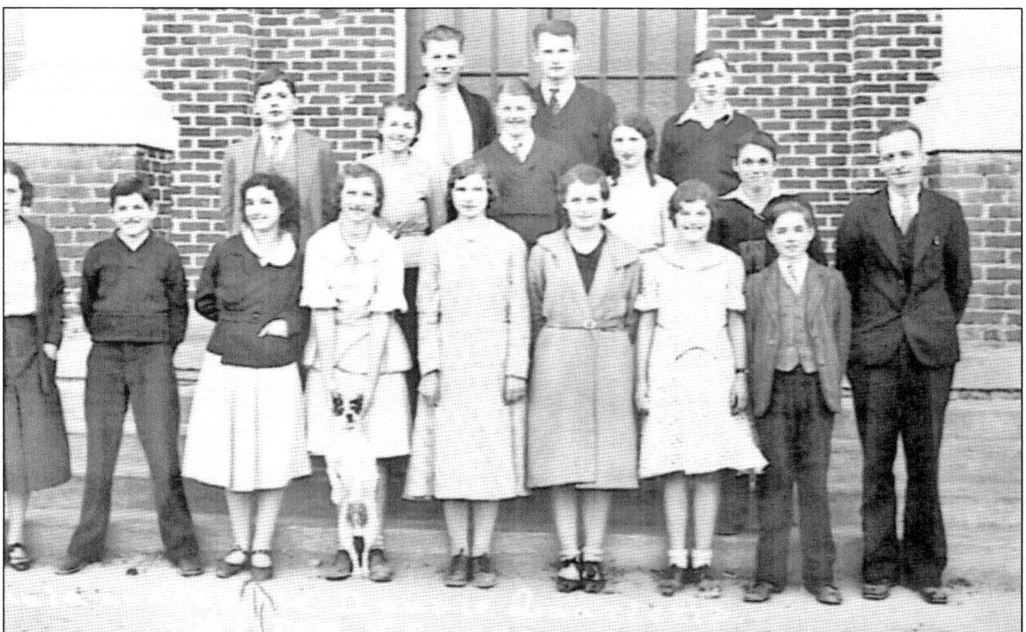

These students (and dog) formed a singing group at Wilton High School in 1931.

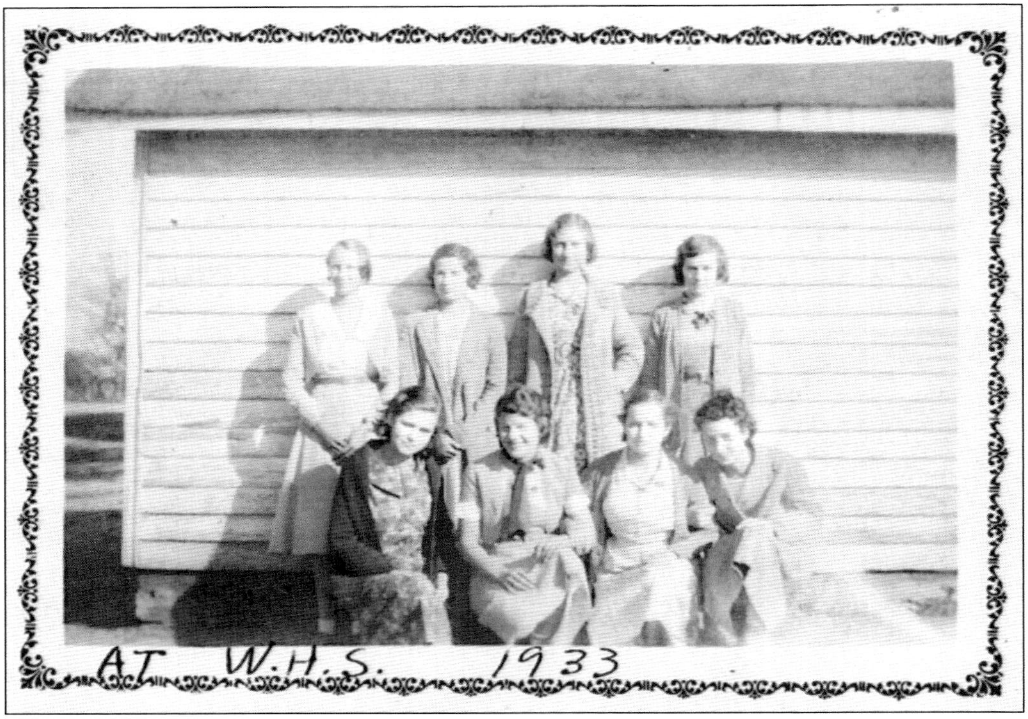

Here are students outside part of Wilton High School in 1933. Wilton Elementary School now stands in this location. (Courtesy of Sybil Lloyd.)

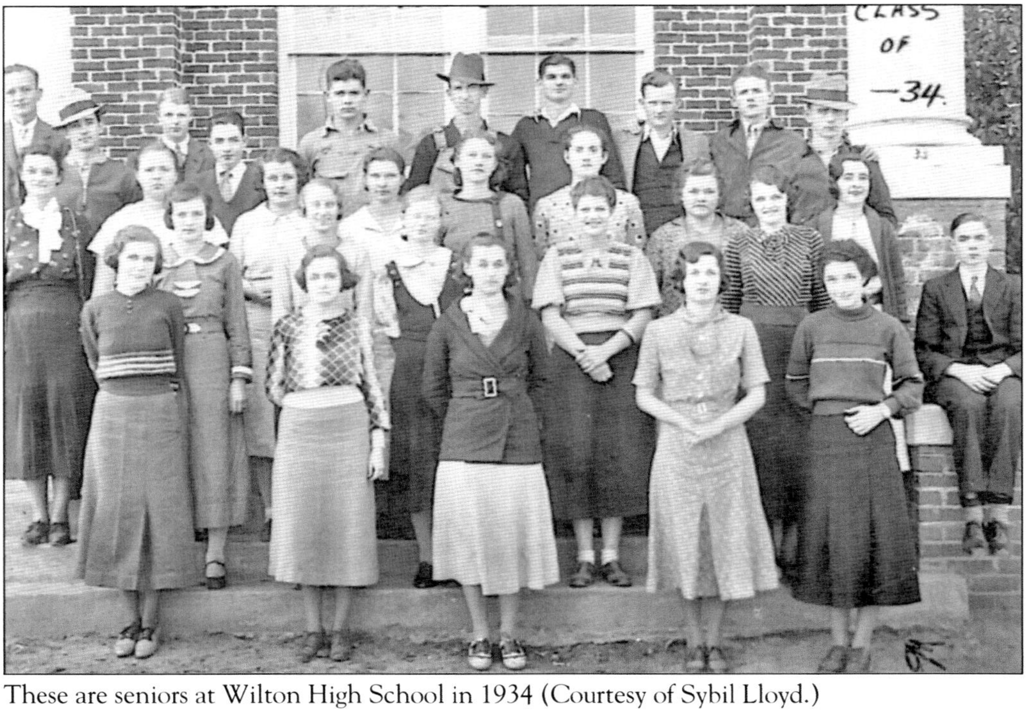

These are seniors at Wilton High School in 1934 (Courtesy of Sybil Lloyd.)

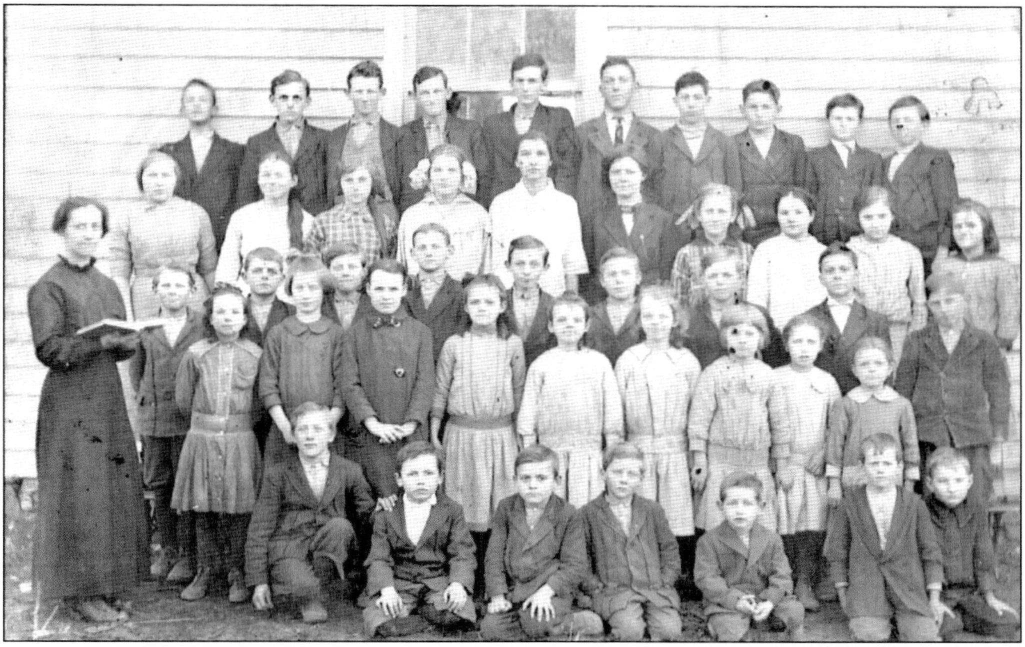

A teacher and students of Penny Hill School assemble for this picture in 1917. This school was located on Chewning Road near Dexter. It operated until the 1930s. (Courtesy of Francis Hart.)

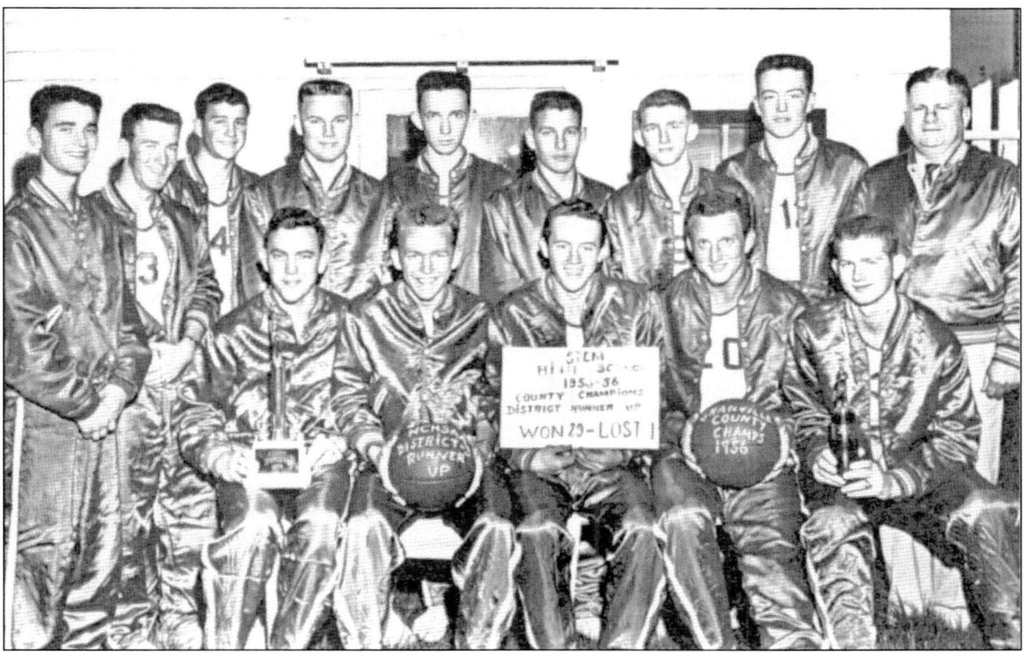

The 1955–1956 boys' basketball team at Stem High School won the Granville County Championship with a record of 23 wins and only 1 loss. They were also state district runners up.

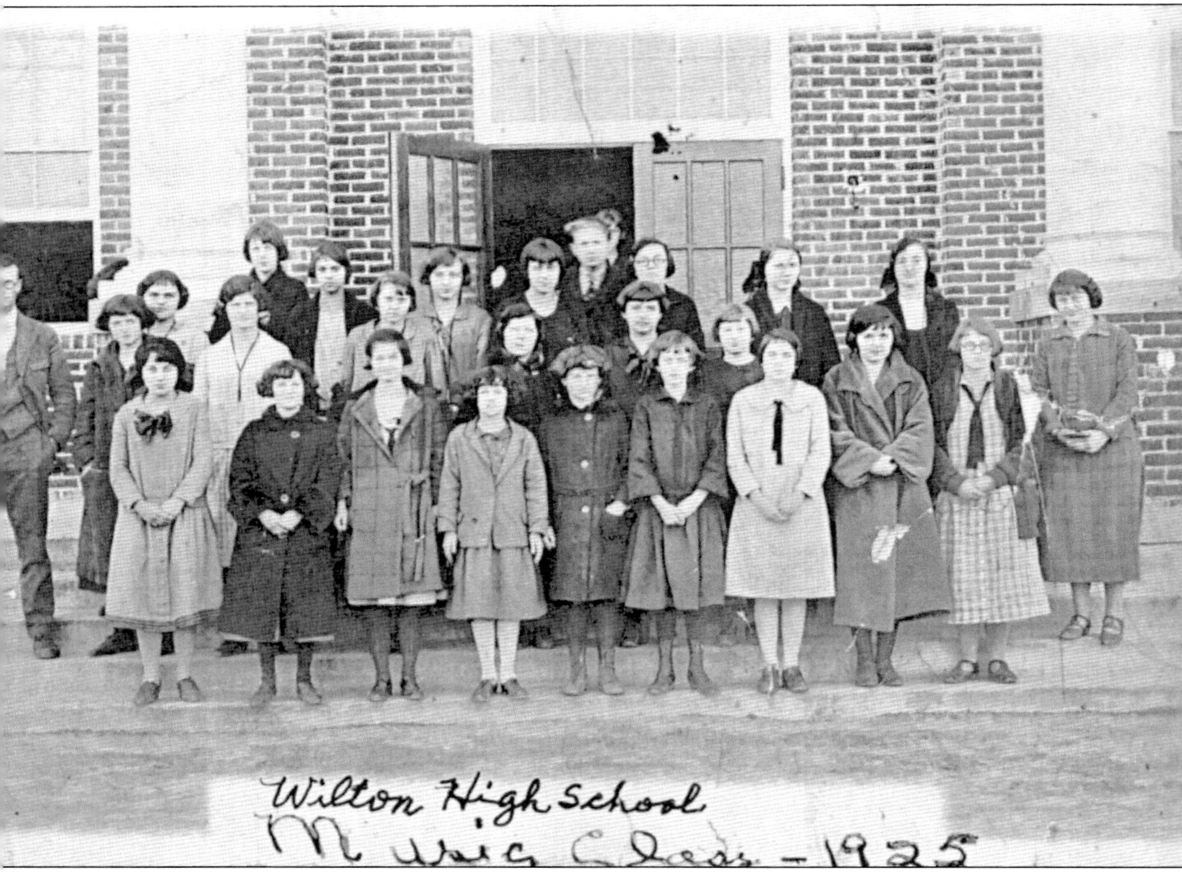

Here is the music class at Wilton High School in 1925. (Courtesy of Sybil Lloyd.)

Four

Farm Life

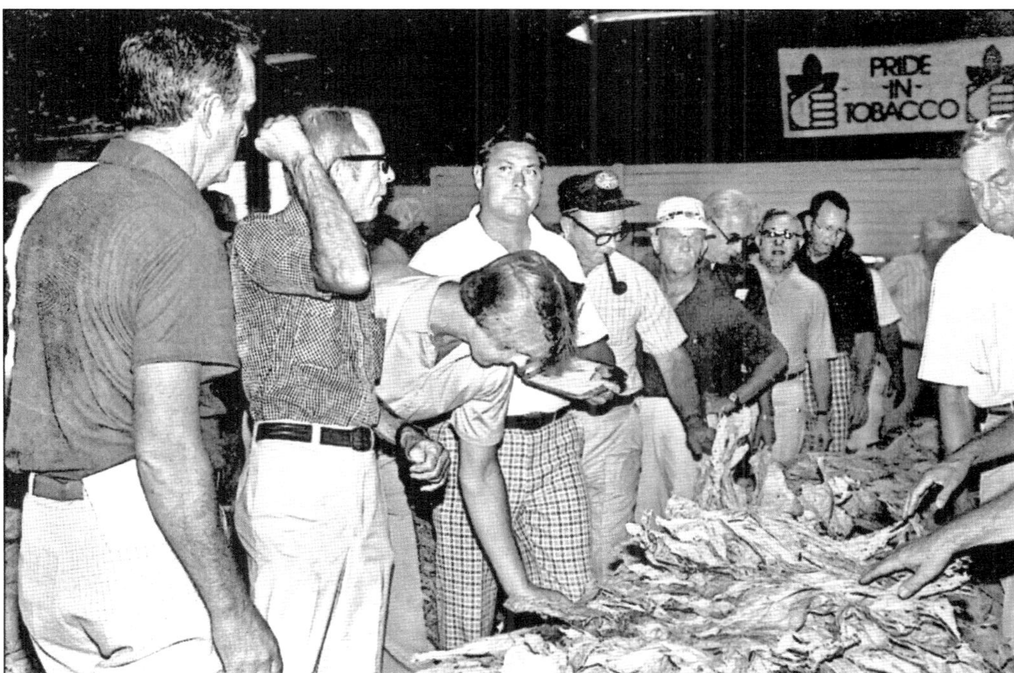

A tobacco auction is taking place inside the Granville Warehouse in Oxford in the early 1970s. (Courtesy of Sam Currin.)

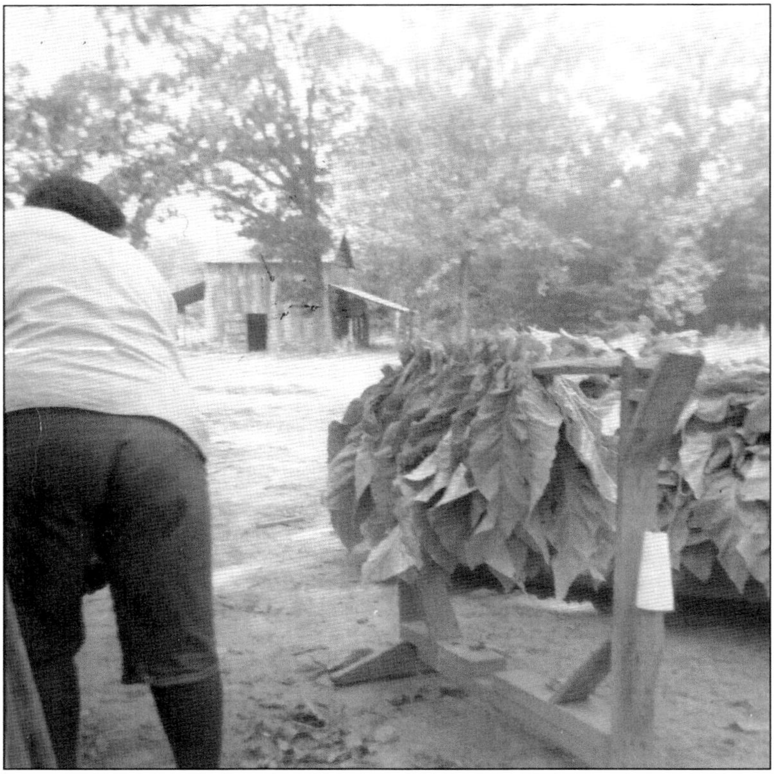

Valnora Morgan is working on a tobacco farm in 1965. (Courtesy of Jean Gill.)

On the floor of Yeargin's Warehouse, tobacco is being sold. Wilbur Yeargin is on the front left, and Taylor Judson is on the front right.

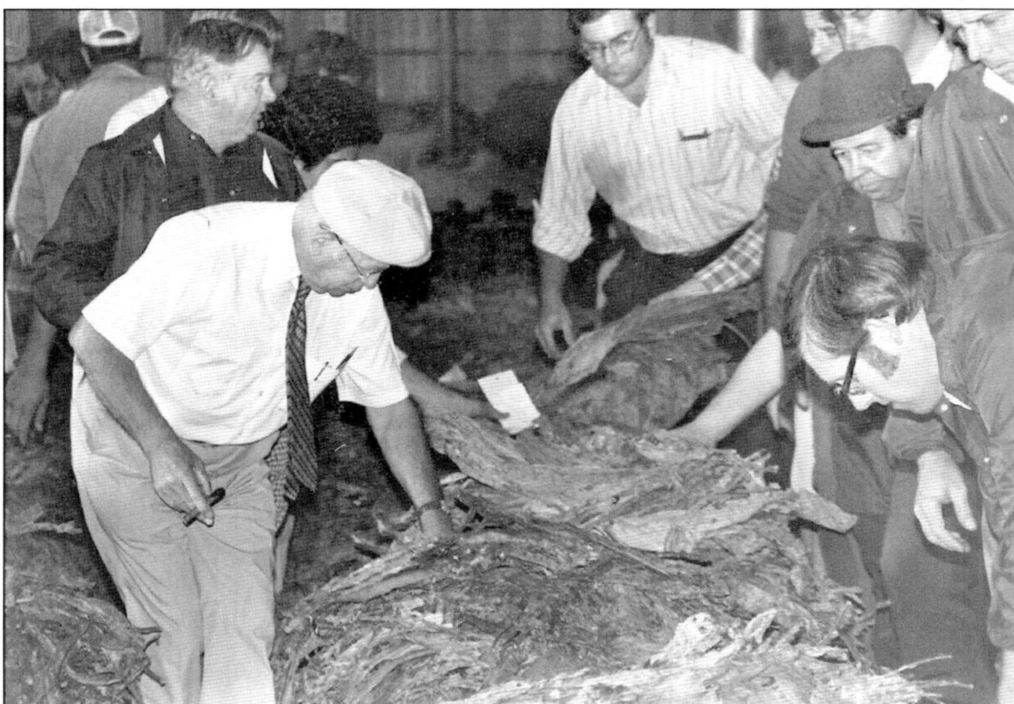

Six-year-old Teresa Blackley holds a stick of tobacco in 1971. Her brother Robert is featured on the cover of this book. (Courtesy of Phyllis Beck.)

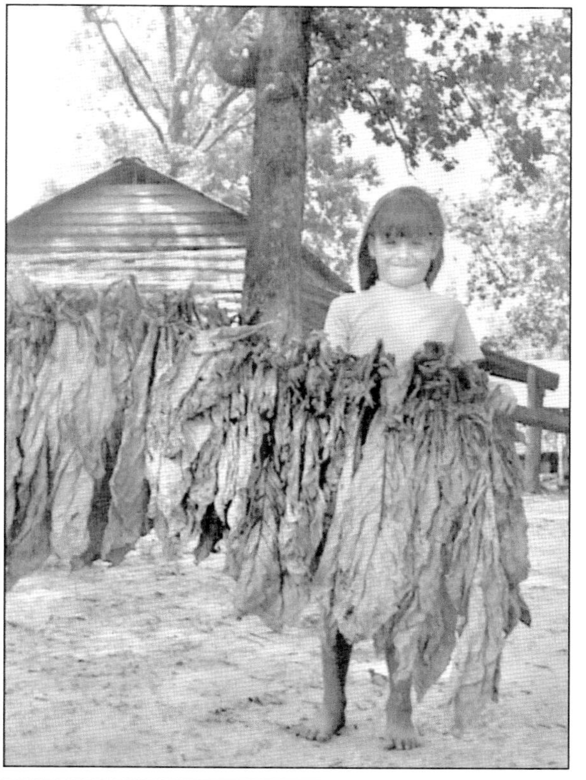

Bruce Montague works his tobacco field, while Robert Blackley drives the tractor. (Courtesy of Phyllis Beck.)

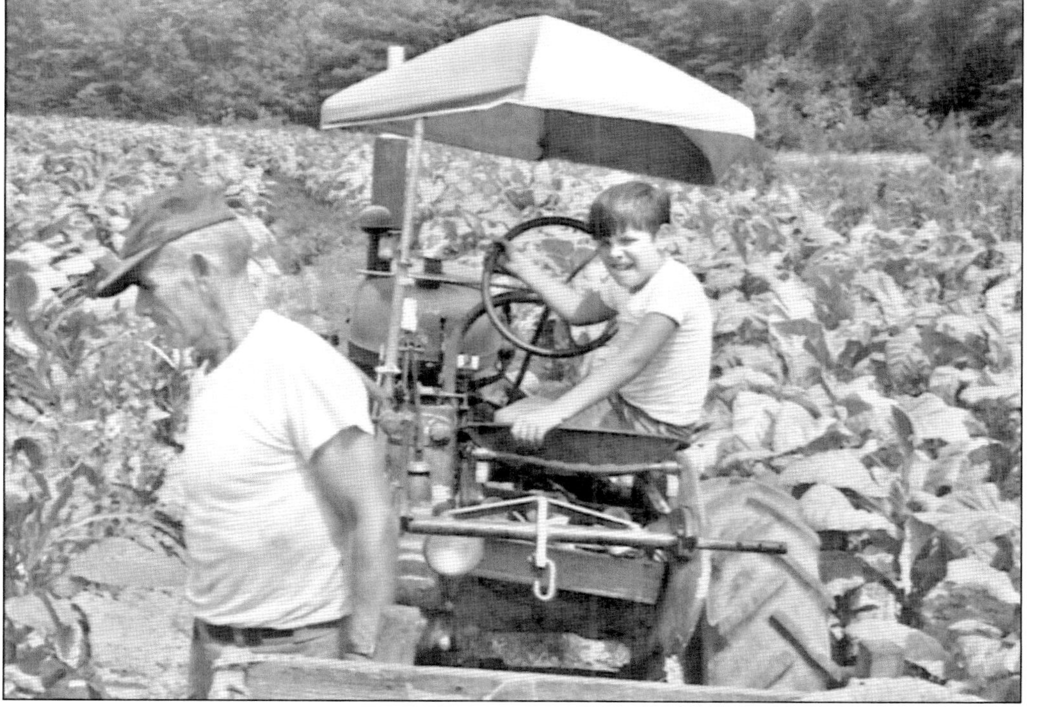

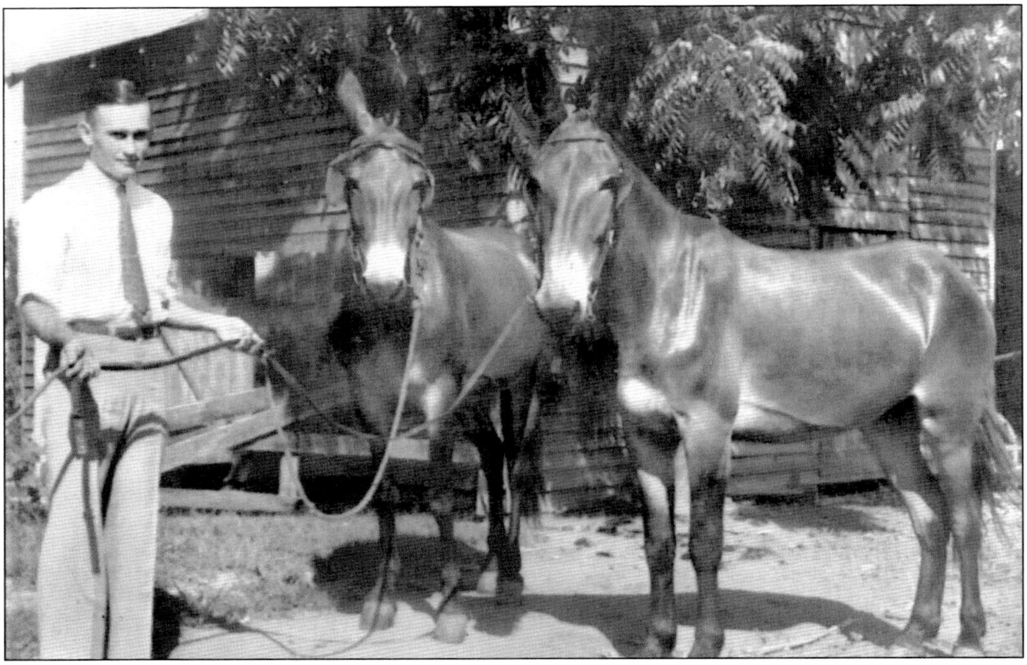
Lucius Wheeler is shown with two of his mules. (Courtesy of Rowena Wheeler.)

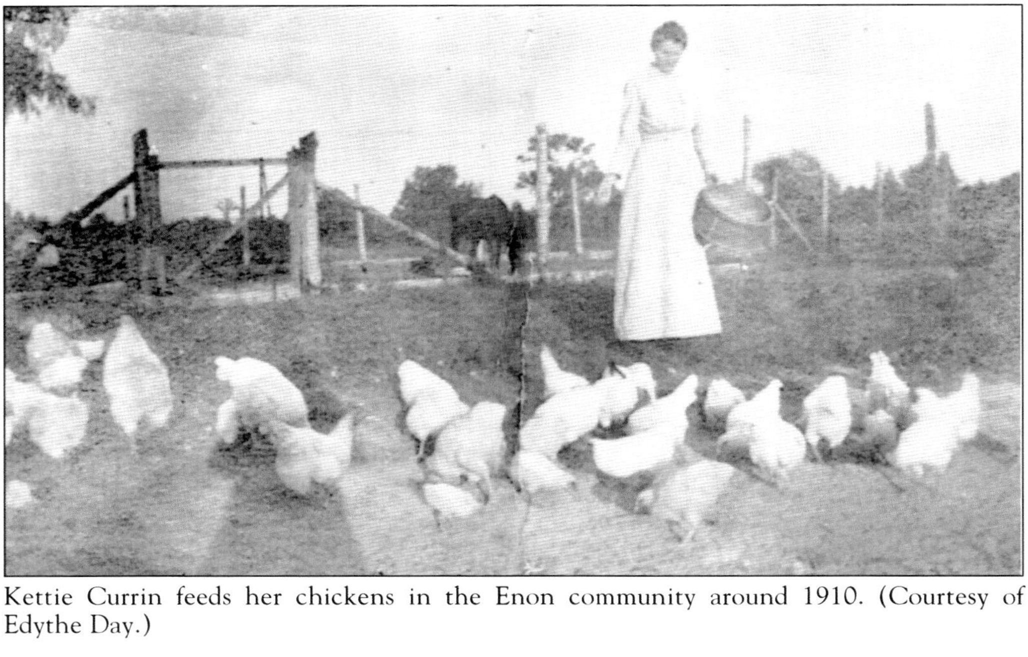
Kettie Currin feeds her chickens in the Enon community around 1910. (Courtesy of Edythe Day.)

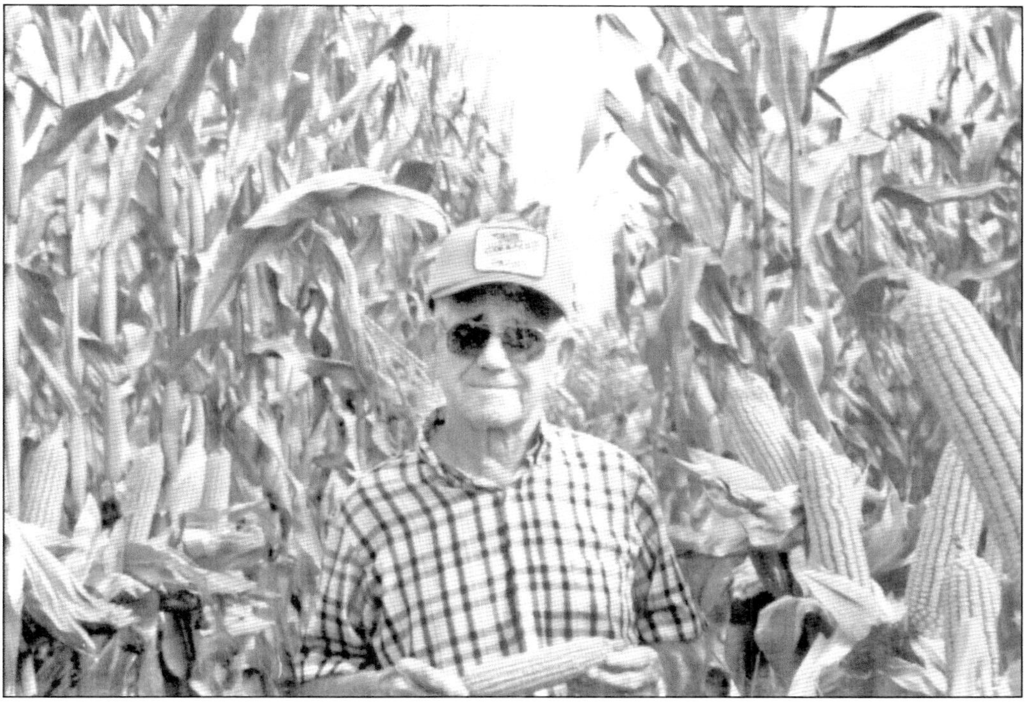

Wilson Day stands next to his large cornstalks on the Day farm on Huntsboro Road. (Courtesy of Edythe Day.)

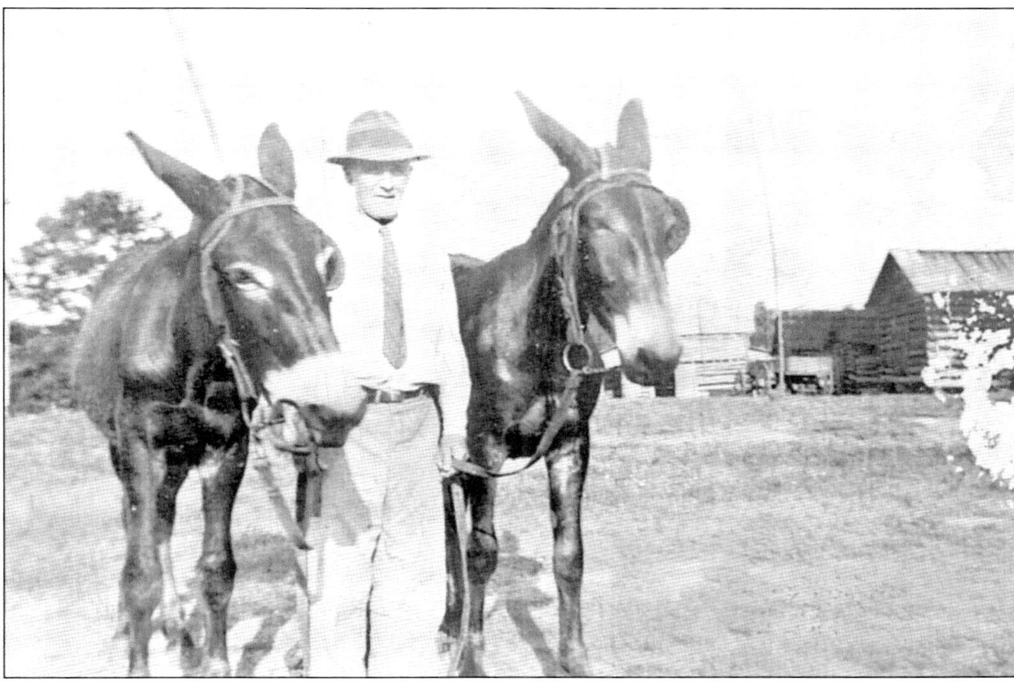

Aucy Leroy Elliott stands next to his mules, Molly and Jericho, on Gela Road in the Mountain Creek community. (Courtesy of Donnie and Linda Milton.)

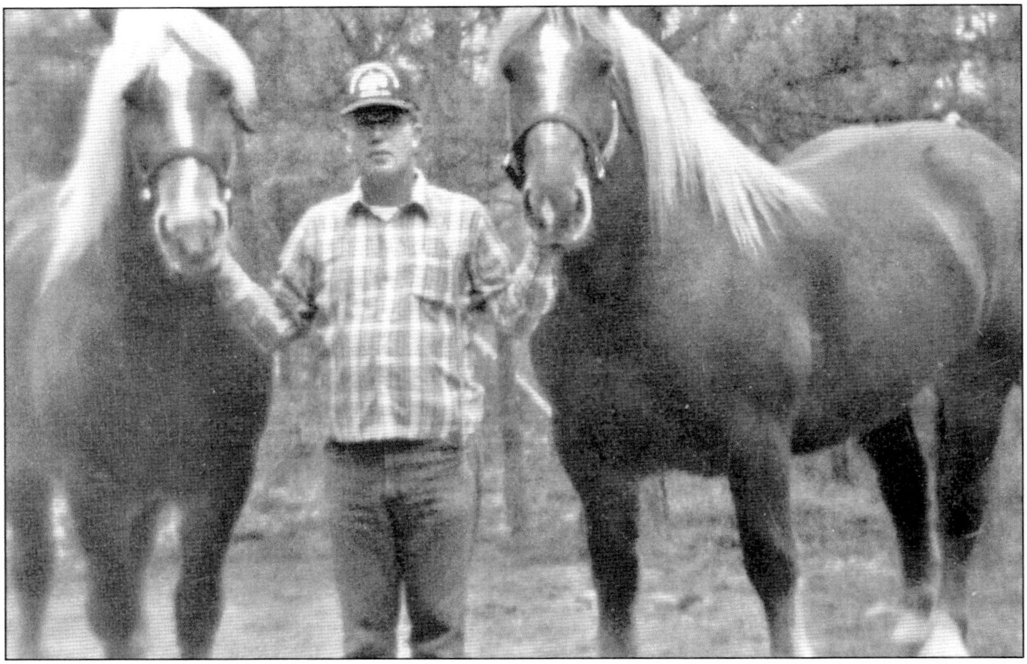

Donald Milton is shown here with two Belgium horses on his farm. Spirit weights 2,210 pounds, and Princess weighs 1,980. (Courtesy of Linda Milton.)

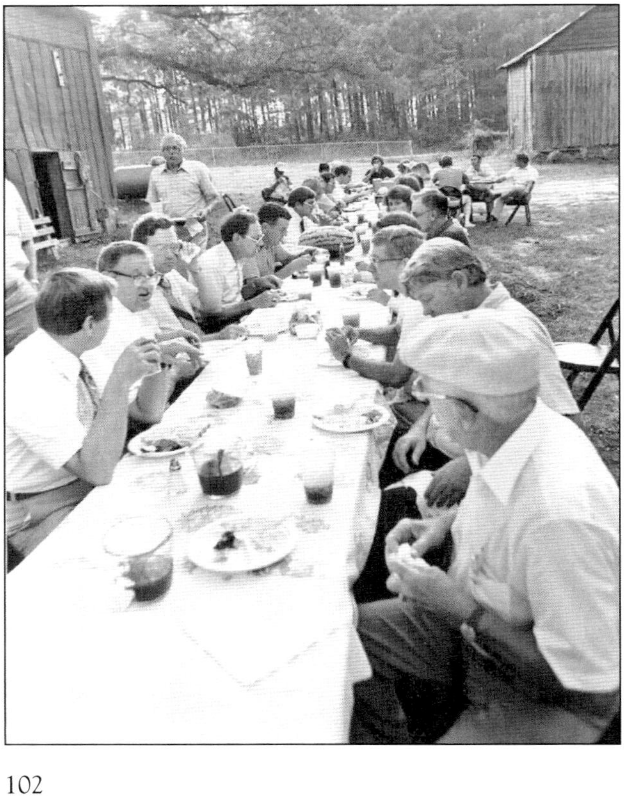

Tobacco officials from around the state and country are given a good old-fashioned picnic lunch on a local farm in Granville County. This occurred in the early 1970s. (Courtesy of Jean Gill.)

Wilbur Yeargin is shown here with two of his true loves, a tobacco field in the background and a tobacco cigar in his hand. (Courtesy of Jean Gill.)

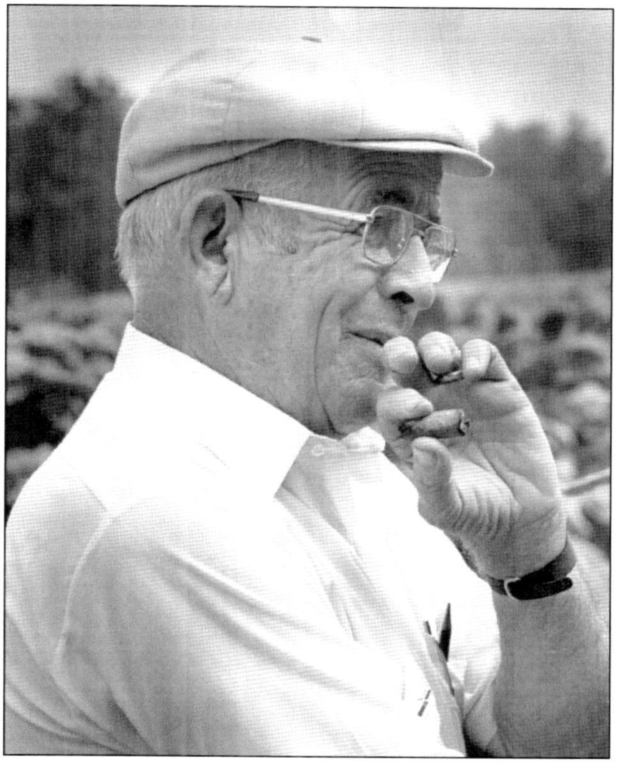

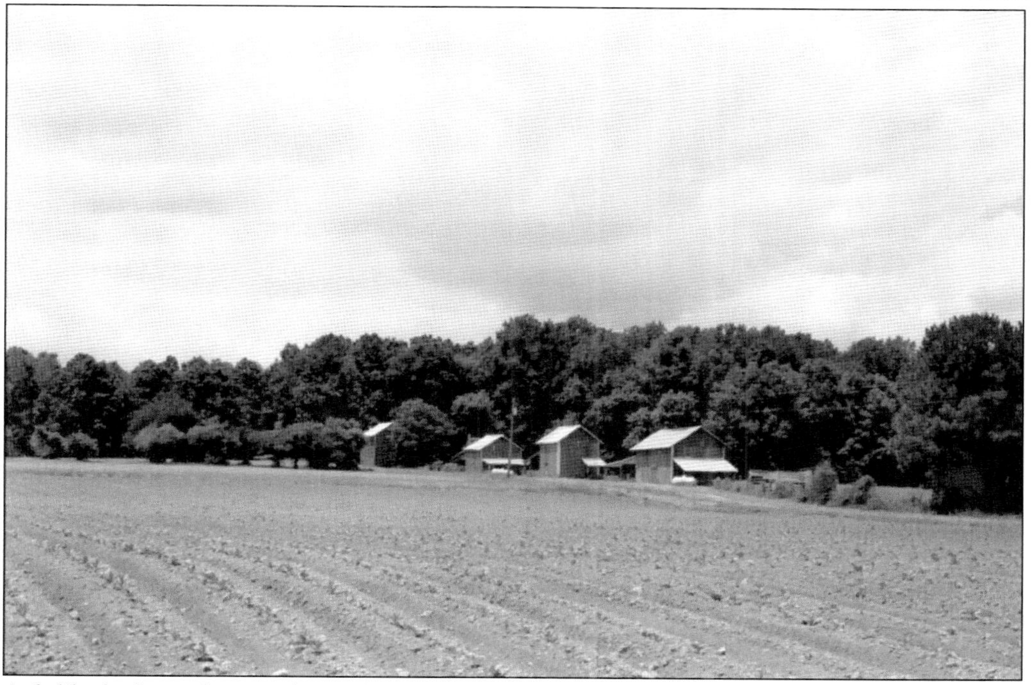

A field of tobacco has just been planted. The barns in the background await the harvest of this crop, which contributed so tremendously to the development of Oxford and Granville County.

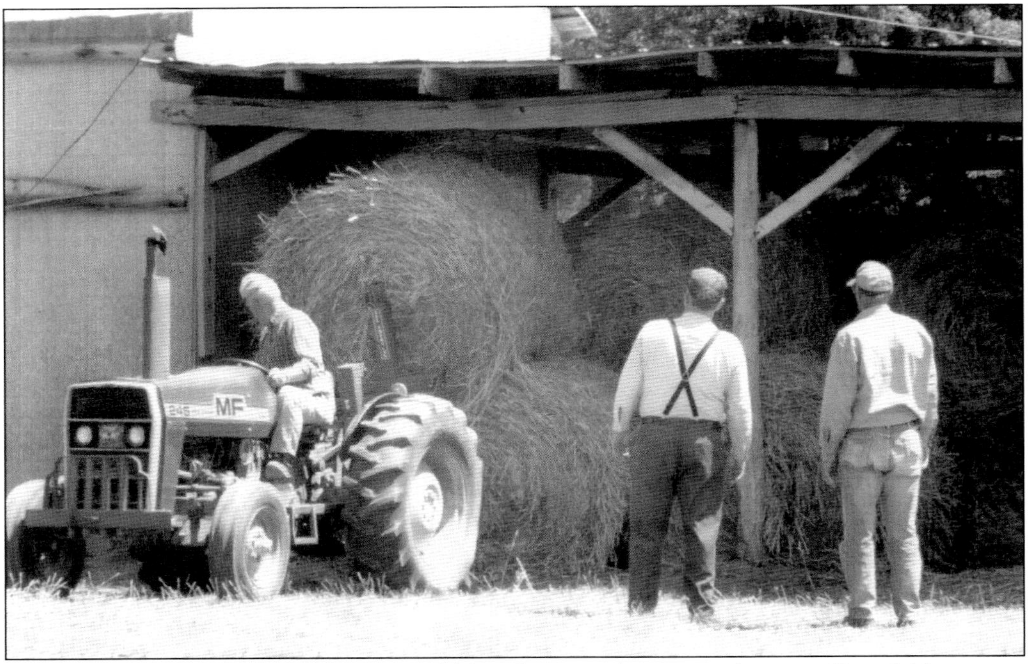

Getting up hay in the spring is an annual labor for many farmers in the area. Gene Milton is on the tractor, while Donnie and Joe Milton supervise. (Courtesy of Donnie and Linda Milton.)

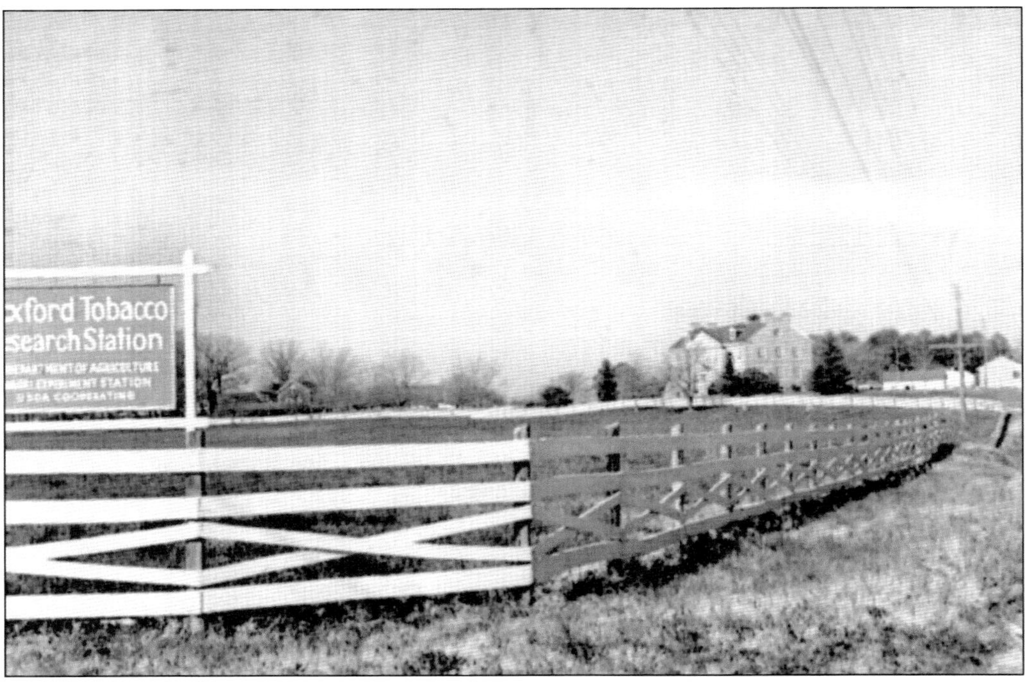

The Oxford Tobacco Research Station was at one time the largest facility of its kind in the world. Built in 1911, this facility has contributed much to tobacco production, not only in Granville County, but everywhere tobacco has been grown.

This is an advertisement for the W.A. Adams Tobacco Company in Oxford.

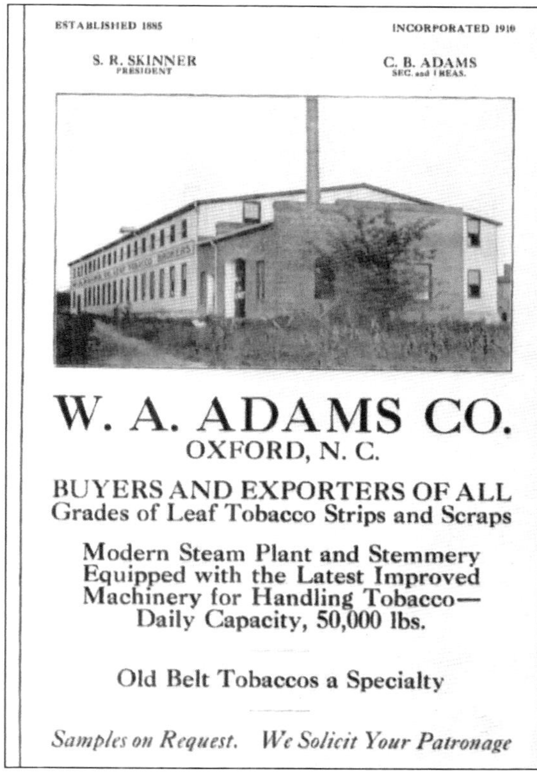

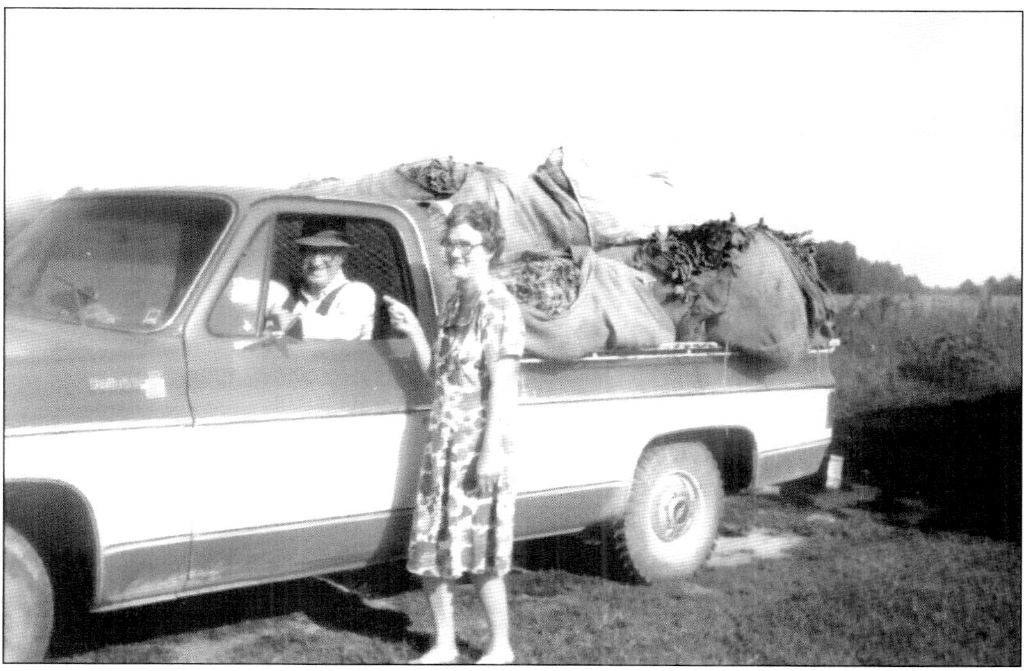

Marie Milton says good-bye to her husband, Jonah, before he heads to the warehouse in 1981. (Courtesy of Donnie and Linda Milton.)

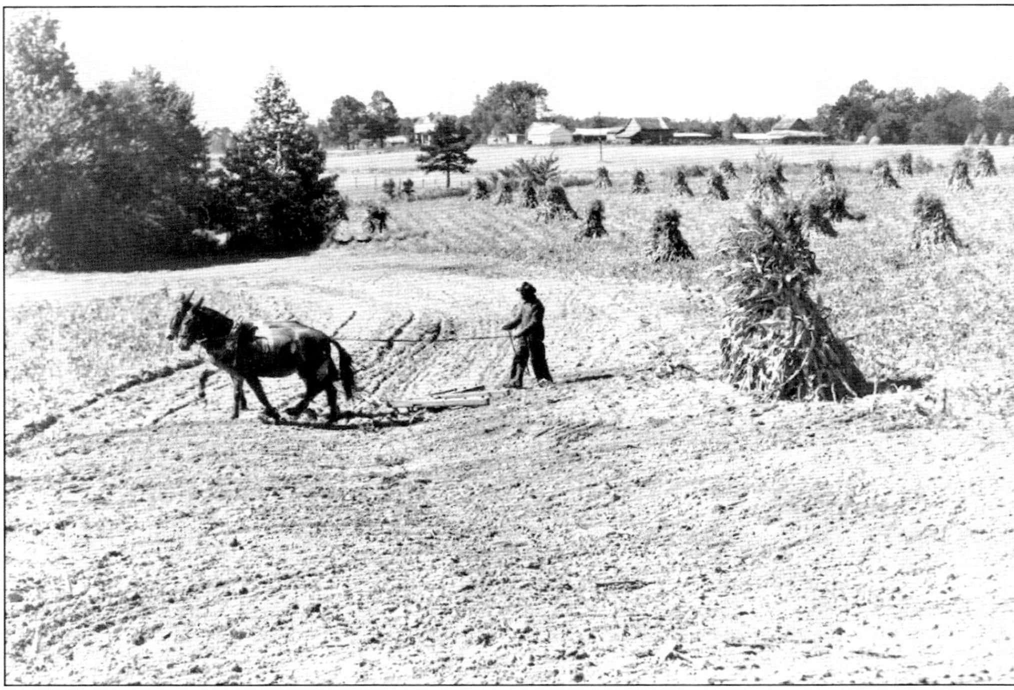

A farmer works his fields with his mules in Granville County in 1939. (Courtesy of Southern Historical Collection, University of North Carolina at Chapel Hill.)

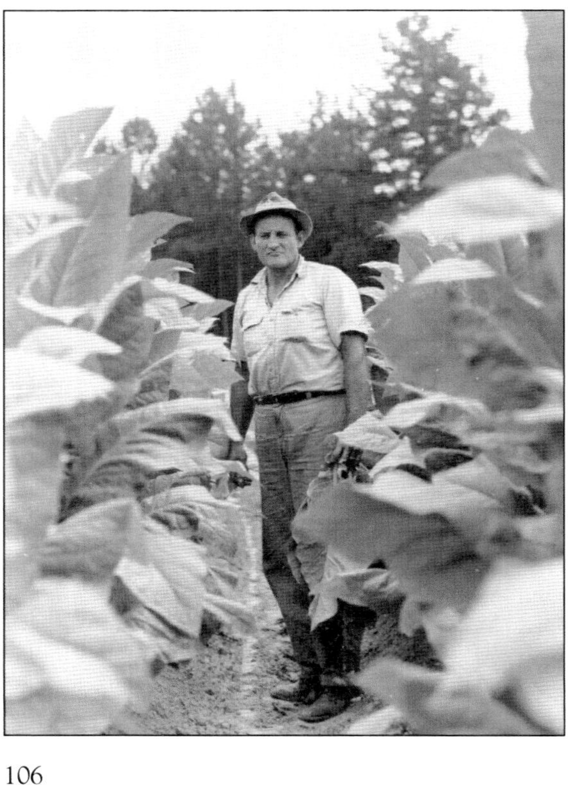

Billy Bowling stands in his tall tobacco field between Stem and Oxford. (Courtesy Mary Wayne Bowling.)

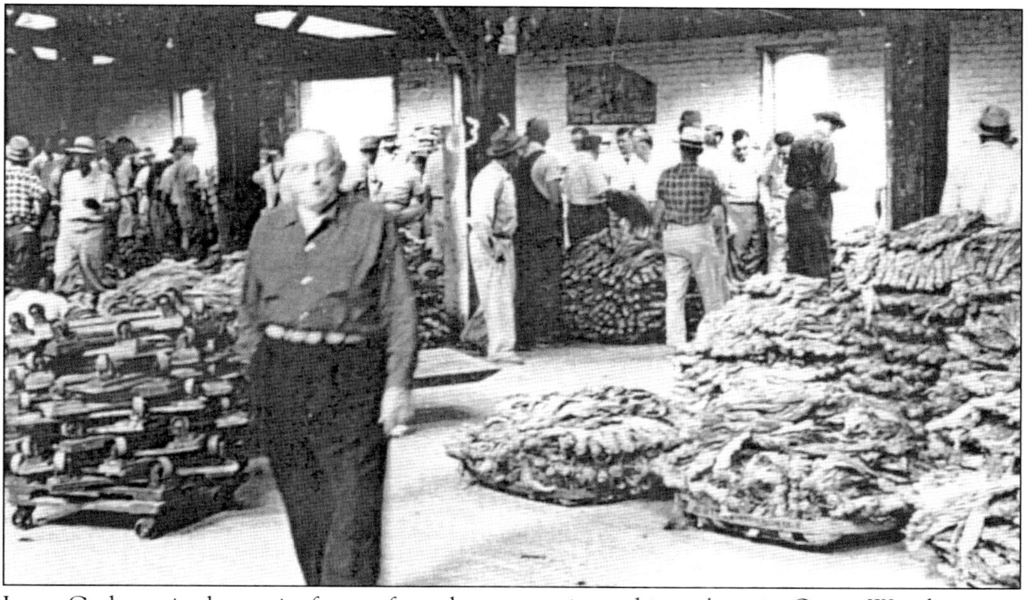

Leon Godown is shown in front of a tobacco auction taking place in Owen Warehouse in Oxford in 1959.

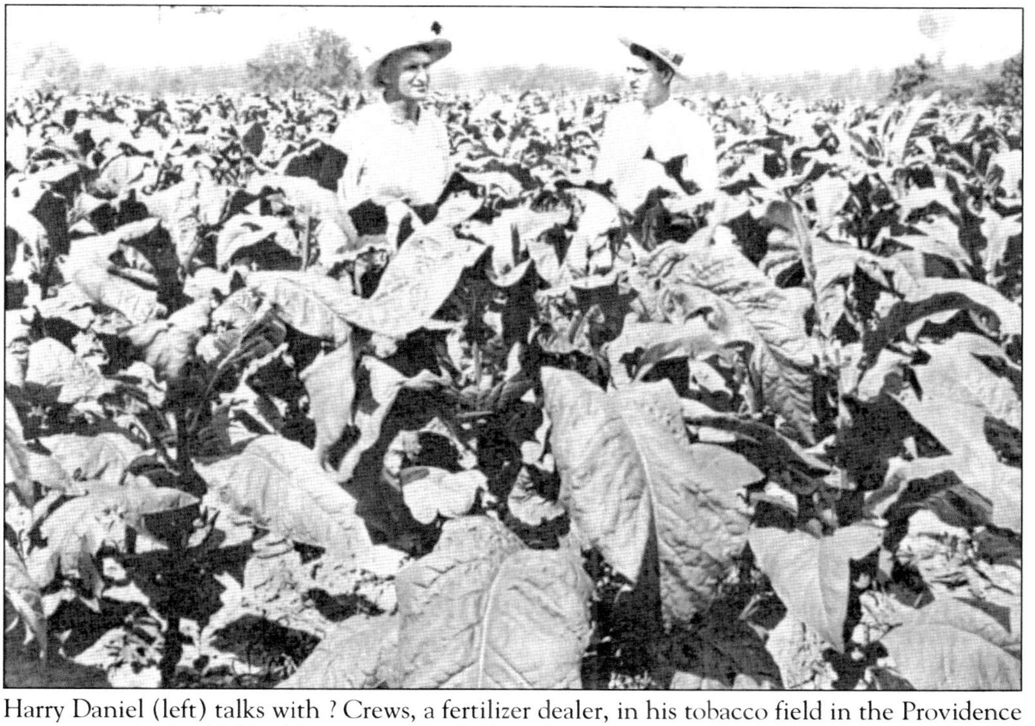

Harry Daniel (left) talks with ? Crews, a fertilizer dealer, in his tobacco field in the Providence community in the 1930s. (Courtesy of Ruth Dean.)

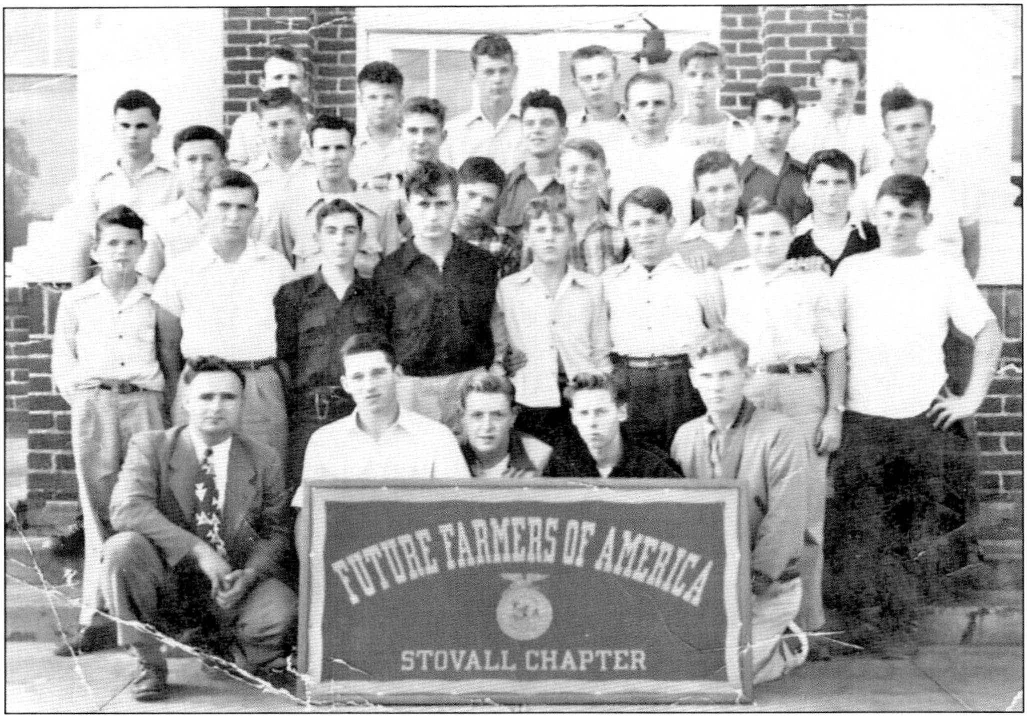

The Future Farmers of America Club of Stovall High School get together for a school picture.

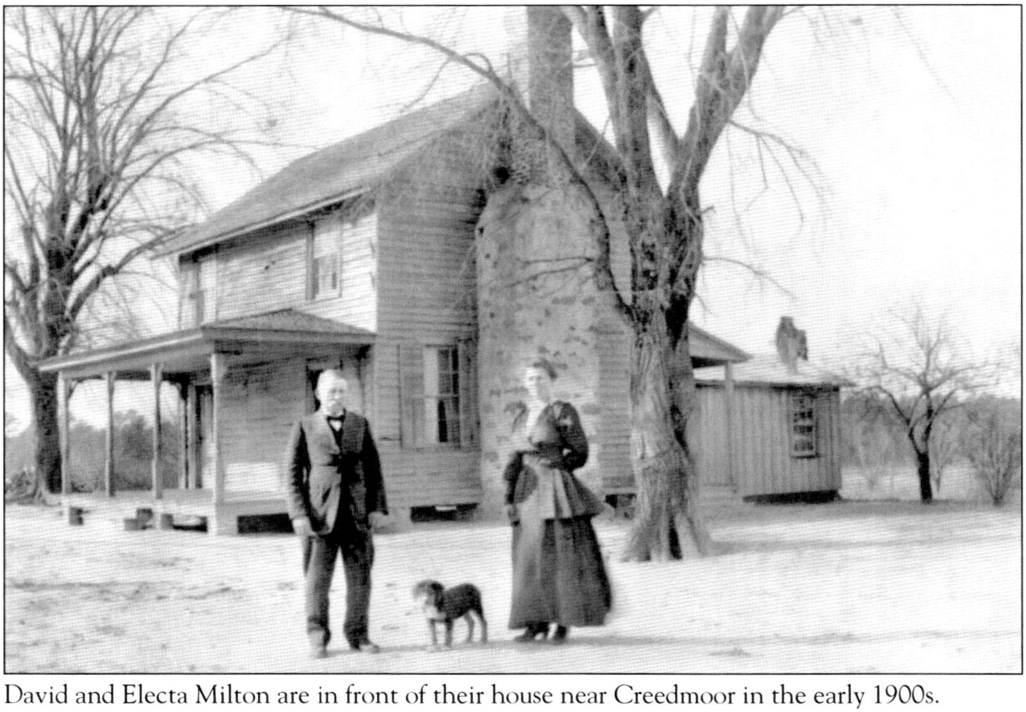

David and Electa Milton are in front of their house near Creedmoor in the early 1900s.

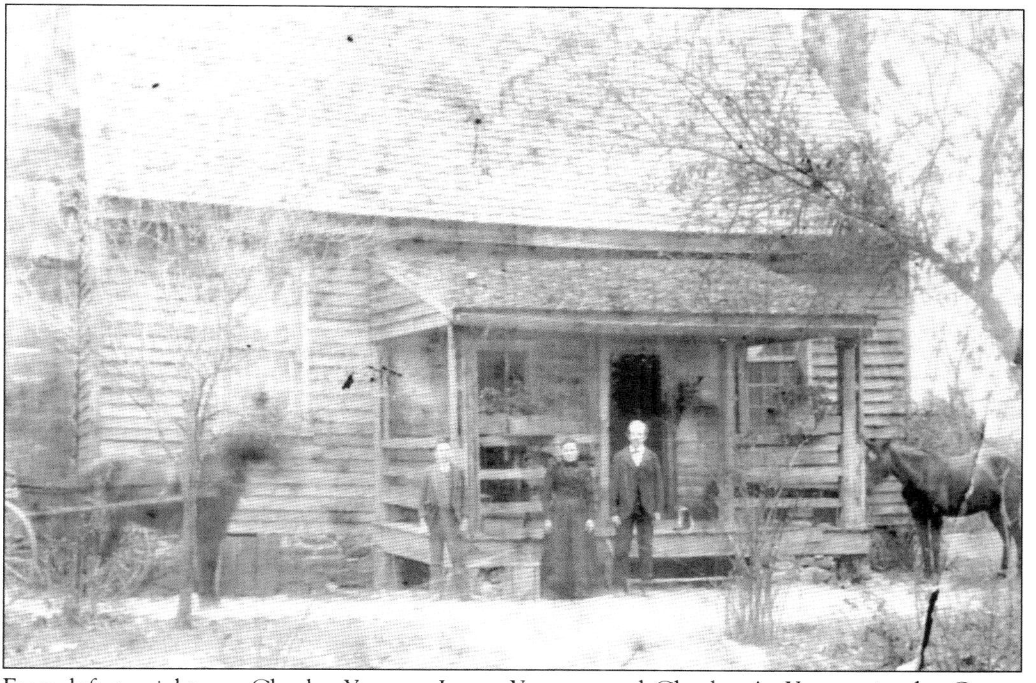

From left to right are Charles Yancey, Laura Yancey, and Charles A. Yancey in the Grassy Creek community in 1895. (Courtesy of Donnie and Linda Milton.)

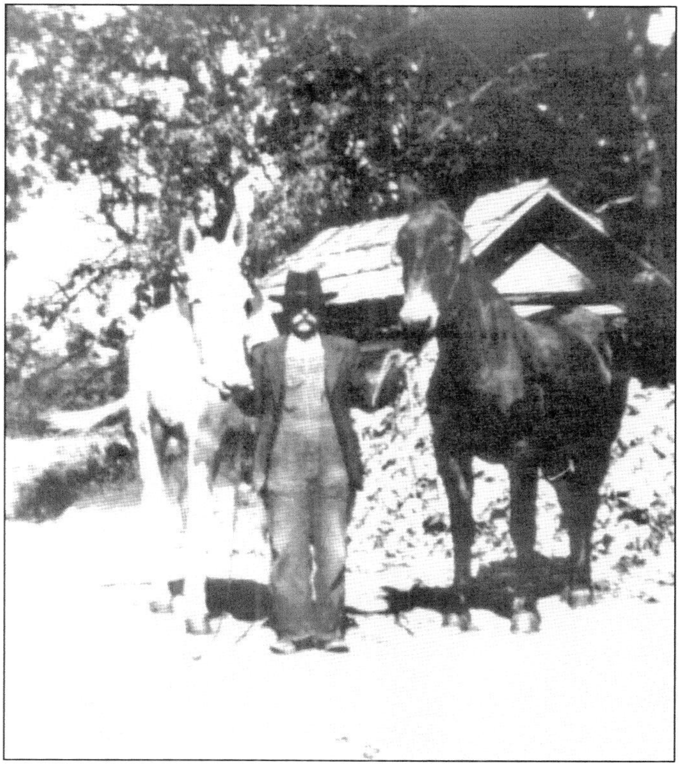

Walter Champion stands with his mules on his farm in the Grassy Creek community in the 1940s. (Courtesy of Emily Champion.)

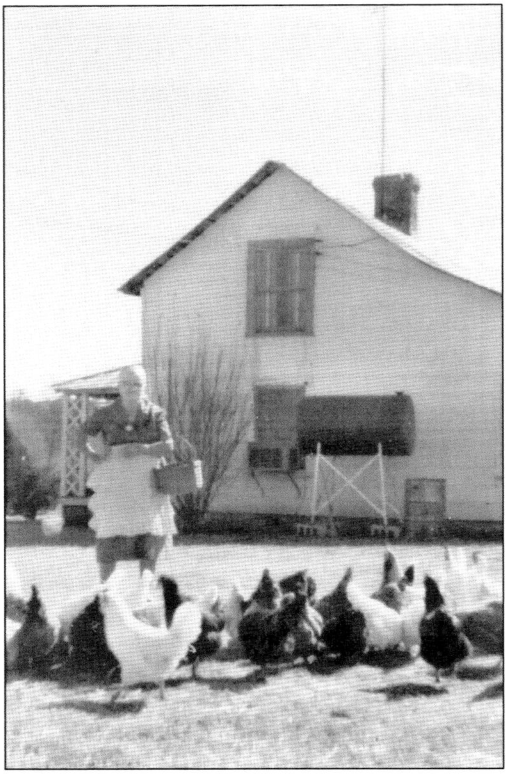

Nona Elliott feeds her chickens behind her and husband Aucy's house in the Mountain Creek community. (Courtesy of Donnie and Linda Milton.)

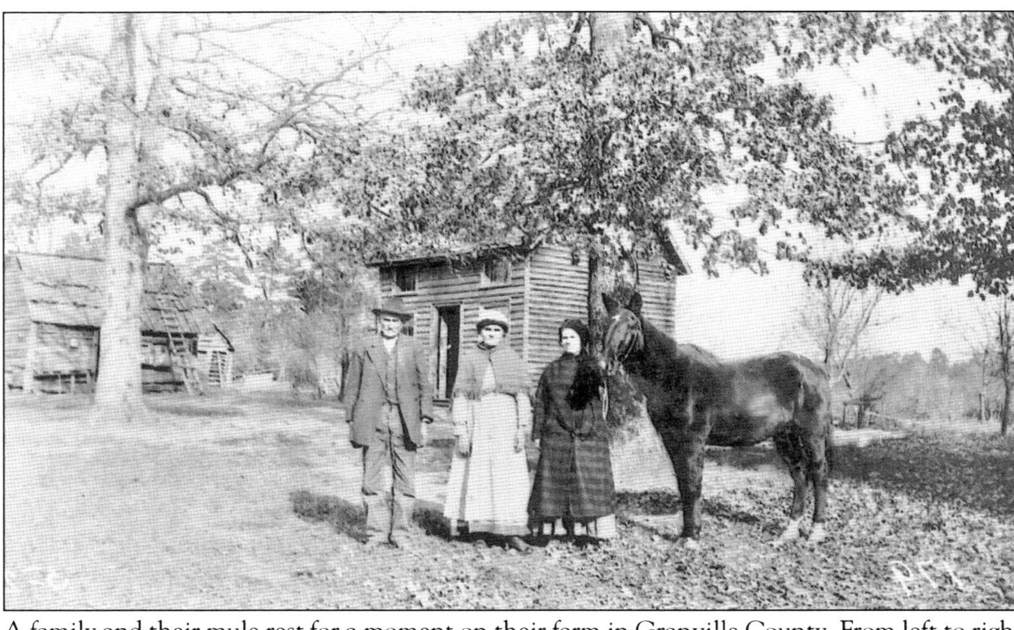

A family and their mule rest for a moment on their farm in Granville County. From left to right are John, Martha, and Sis Wilson. (Courtesy of Birk Lunsford.)

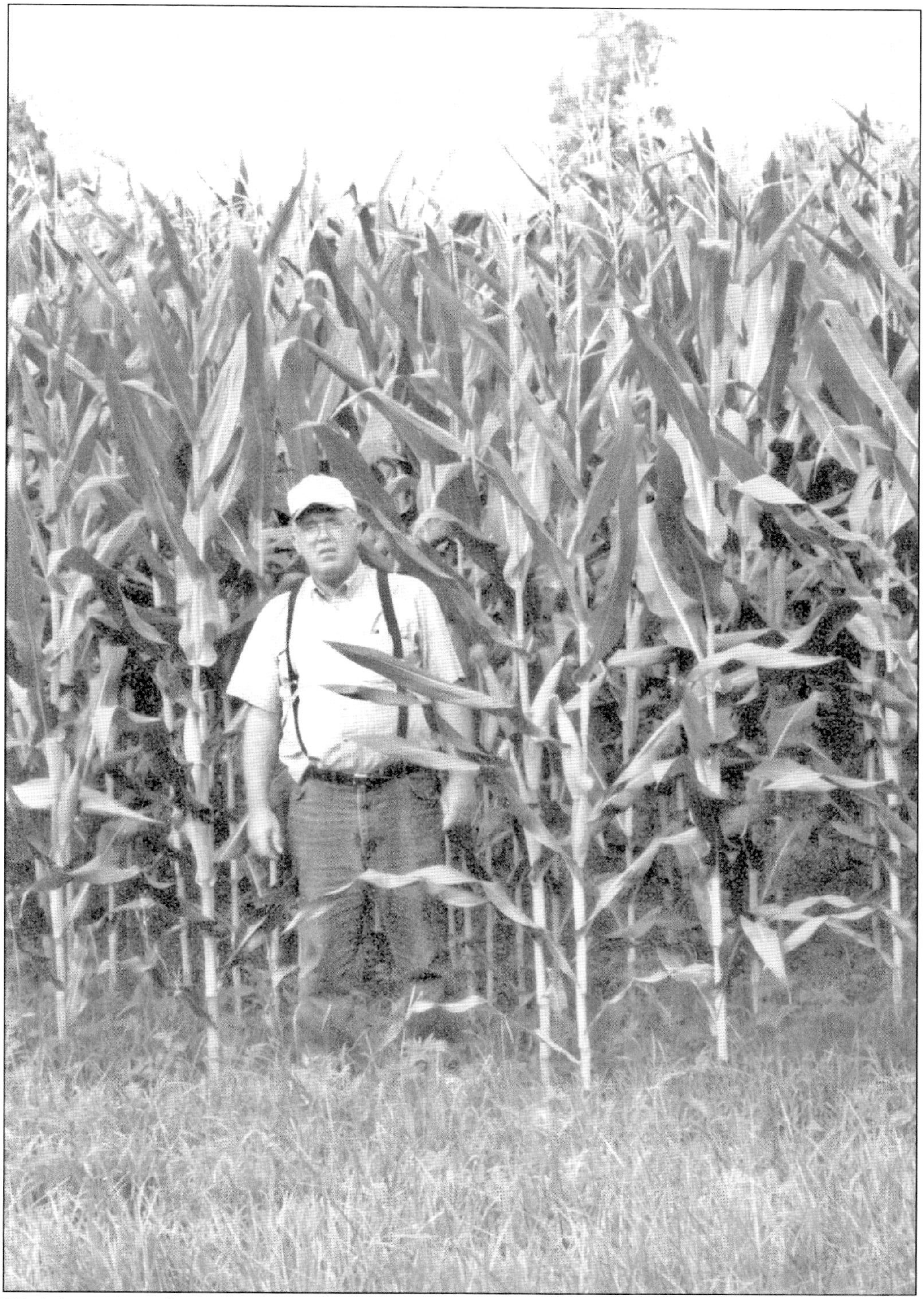

With his cornstalks towering above him, Donnie Milton shows other farmers in the area how to grow a bountiful crop. (Courtesy of Linda Milton.)

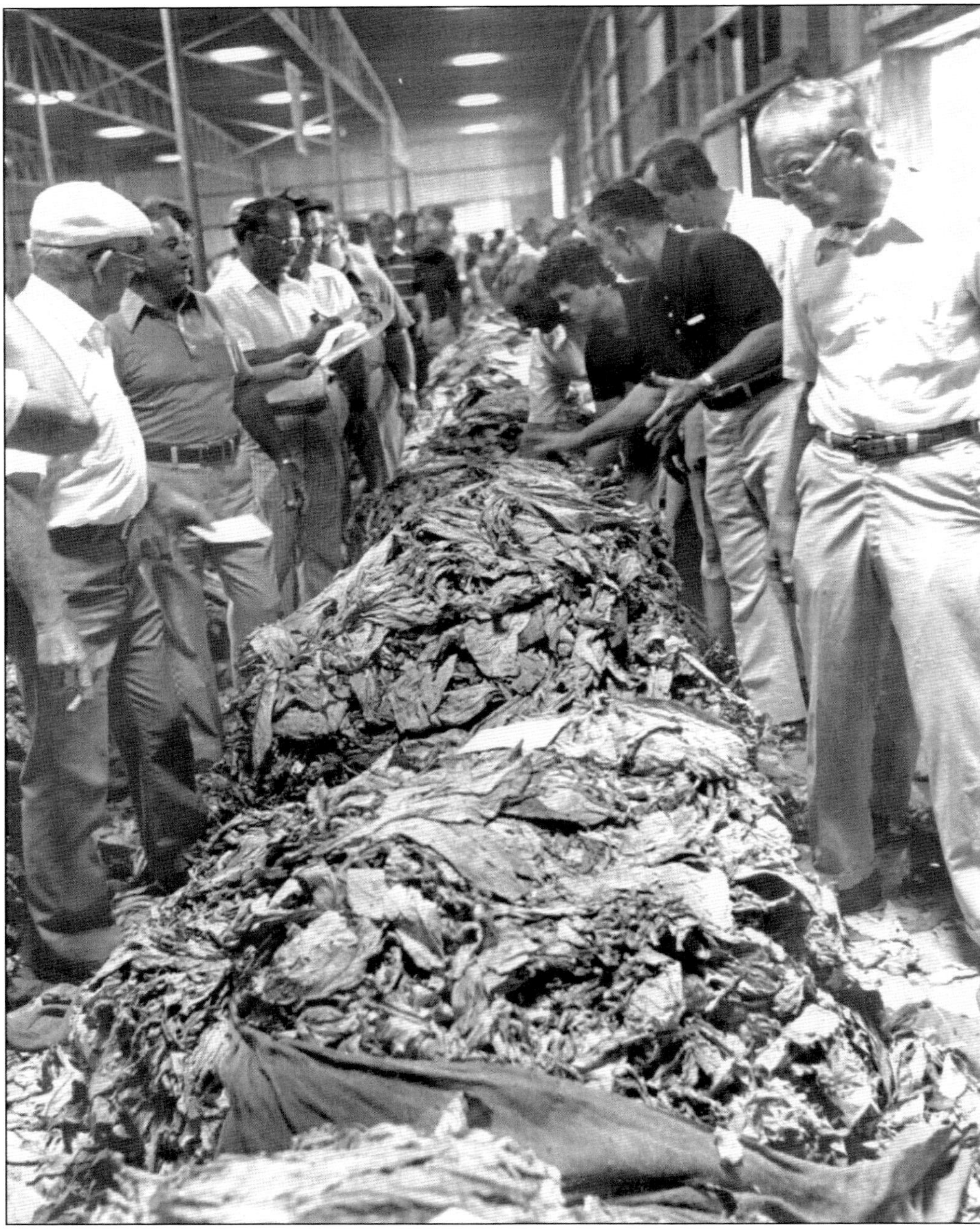

A long row of tobacco ready for sale can be seen inside Yeargin's Warehouse in the early 1970s. (Courtesy of Jean Gill.)

Five

Surrounding Communities

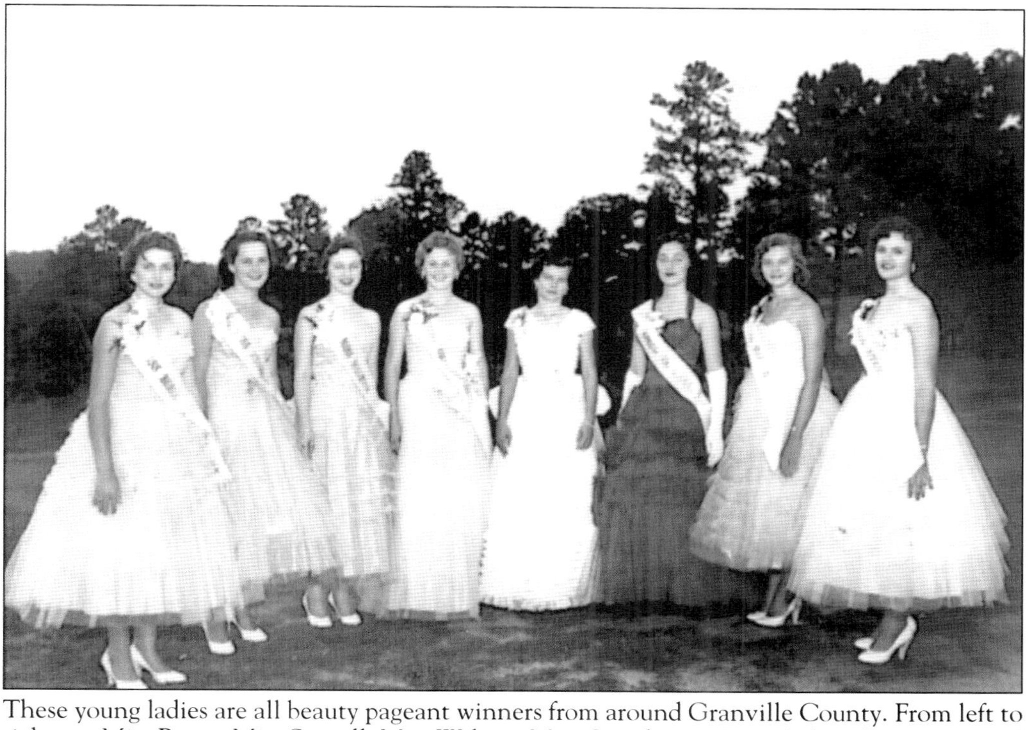

These young ladies are all beauty pageant winners from around Granville County. From left to right are Miss Berea, Miss Stovall, Miss Wilton, Miss Creedmoor, Miss Oak Hill, Miss Oxford Orphanage, Miss Oxford, and Miss Stem. This picture was taken in the 1950s. (Courtesy of Lisa Oakes.)

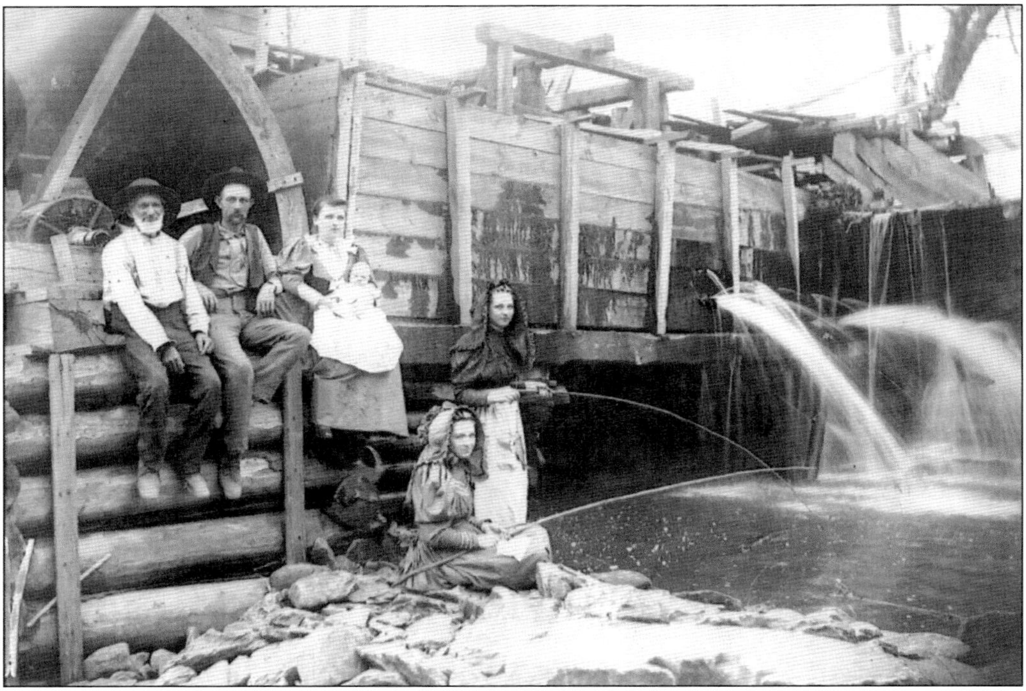

Let's fish for a while at Lyon's Mill in southern Granville County. This picture is from the 1890s. (Courtesy of Carolyn Moss.)

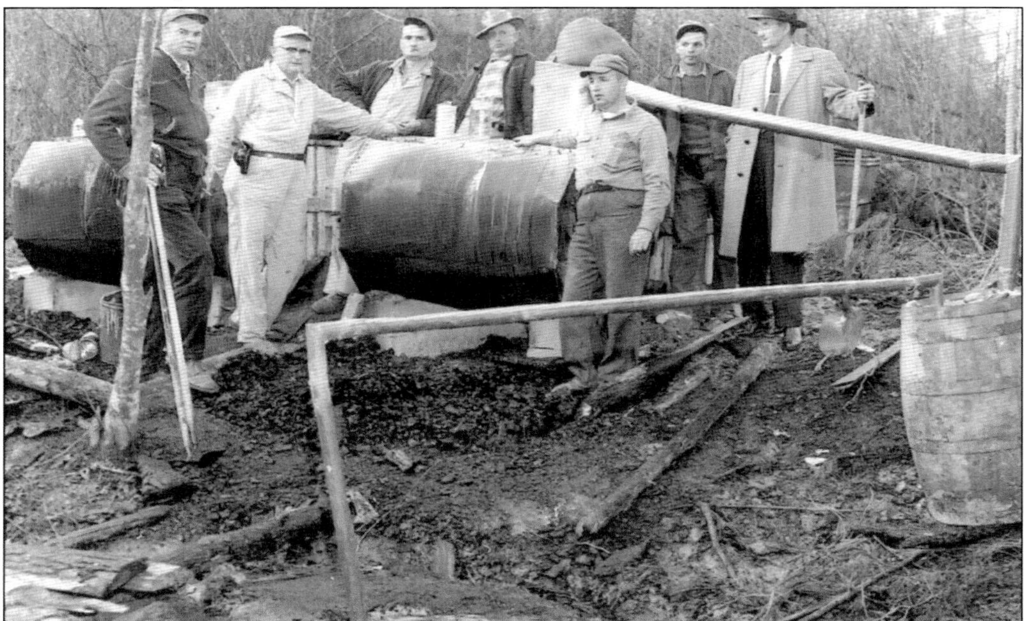

After busting a whiskey still, members of the Granville County Sheriff's Department catch their breath. From left to right are Wallace Bowling, J.C. Cash, Arthur Ray Currin, Bernard Newton, Pluter Morris, Archie Wilkins, and Sheriff Roy Jones. This picture was taken in the 1950s. (Courtesy of Danny Bowling.)

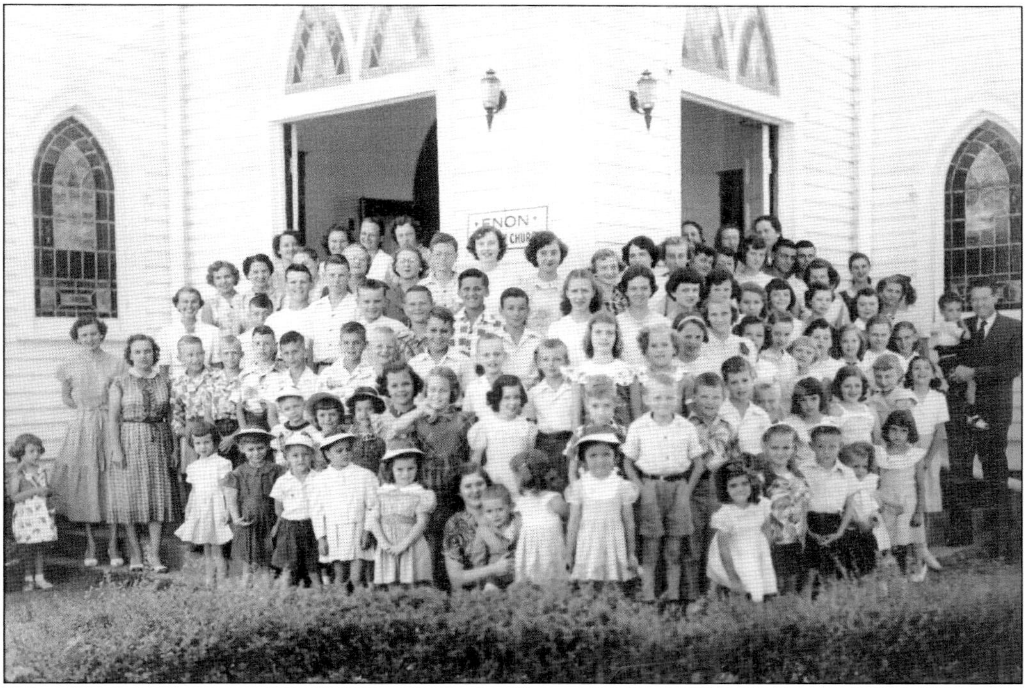

Members of Enon Baptist Church are shown here in the early 1950s. (Courtesy of Jennie O'Brian Schilagi.)

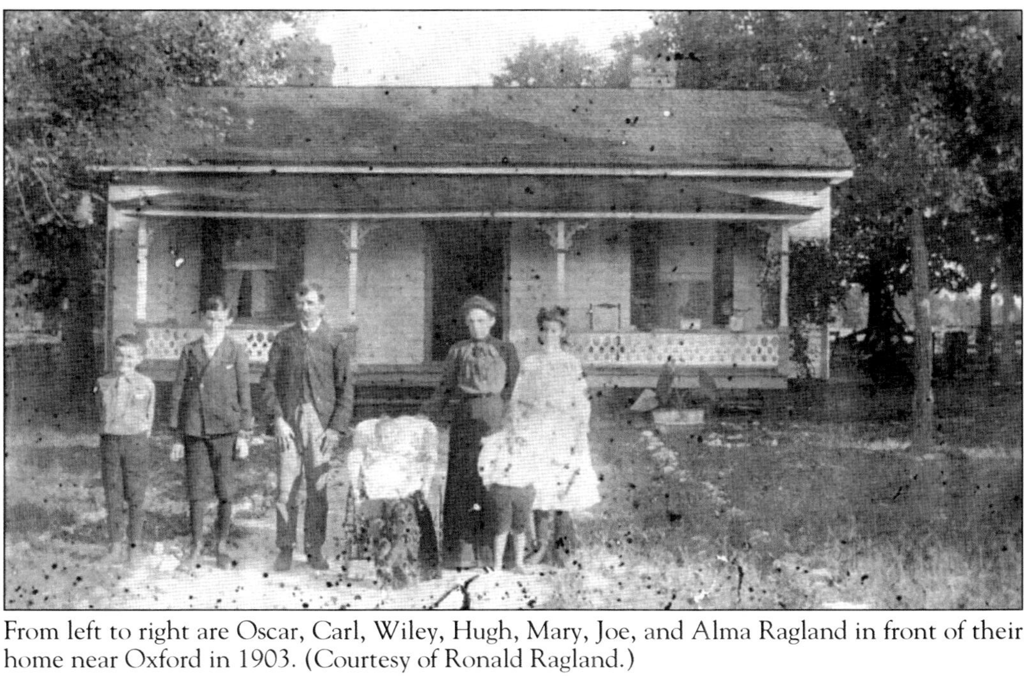

From left to right are Oscar, Carl, Wiley, Hugh, Mary, Joe, and Alma Ragland in front of their home near Oxford in 1903. (Courtesy of Ronald Ragland.)

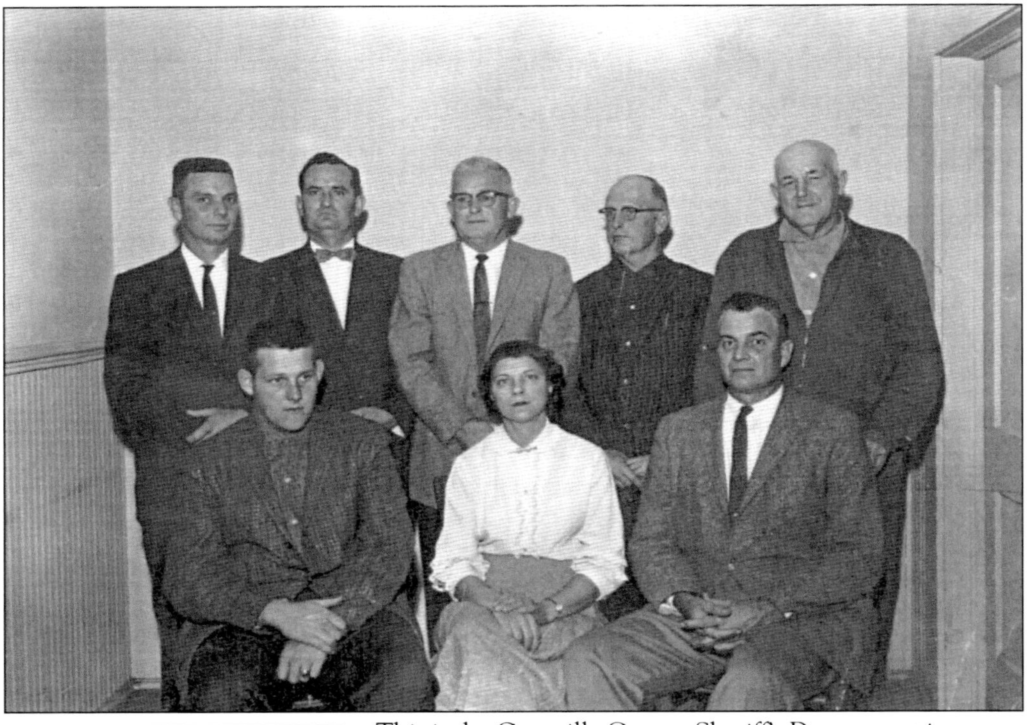

This is the Granville County Sheriff's Department in the early 1960s. From left to right are (front row) Taylor Jackson, Janie Day, and Wallace Bowling; (back row) Archie Wilkins, Arthur Ray Currin, Julius Cash, Bernard Newton, and Joe Pruitt. (Courtesy of Taylor Jackson.)

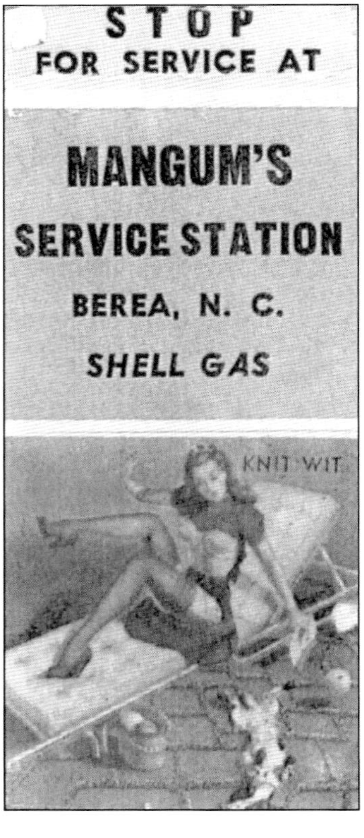

This was a matchbox cover offered to customers from Mangum's Service Station in Berea. It came with a purchase of cigarettes.

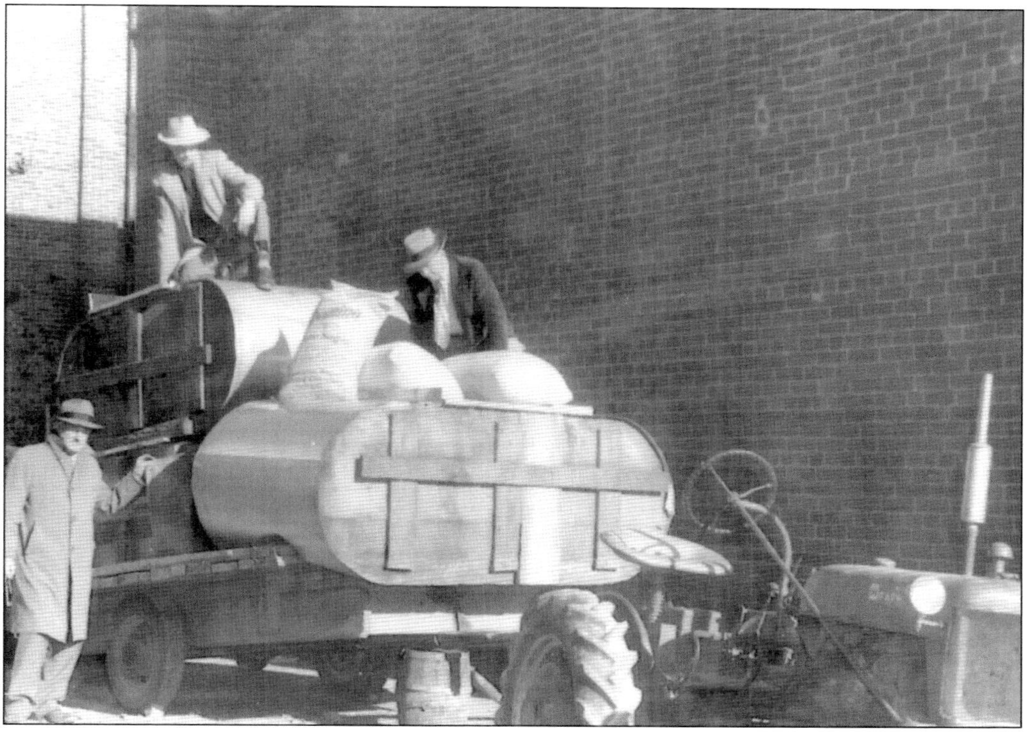

A whiskey still is being loaded at Berea High School in the 1950s. From left to right are Joe Pruitt, Archie Wilkins, and Bernard Newton. (Courtesy of Brin Wilkins.)

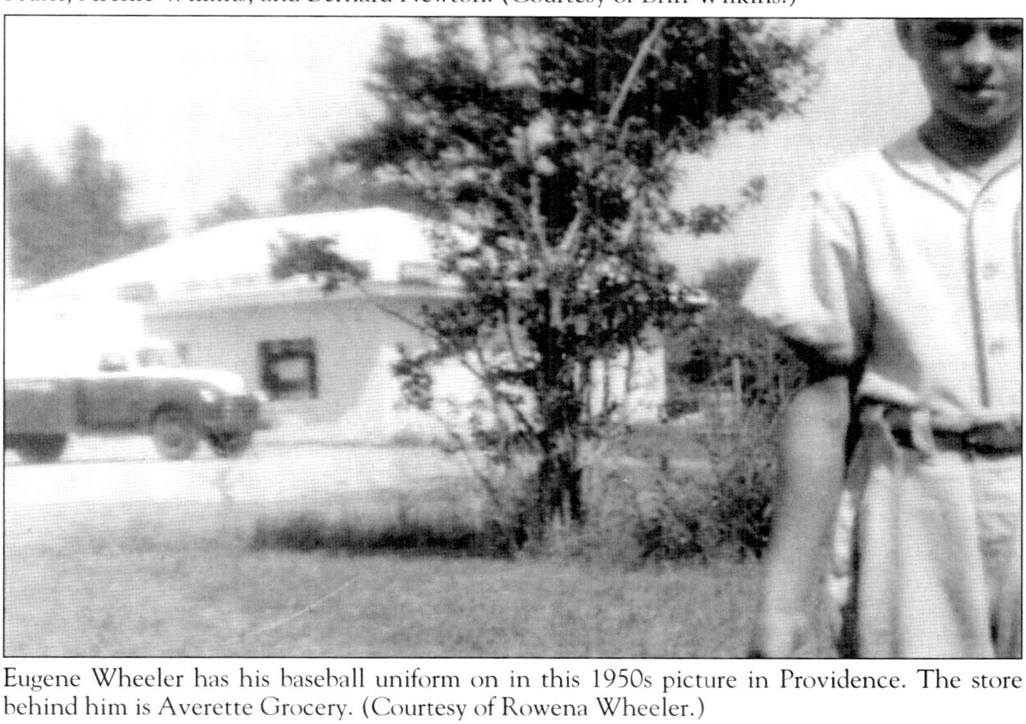

Eugene Wheeler has his baseball uniform on in this 1950s picture in Providence. The store behind him is Averette Grocery. (Courtesy of Rowena Wheeler.)

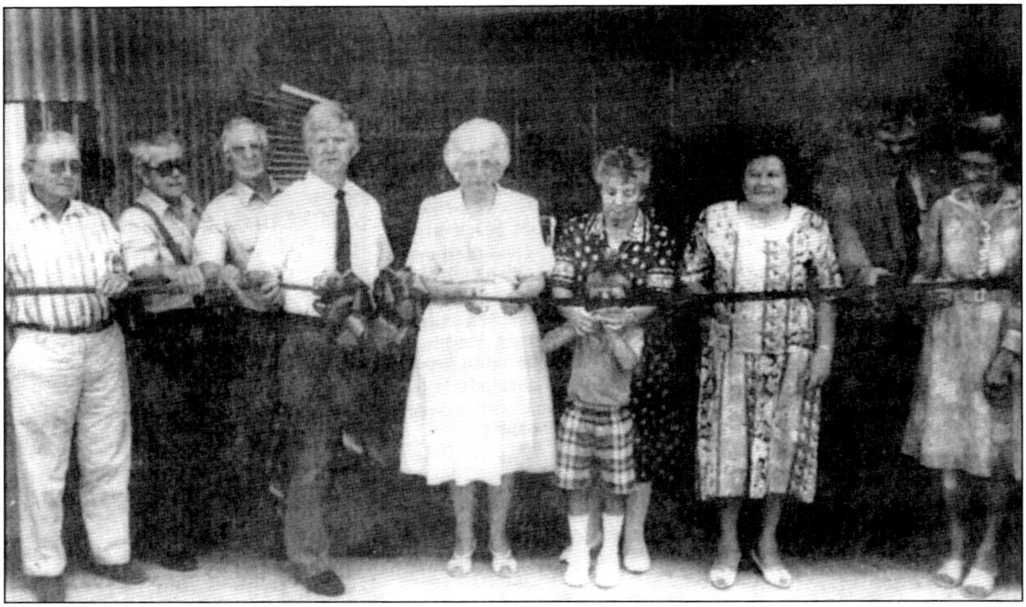

A ribbon-cutting ceremony to dedicate the new Providence Fire Department was held in 1993. From left to right are Mack Ramsey, Frank Arrington, Robert Thomas, Chief Amos Harris, Pat Wilkins, Ollie Bowling (grandson of the first president of the department, O.L. Bowling Jr.), Mary Bowling, Gertrude Satterwhite, Ricky Satterwhite, and Violet Woodlief.

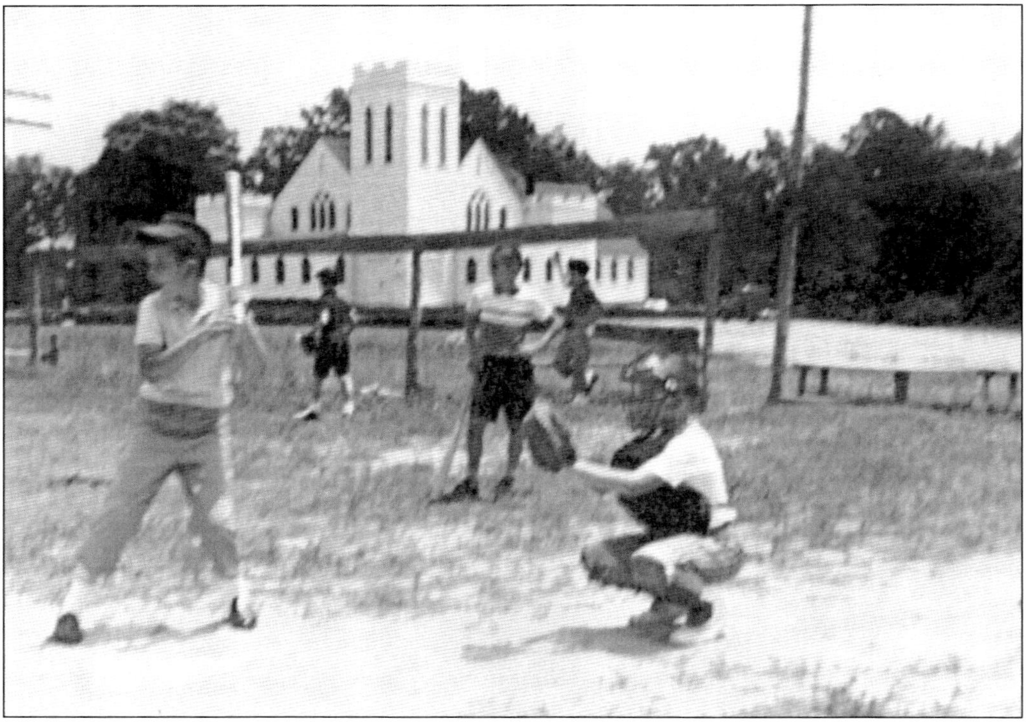

A game of baseball is enjoyed in front of Enon Baptist Church in 1960. (Courtesy of Taylor and Martha Jackson.)

A group of children relax outside Enon Baptist Church in 1960. (Courtesy of Taylor and Martha Jackson.)

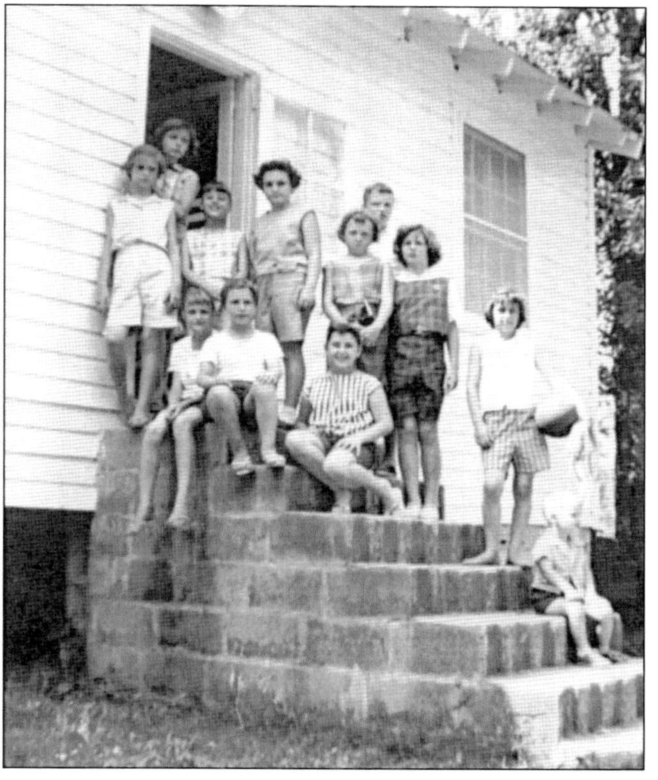

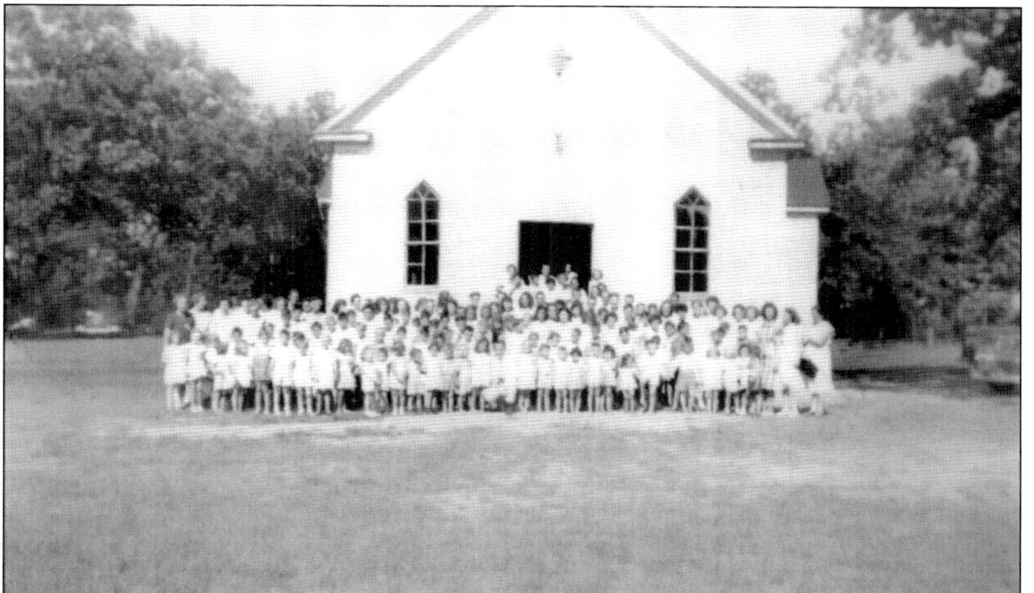

Standing in front of Providence Baptist Church in 1947 is the Bible class. This church was first called Beulah Baptist Church when it was built in 1907.

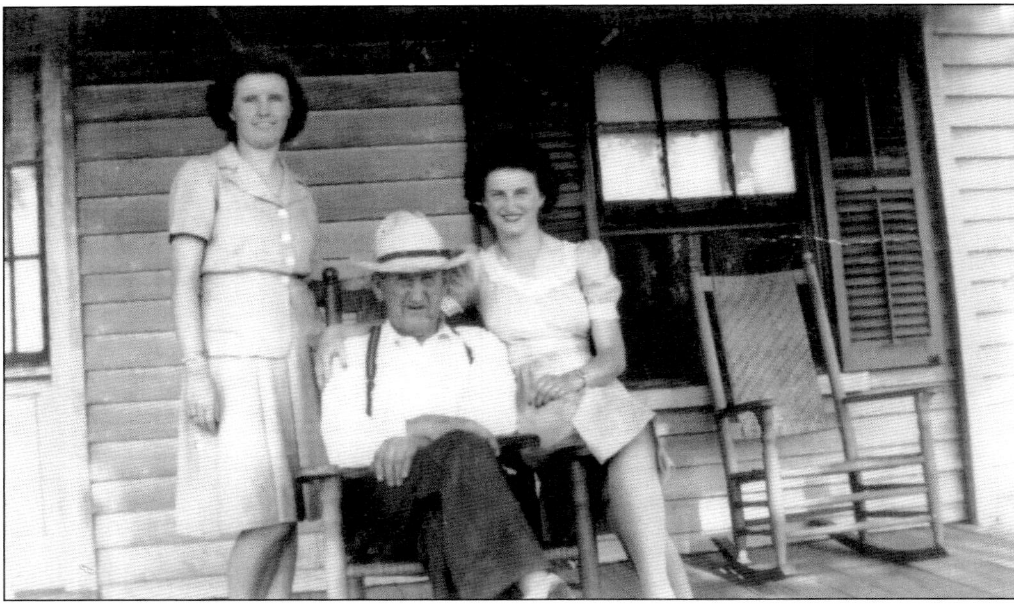

From left to right are Estelle Critcher Woody, Bose Critcher, and Catherine Critcher Laws at their house on Hallie Burnette Road in Providence.

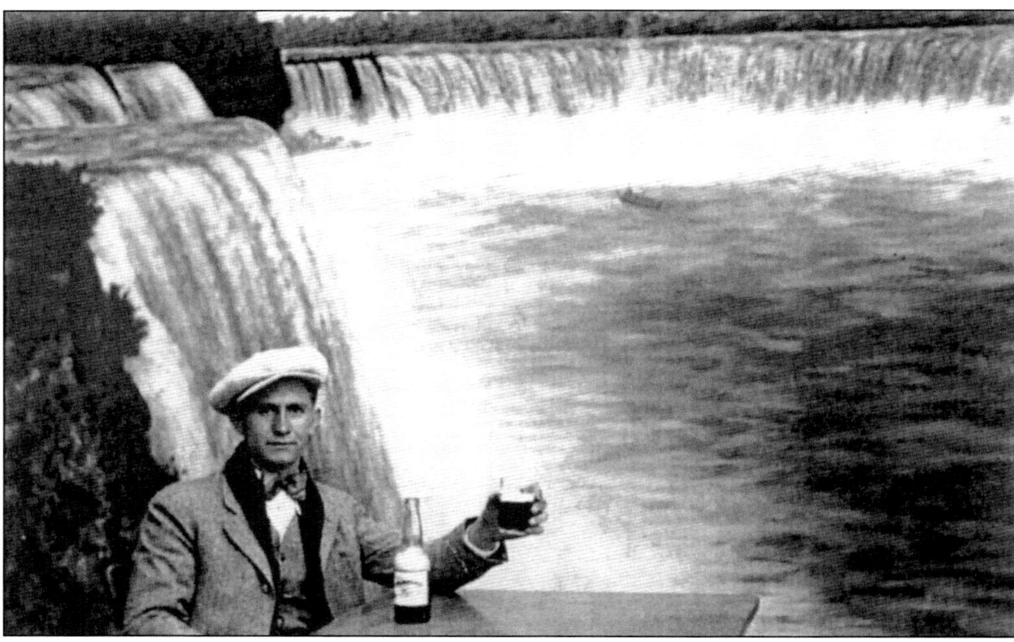

James Woodlief of Providence is pictured at Niagara Falls in 1914. (Courtesy of Josh Mangum.)

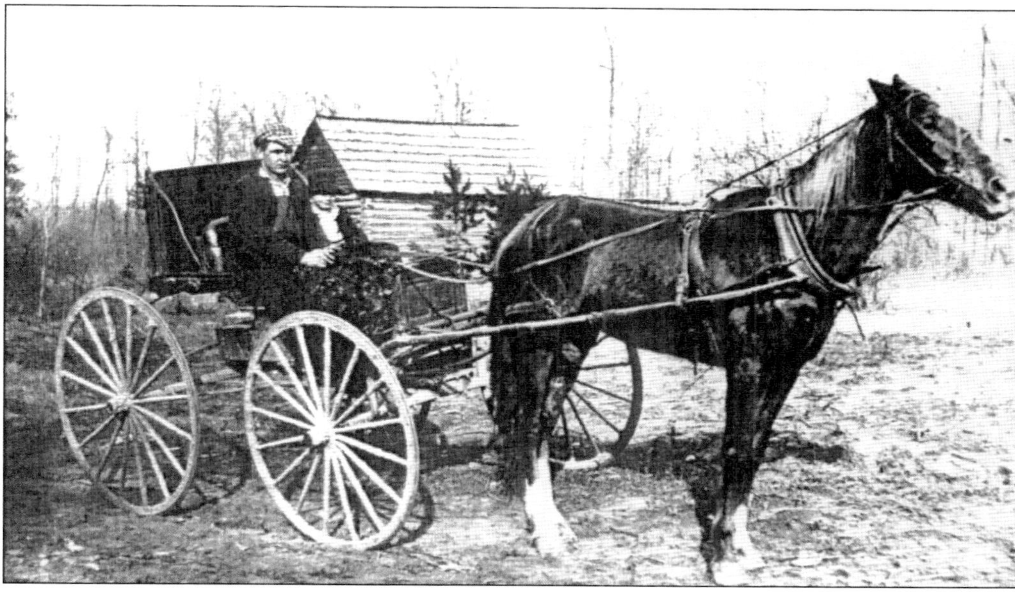

James and Charlie Woodlief prepare for a ride in Providence in 1915.

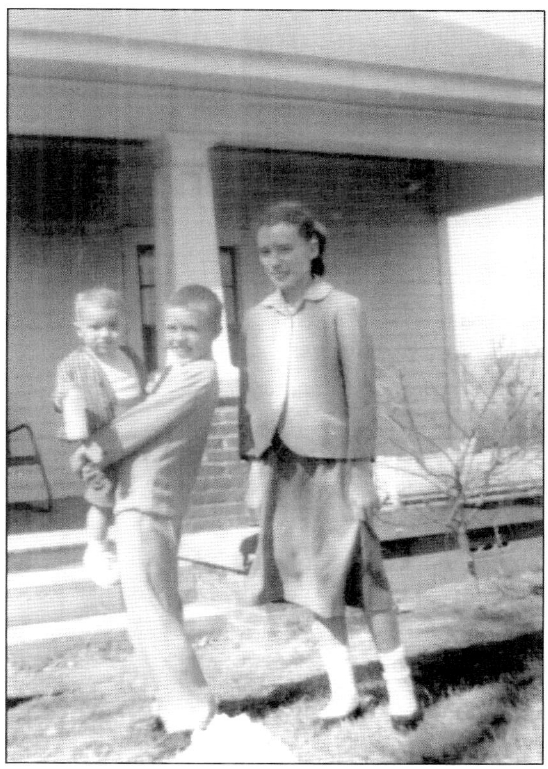

From left to right are Wade Milton, Donnie Milton, and Brenda Milton Frazier at their home in Providence. (Courtesy of Donnie and Linda Milton.)

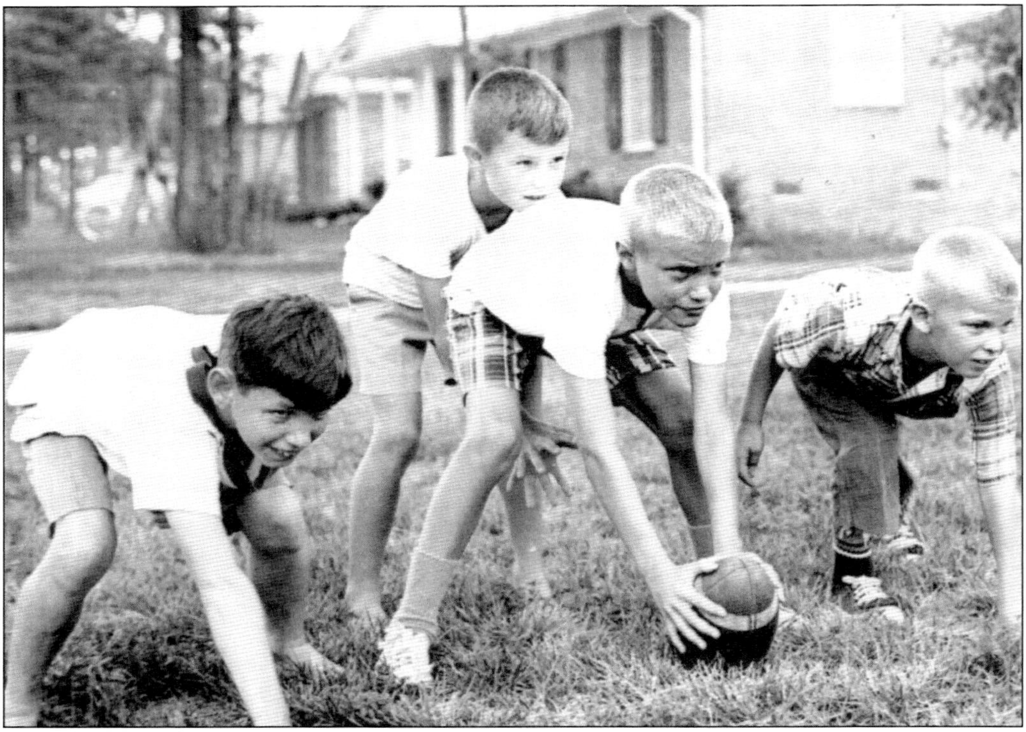

Possibly with dreams of the NFL, some young boys play football in the Butner area.

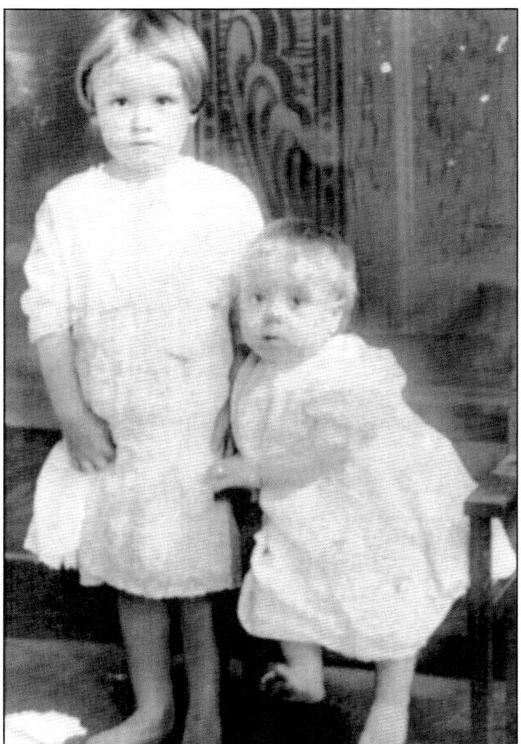

Ada Lee Walker Cozart and Linwood Walker lovingly embrace in 1917. (Courtesy of Mary Bowling.)

The Grissom family is shown here in the 1910s. Seated from left to right are Martha Grissom, Rosa Grissom (young lady), and Elsie Grissom. Standing are J.E. Emmitt Grissom, William Grissom, and J.E. Grissom. (Courtesy of Herbert Grissom.)

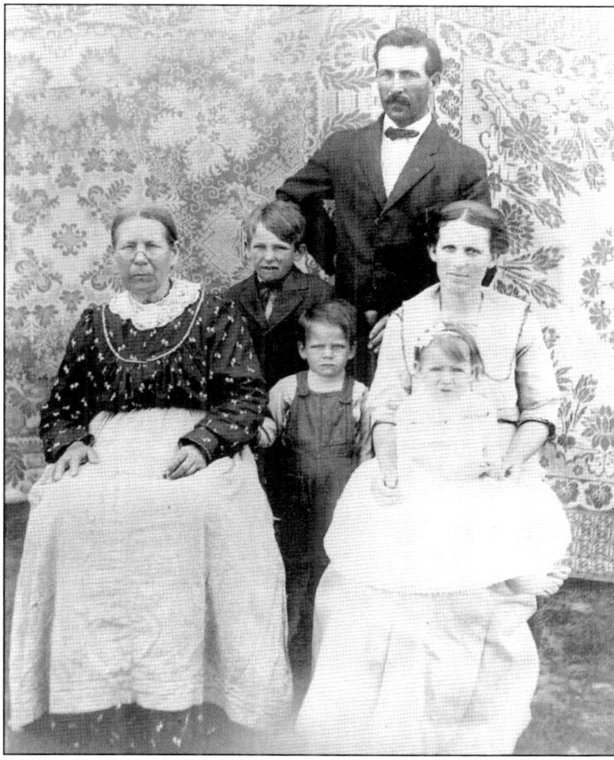

Billy Mangum proudly displays his race car in Berea in the 1940s. (Courtesy of Josh Mangum.)

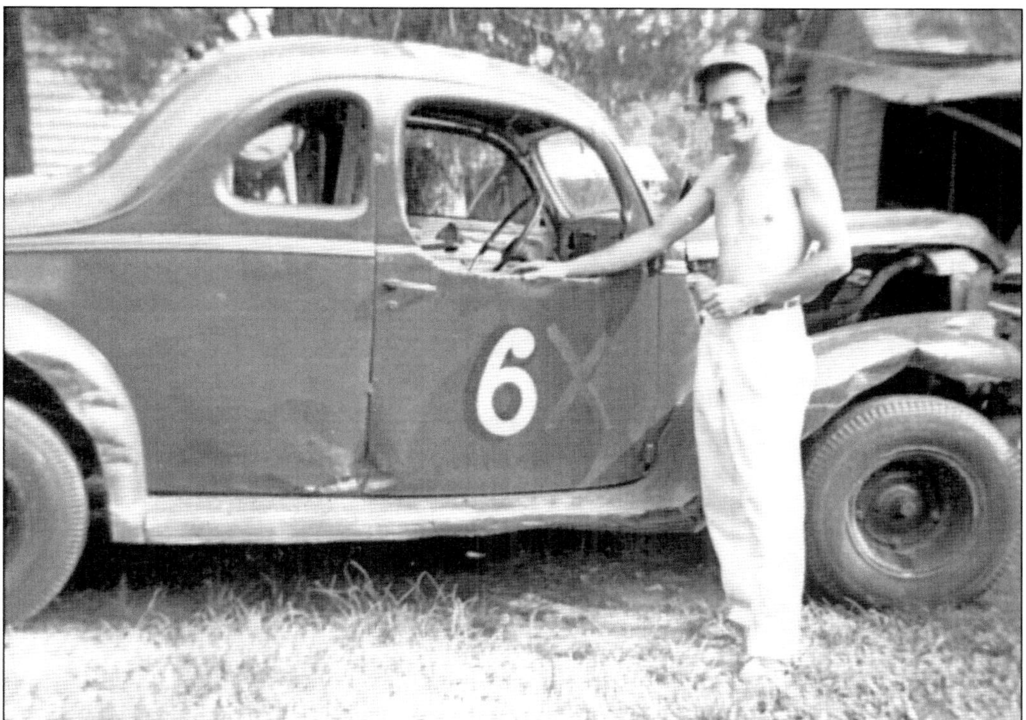

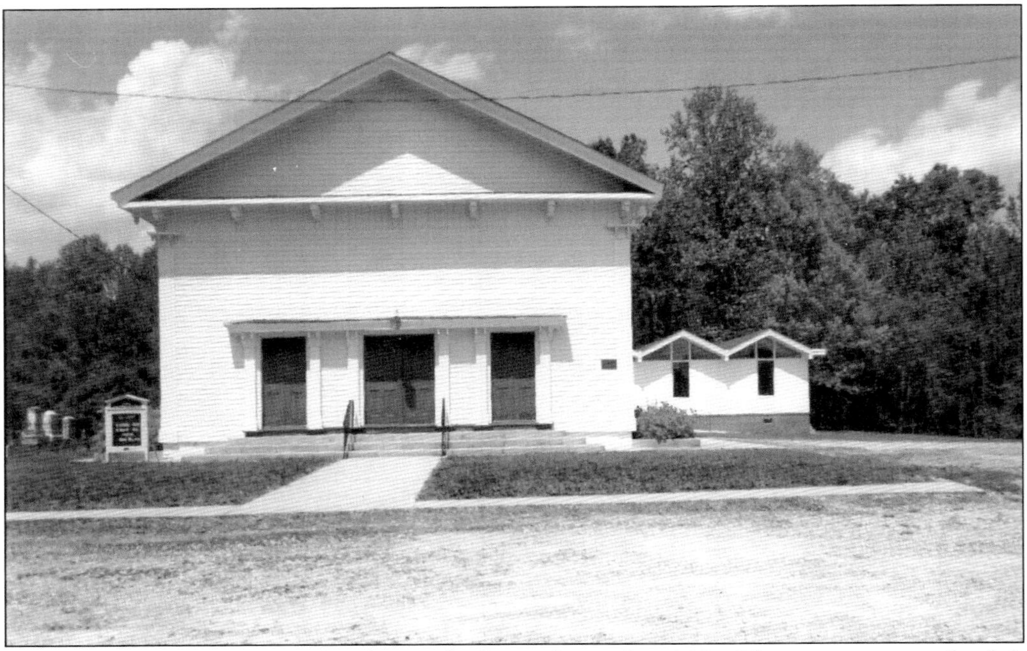

Salem United Methodist Church was built in the early 1860s. The cemetery to the left contains the graves of many of its founders. This church is located in Huntsboro. (Courtesy of Edythe Day.)

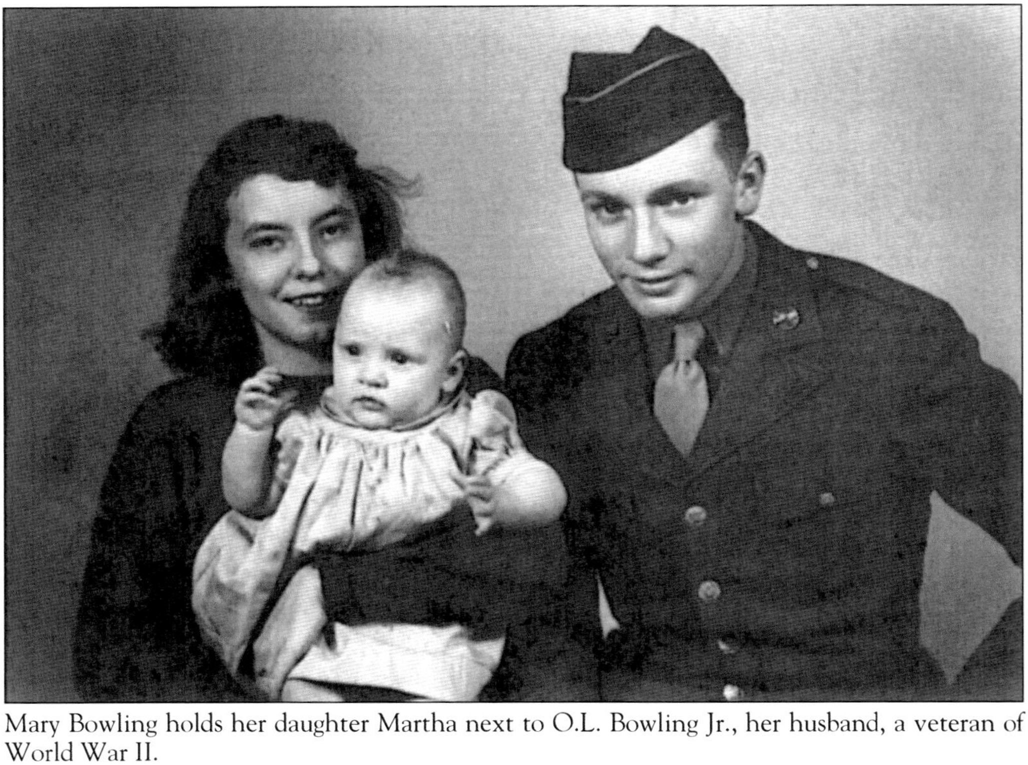

Mary Bowling holds her daughter Martha next to O.L. Bowling Jr., her husband, a veteran of World War II.

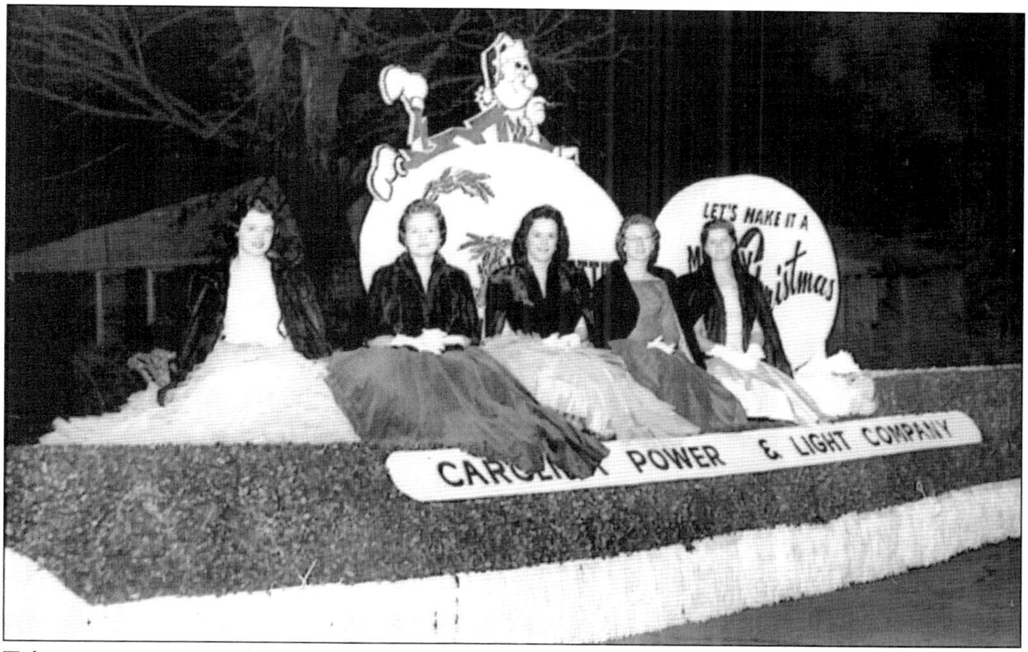

Taking part in a parade in 1958 are, from left to right, unidentified, Marilyn Spencer, Betty Currin, Eugina Brummit, and Jo Ann Hatton. (Courtesy of Lisa Oakes.)

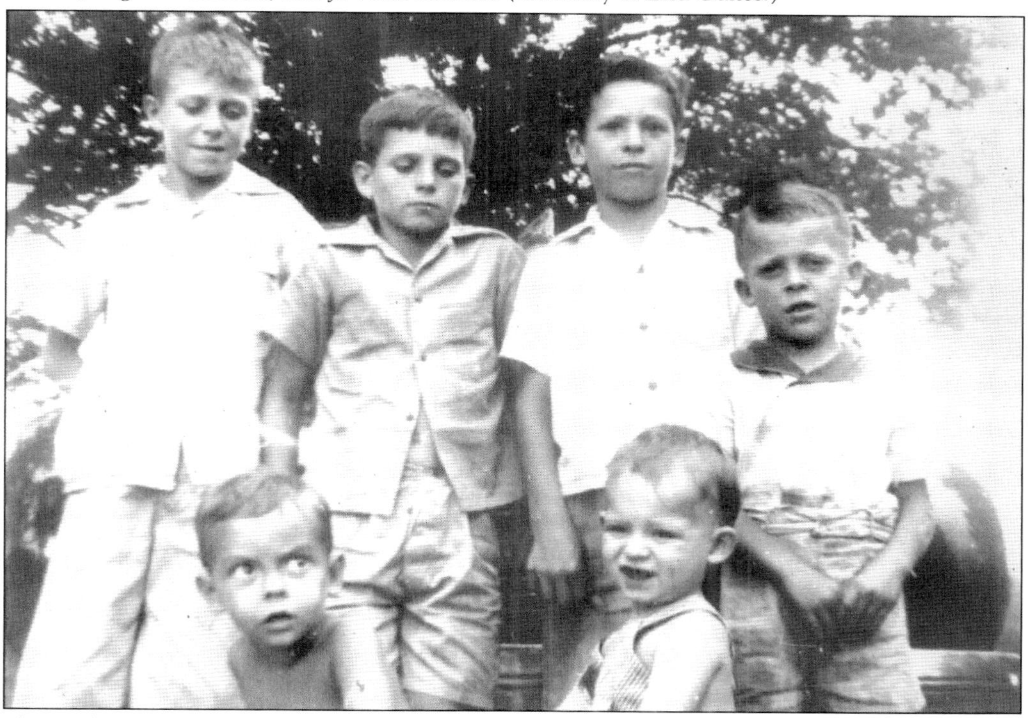

Shown here from left to right are (standing) Herbert, Melvin, Marion, and Ben Grissom; (sitting) Billy Grissom and Jimmy Elliott. Marion later served as Granville County sheriff for many years. (Courtesy of Herbert Grissom.)

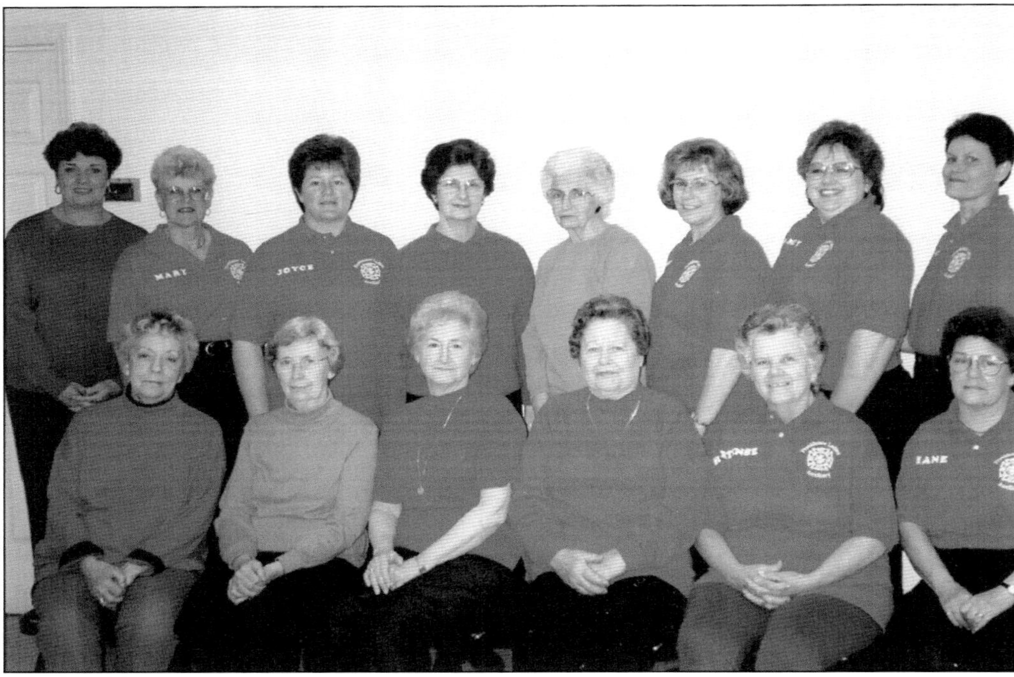

The ladies of the Providence Fire Department Auxiliary meet in the 1970s. From left to right are (front row) Mary Bowling, Candace Burnett, Margaret Tilley, Gertrude Satterwhite, Hortense Ramsey, and Diane O'Briant; (back row) Martha Owens, Mary Elliot, Joyce Ellington, Sandra Green, Pat Wilkins, Jean Huff, Nancy Thomas, and Pat Satterwhite.

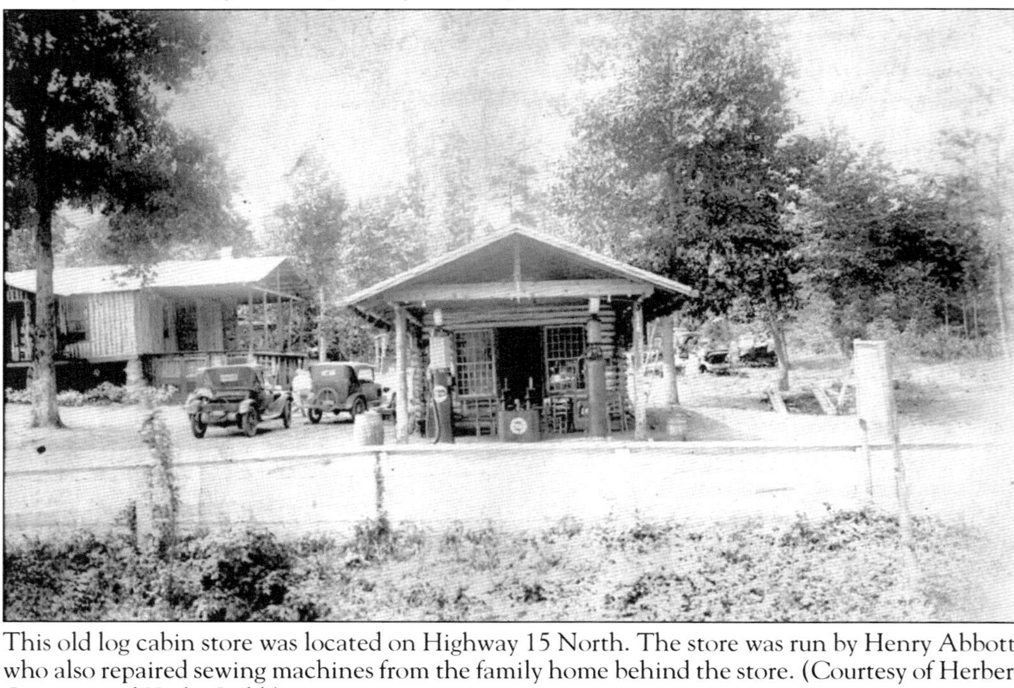

This old log cabin store was located on Highway 15 North. The store was run by Henry Abbott, who also repaired sewing machines from the family home behind the store. (Courtesy of Herbert Grissom and Kathy Judd.)

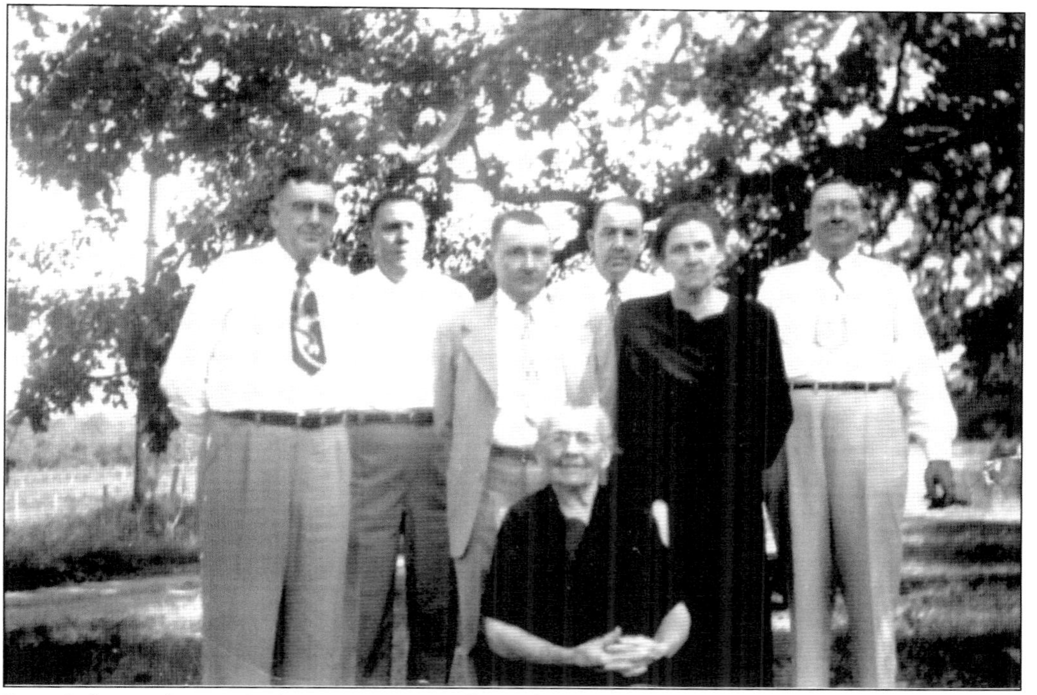

From left to right are Graham, Lonnie, Willie, John, Maude, and Roy Breedlove. Seated is Ida Breedlove. The family gathered for this picture in the Lewis community on Chewning Road. (Courtesy of Woody Breedlove.)

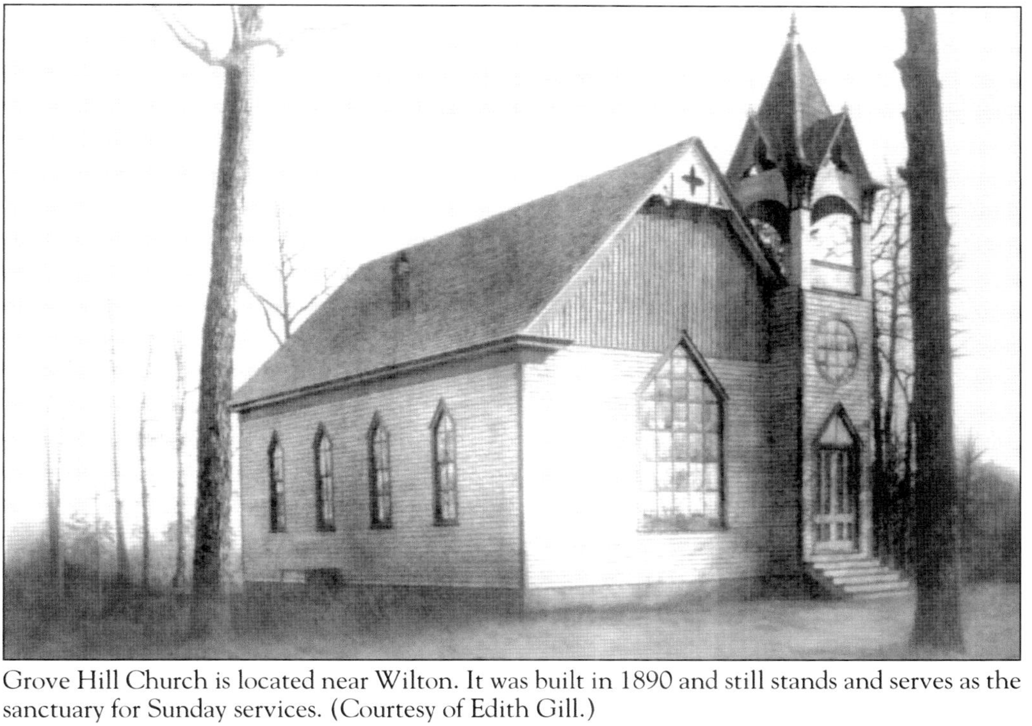

Grove Hill Church is located near Wilton. It was built in 1890 and still stands and serves as the sanctuary for Sunday services. (Courtesy of Edith Gill.)

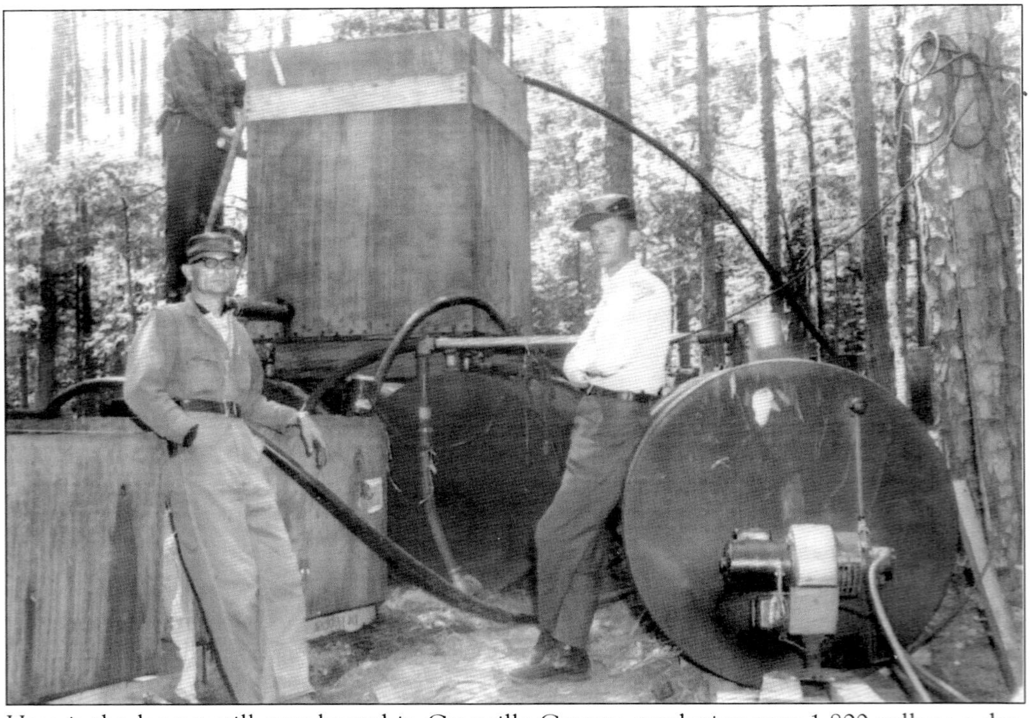

Here is the largest still ever busted in Granville County, producing over 1,800 gallons a day. This was in the Enon community. Shown are Arthur Ray Currin (on top), H.T. Brame (left), and Jack Parrish. (Courtesy of Brin Wilkins.)

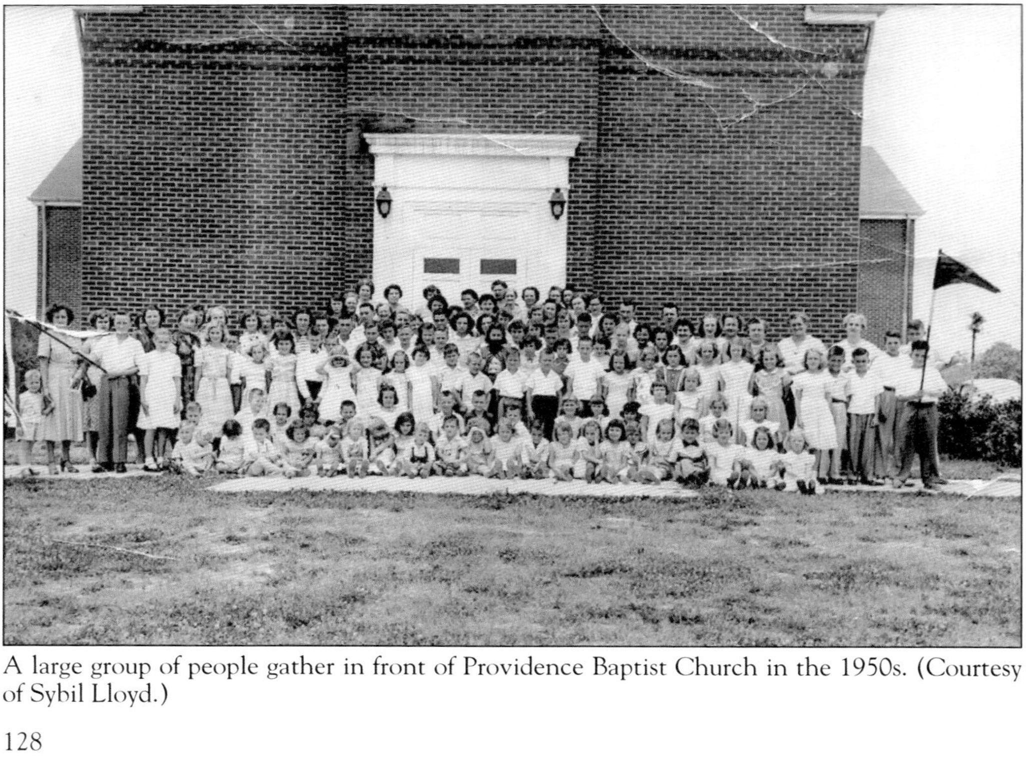

A large group of people gather in front of Providence Baptist Church in the 1950s. (Courtesy of Sybil Lloyd.)